IN THE SHADOW OF WORLD LITERATURE

translation

TRANSNATION

SERIES EDITOR **EMILY APTER**

A list of titles in this series appears at the back of the book

IN THE SHADOW OF WORLD LITERATURE

SITES OF READING IN COLONIAL EGYPT

MICHAEL ALLAN

PRINCETON UNIVERSITY PRESS
PRINCETON AND OXFORD

Published by Princeton University Press,
41 William Street, Princeton, New Jersey 08540
In the United Kingdom: Princeton University Press,
6 Oxford Street, Woodstock, Oxfordshire OX20 1TR

press.princeton.edu

Cover photograph: Rosetta Stone, by Okko Pyykkö

ISBN 978-0-691-16782-4

ISBN (pbk.) 978-0-691-16783-1

Library of Congress Control Number: 2015958283

British Library Cataloging-in-Publication Data is available

This book has been composed in Linux Libertine O and Lato

Printed on acid-free paper ∞

Printed in the United States of America

10 9 8 7 6 5 4 3 2 1

CONTENTS

ACKNOWLEDGMENTS

On my shelf when I was a child was a seemingly antique edition of a book whose contents I knew as much from the smell of its musty pages as from the fading gold lettering embossed on its cover. I recall that the book had color plates and an inscription written in ink acknowledging that it belonged to my grandfather. He was both a smoker and an avid reader, and all of his books seemed to possess the odor of the tobacco exhaled from his pipe. With its strong scent, yellowed pages, and leather cover, this particular book came to embody my grandfather for my young imagination. It spoke to his library and the manner in which he possessed and consumed books. Its pages contained stories that touched my eyes differently than his, and yet both my grandfather and I incorporated this book into our lives and our collections. Each of us let the book matter as much through how we loved it as through anything written on its pages.

That the musty book was a copy of *One Thousand and One Nights* only reveals the extent of a transformation from one generation to the next. This was a book that meant something quite different to my grandfather as a child in Montreal than it did to me years later in Northern Virginia. What I loved and what I held in my hands was an index of my grandfather and his library. The repository of stories contained on the pages was somehow eclipsed by the status of the book as an artifact, an object, and a trace of my grandfather's life. And years later, these pages came alive for me again as a sign of my grandfather and his imagination, his world, and his books, alongside my own voyage through language, literature, and philosophy in Canada, the United States, the Middle East, and Europe. Holding his book in my hands, I questioned what compelled my grandfather to this text and the stories on its pages. On shelves otherwise filled with Quebec and Canadian history, what did a book like *One Thousand and One Nights* mean to him? How did this text fit his collection?

In the Shadow of World Literature explores the relationship between readers and texts across traditions, but it relies as much on the terms in which books come to matter as on the primacy of writing. For my grandfather, a collection of books bespoke the value of education, intellect, and curiosity beyond the scope of a linguistic or national tradition. Even if each particular book in his library had a story, its status as a book lent it significance within the broader collection and all that it stood for. Reading for my grandfather was a practice linked to his armchair and his pipe, and stories mattered as they allowed him to envision a world and its past—and to imagine his place within it. For me, reading as a practice has become the site of this study, and this basic framework shifts my attention from books to readers and from objects to interpretative communities. In the following chapters, I undertake an encounter with various sites for thinking about what literature means, for whom, and in what ways.

The learning that leads me to find value in these questions, to care about how literature matters, and to consider historical and linguistic formations as integral to the sensorium is something that derives from interactions with others. And in this regard, I am deeply indebted to those who have helped to form my relationship to texts, readers, and the world. From sunny days in Berkeley, Cairo, and Tangier to rainy days in Eugene, New York, and Berlin, this book has been shaped by almost a decade of conversations, collaborations, and friendships.

Foremost in a list of friends to thank are the mentors whose work has proven an inspiration to me throughout the entire composition process. I thank Judith Butler, whose scholarship drew me to Berkeley and whose subsequent guidance and thoughtful engagement demonstrated for me the intricate connections of literature, language, and philosophy; Saba Mahmood, who provided me a generous form of interlocution at once compassionate and critical, and whose attention to ethics, sensibilities, and anthropology transformed how I read and relate to words; and Karl Britto, who modeled for me the fusion of history, language, and literary reading with his attentive insights on colonialism and literary form. What follows benefits from the attention, care, and potential that these three saw in the arguments and issues at stake in this work. The questions that inform the seed of this project draw both directly and indirectly from the environments they fostered in their classrooms and in friendships that grew out of intellectual exchanges they offered.

Along the path to completing the project, I have also benefitted from a number of institutional sources of support. In Berlin, I was grateful to participate in the Forum for Transregional Studies as a fellow of Europe in the Middle East/the Middle East in Europe (EUME) from 2011 to 2012. My indebtedness to EUME extends back to my time as a graduate student, when I had the occasion to attend two Summer Academies: one in Alexandria, Egypt, in 2003, and the other in Beirut, Lebanon, in 2006. On both of these occasions and during my year in Berlin, I learned richly from the friendship, intellect, and guidance of Georges Khalil, who modeled innovative and imaginative ways of understanding politics, history, and literature. The support of the Friedrich Schlegel Institute for Literary Studies at the Freie Universität in Berlin allowed me a space to write, and I thank my friends and colleagues, in particular Gish Amit, Elisabetta Benigni, Julie Billaud, Ahmed Fekry Ibrahim, Hafid Ismaili, Prashant Keshavmurthy, Gijs Kruijtzer, Adam Mestyan, Mostafa Minawi, Ihab Saloul, Saeko Shibayama, and my dear office mate Adania Shibli. Many of the questions explored in the various chapters of my book follow from discussions, readings, and conversations from the lecture-cum-seminar series of Zukunftsphilologie, EUME Summer Academies and the EUME Berliner seminar. I thank Manan Ahmed, Islam Dayeh, Angelika Neuwirth, Rachid Ouaissa, Friederike Pannewick, and Samah Selim for their contributions in these various settings.

My time as part of the Society of Fellows at Columbia University offered me a rich environment to think critically about literary history, textuality, and colonialism. Afternoons spent in the Heyman Center for the Humanities and conversations with Katherine Biers, Josh Dubler, Marwa Elshakry, Eileen Gilooly, Kevin Lamb, David Novak, Patrick Singy, Joseph Slaughter, Will Slauter, and Gauri Viswanathan made the year incredibly rewarding. At Berkeley, I enjoyed the support of the Townsend Center for the Humanities. I owe a debt of gratitude to Anthony Cascardi and Teresa Stojkov, and to my dear colleagues Samera Esmeir, Michael Kunichika, and Kris Paulsen. The following year, I had the good fortune to participate in the Religion, Secularism and Modernity Working Group, and I thank Charles Hirschkind, Victoria Kahn, Niklaus Largier, Saba Mahmood, Robert Sharf, and Matthew Scherer for the conversations and insights they offered. I appreciate the support of the Sultan Fellowship at the Center for Middle Eastern Studies at Berkeley that made possible additional visits to Cairo as I composed my chapters.

Friends and colleagues working on the Middle East have helped to constitute my sphere of interlocutors, and much of what follows benefits directly from the sorts of questions that their work makes thinkable. I am grateful for the friendship of On Barak, Elizabeth Bishop, Emily Drumsta, Tarek El-Ariss, Hoda El Shakry, Omnia El Shakry, Sarah Eltantawi, Samuel England, Samera Esmeir, Mayanthi Fernando, Gretchen Head, Elizabeth Holt, Lital Levy, Peter Limbrick, Amir Moosavi, Ibrahim Muhawi, Milad Odabei, Noha Radwan, Martina Rieker, Janell Rothenberg, Irene Siegel, Shaden Tageldin, Adam Talib, Kabir Tambar, and Nirvana Tanoukhi. I thank as well my friends at CLS Tangier: Kerry Adams, Abdelhak Akjeje, Yhtimad Bouziane, Youniss El Cheddadi, Anita Husen, Khaled Al Masaeed, and Sonia S'hiri, and the numerous students I had the pleasure of working with and learning from during my two summers in Morocco.

Professors, friends, and interlocutors past and present have also helped to enrich this project. I thank Anton Kaes for teaching me about connections between history and aesthetic form, and Muhammad Siddiq for a commitment to language, literary traditions, and the art of reading. I also thank Christian Amondson, Anjali Arondekar, Geoff Baker, Nima Bassiri, Réda Bensmaïa, Ayelet Ben Yishai, Hicham Bouzid, Natasha Burger, Juan Caballero, Manuela Campos, Yoon Sook Cha, Faye Chaio, Laura Chrisman, Kegham Djeghalian, Alex Dubilet, Karen Emmerich, Aaron Fai, Taron Flood, Hannah Freed-Thall, Jason Friedman, Benj Gerdes, Victor Goldgel-Carballo, Amanda Goldstein, Margarita Gordon, Redouane Hadrane, Katharine Halls, Jen Hayashida, Daniel Hoffman-Schwartz, Satyel Larson, Katherine Lemons, Emma Libonati, Tom McEnaney, Chris Nealon, Nimrod Reitman, Felix Rhein, Allison Schachter, Stephan Schmuck, Thea Schwarz, Katie Skibinski, Ann Smock, Richard So, Jordan Alexander Stein, Judith Surkis, Annika Thiem, Ben Tran, Toby Warner, Andrew Weiner, Sarah Wells, Travis Wilds, Yves Winter, Benjamin Wurgaft, and Karen Zumhagen-Yekplé.

In Comparative Literature at the University of Oregon, I feel grateful to be surrounded by such intellectually supportive faculty and students. Thank you to my colleagues Jennifer Bright, Steven Brown, Katherine Brundan, Kenneth Calhoon, Lisa Freinkel, Warren Ginsberg, Sangita Gopal, Katya Hokanson, Dawn Marlan, Leah Middlebrook, Jenifer Presto, and Tze-Yin Teo. I owe a special thank you to Cynthia Stockwell for her wisdom, guidance, and support in all aspects of my working life. The graduate and undergraduate students in Comparative Literature have helped to make my time in Eugene as rewarding as it has been, and some questions addressed in the following chapters come from conversations conducted in the context of seminars, directed readings, or informal discussions in the hallways of Villard. I have learned from my colleagues, especially Lara Bovilsky, Roy Chan, Anita Chari, Mai-Lin Cheng, Amanda Doxtater, Chris Eckerman, Alisa Freedman, David Hollenberg, Angela Joya, David Li, Katharina Loew, Lanie Millar, Quinn Miller, Fabienne Moore, Malek Najjar, Paul Peppis, Forest Pyle, Sergio Rigoletto, Daniel Rosen, Lynne Rossi, George Rowe, Ben Saunders, and Bish Sen. And to Colin Koopman, Stephanie LeMenager, and Rocío Zambrana, I thank you for helping constitute my family in Eugene.

Numerous friends and colleagues have played a direct role in reviewing sections of the book. I am indebted to the anonymous readers of my manuscript as well as to Sunayani Bhattacharya, Tarek El-Ariss, Karen Emmerich, Katharine Halls, Jean-Michel Landry, Jeffrey Sacks, Jerilyn Sambrooke, and Adam Talib for the care they offered reading my work from beginning to end. Sarah Burgess, Kenneth Calhoon, Omnia El Shakry, Gretchen Head, Elizabeth Holt, Leah Middlebrook, Jenifer Presto, Rouven Gueissaz, and Allison Schachter have provided me with thoughtful feedback at various stages, and I have been grateful for their insights and encouragement. I owe my editor, Anne Savarese, as well as Joseph Dahm, Juliana Fidler, Heather Jones, Jenny Wolkowicki, and the staff at Princeton University Press my thanks for their support and professionalism through the publication process.

My book has benefited from questions, comments, and audiences at St. Andrews University, Columbia University, Cornell University, the Max Planck Institute in Berlin, Philipps-Universität in Marburg, Princeton University, the University of California, San Diego, the Berliner Seminar at the Wissenschaftskolleg zu Berlin, as well as audiences at panels for the American Comparative Literature Association, the Middle East Studies Association, the Modern Language Association, and the Modernist Studies Association. Excerpts of chapter 4 first appeared under Michael Allan, "How Adab Became Literary: Formalism, Orientalism and the Institutions of World Literature," *Journal of Arabic Literature* 43 (2012) 172–196, and excerpts of chapter 5 are from Michael Allan, "Re-Reading the Arab Darwin: The Lewis Affair and Naguib Mahfouz's *Palace of Desire*," *Journal of Modernism/Modernity*, (forthcoming). I thank Koninklijke Brill NV, Leiden and Johns Hopkins University Press respectively for permission to publish this material here. I also appreciate the generous subvention provided by the Oregon Humanities Center and the College of Arts and Sciences at the University of Oregon to assist with the costs of indexing.

To D. J. Allan, Sarah Burgess, Erica Dillon, Tadashi Dozono, Rouven Gueissaz, Lars Kim, Melanie Krebs, Armando Manalo, David Marks, and family in Chicago, Montreal, Seattle, and Virginia, I thank you for years of encouragement, conversation, and distraction. To Keith Lichten, I am especially grateful for your remarkable tenderness, good nature, and laughter across the many years of our friendship. And to those friends—human and otherwise—whose names are traced in the pages that follow, I thank you for the richness you provide to my everyday life.

My grandfather's classic book reemerged for me as I packed boxes in the basement of my childhood home on the occasion of my mother's death. If from my grandfather I inherited fragments of a library, then from my mother I inherited a manner of relating to the world. She passed away halfway through the completion of this book, and the break in chapters bears testimony to a sort of transformative loss that left me reading, feeling, and responding differently. Her friendship traverses the pages I write and inspires how I hope to relate to all that surrounds me. A concern for others, compassion in listening, and social awareness were all attributes that I admired deeply in her. She was selfless, determined, and quietly driven. She would undoubtedly recoil at this dedication, but I cannot help but credit her, thank her, and miss her in all that follows.

NOTES ON TRANSLITERATION

I have opted here for a system based on the *International Journal of Middle Eastern Studies* (*IJMES*) for the transcription of Modern Standard Arabic. Across the various chapters, I follow the conventional spelling of names and titles readily available in English (e.g., Taha Hussein, Naguib Mahfouz), and I follow the simplified transliteration of characters' names available in published translations. I have also chosen not to transliterate lengthier citations and instead to quote directly in Arabic, particularly in chapters 5 and 6. Readers familiar with Arabic will find fully transliterated names and titles available in the notes and bibliography.

IN THE SHADOW OF WORLD LITERATURE

INTRODUCTION

OF WORDS AND WORLDS

In a striking passage from *al-Ayyām* (The Days), the Egyptian writer Taha Hussein (Ṭāhā Ḥusayn) narrates a time in his life before he knew how to read or write. The opening pages describe in detail his memories of childhood, his schooling, and his relationship to those who introduced him to a world of words. His account both depicts scenes from his local village and reflects abstractly on the act of remembering: "The memory of children [*dhākirat al-aṭfāl*] is indeed a strange thing, or shall we say that the memory of man plays strange tricks when he tries to recall the events of his childhood; for it depicts [*tatamaththal*] some incidents as clearly as though they only happened a short time before, whereas it blots out [*yamḥī*] others as though they had never passed within his ken."[1] Noting what he can and cannot recall, Hussein's opening reflections poetically conjure moments from his past with a series of impressionistic objects and details: a fence, a canal, the schoolmaster's orchard, and the slope of an embankment. He writes sentence after sentence repeating the words, "He remembers [*yadhkuru*]," to frame what he brings to life for us as readers, and he does so in a work that would become not only a landmark in modern Arabic literature, but a contribution to world literature more generally. And yet, I begin with this extraordinary book as much for how it depicts Hussein's nascent literary education as for what it blots out. In this grandiose account of a life in letters, the beginning—the moment of a life before literacy—is simultaneously remembered and forgotten, captured in literary form and somehow lost.

We confront in these opening pages a challenge of reading. In Hussein's autobiography is born not only the story of an author coming into literacy, but an entire way of being in language. He tells the story of a life that would have been unnarratable were it not for the education he came to acquire—an education split between the Qur'anic learning of his years at al-Azhar and his literary training in France. He inscribes with his words memories of times gone, and he constructs a literary world that shrouds his preliterate childhood with impressions, objects, and details from his past. These early years—his time prior to his exposure to scripture, to the alphabet, to the laws of grammar, genre, and form—emerge through a narrative recognizably literary. And once the writer comes into literacy, there is almost no limit to the contents of his narration and no escape from the world it makes thinkable. What is lost, or blotted out, is a way of being in language before knowing how to read and write. What is lost, in other words, is the very way to imagine a world without literature. And what literature means for Hussein—as for a whole range of readers trained in the modern literary disciplines—is something quite specific.[2]

For scholars of world literature, it would be tempting to understand Hussein's autobiography in terms of its transnational dimension—its movement from a village in Upper Egypt to al-Azhar in Cairo and to Montpellier, France; or its passage from Arabic into French literary circles at the hands of André Gide. But beyond charting a movement between nations and languages, I highlight the beginning of the autobiography for what it reveals of an alternate sort of travel, one that points less to geographical places than to ways of reading, knowing, and apprehending the world. With its accumulated impressions of objects and details, the opening section is seemingly nostalgic for a mode of experience now eclipsed by the literacy of its narrator, who, like Walter Benjamin's famous storyteller, hovers ambivalently between past and present.[3] On the pages of his book are traces of other literary sources that both form and render possible his training as a writer, making what we read an account and a curriculum, an autobiography and an archive. His book describes not only texts, but the disciplined training of his literary mind, one whose education turns on a capacity to read, appreciate, and comment on the subtleties of literary form. And this disciplined training is initially forged in Qur'anic schools and further developed through literary study in France and Egypt, complicating any perceived opposition between secular humanism and religious education.

There is more, though, to this account of a coming into literacy. Beyond the pages of his life in letters, Hussein labored institutionally, serving as a professor, a dean, and a key figure in the crafting of literary curricula for the modern Egyptian state. In this endeavor, he helped to place Arabic literature, which he knew so well and on behalf of which he labored so intently, among the literary traditions of an emergent world literature. To the literary models seen in Greek, Latin, French, English, and German, he added Arabic—a language he understood to embody a Mediterranean and cosmopolitan heritage. In his work, both as a writer and as a public intellectual, a circular performance of reading, writing, and cultivating scholars was born. His writings would bring poetic traditions to bear on an emergent literary paradigm that he was himself to help forge. As with childhood in his autobiography so too with early poetic traditions in his literary history, all would contribute to the formation of a seemingly continuous literary world and a curriculum. As the dean of Alexandria University and one of the most prominent public intellectuals of his generation, Hussein would be inseparable from the institutional framework integral to defining not just *what* but *how* to read.

I take Hussein's autobiography as my beginning for how it points us simultaneously to the formal conditions of literary education and to the limits of an emergent literary world.[4] Taking seriously the dynamic of remembering and forgetting, *In the Shadow of World Literature* is an effort to consider transformations that both create the modern literary disciplines and define the contours of a reading public. What follows is an account concerned as much with the conditions and exclusions of literacy as with the national and linguistic geography of a world republic of letters. As you will see, this undertaking is both theoretical in its general engagement with world literature, literary theory, and postcolonial studies, and historical in taking Egypt as a paradigmatic site from which to consider literary publics, textual cultures, and the history of reading. The six chapters deal with two convergent and enmeshed narratives: on the one hand, the formation of a modern literary paradigm linked to education reform, the rise of a reading public and modern Arabic literature, and on the other hand, the story of what gets blotted out, religious institutions and practices that come to be understood as traditional. In this process, I deal with the emergence of literature as the domain for the cultivation of aesthetic sensibilities and the development of character, and I address how an emergent literary culture redefines religious practices and textual traditions once deemed crucial to the formation of an ethical subject.[5]

Throughout this book, I focus on the putative opposition between a practice of reading based on memorization, embodiment, and recitation in Qur'anic schools (*katātīb*; *kuttāb*, sing.) and another practice based on reflection, critique, and judgment, increasingly integral to what gets defined as literacy in the modern Egyptian state.[6] My goal is to consider how this opposition is secured, to assess its purchase within world literature, and to question its limits for understanding the dynamics of literary publics. For my purposes here, literary reading is not some theoretically detached object, but an embodied practice integral to being recognizably educated in the modern state; and world literature is not the all-inclusive meeting place of national literary traditions, but the emergent distinction between those deemed literate, cosmopolitan, and modern, and those others who are not. What follows, then, is an account of world literature as it transforms textual practices, defines the borders of a world republic of letters, and distinguishes the literate and the illiterate, the modern and the traditional, the tolerant and the intolerant, the ignorant and the enlightened.

Allow me to tell you preliminarily what this book is not. An area studies specialist expecting a meticulous historical account of a social world will be remiss to find little of the sort here. What I offer instead is a series of readings that circle back on the relationship between words and worlds. Although I take the social world of texts quite seriously, I do so to consider the imaginative force of words in configuring worlds. In this sense, I consider worlds foreclosed by particular modes of reading. I admit here the circularity of this endeavor—reading about the vanishing point of reading, the horizon of the literary itself. It is an endeavor, though, meant to allow for the consideration of literature not as a neutral medium through which stories materialize, but as a practice that comes to dictate how to read, respond to, and understand the world. As we see with the opening of Hussein's autobiography, what remains in the shadow of world literature are textual forms and modes of experience no longer thinkable in a modern literary paradigm.

Looking at the interwoven strands of modernization, literature, and secularism, this book ultimately raises a number of questions concerning the assumed universalism of world literature. The sections that follow here in the introduction trace three different axes of inquiry: literary modernity in Egypt, reading worlds, and secularism. The first axis of the book considers *how* literature comes to be read with the rise of the modern Egyptian state, pedagogical reforms, and demands for critical literacy. Who or what authorizes what it means to read properly? What relationship between a reader and text does literature imply? How does literary reading differ from memorization? The second axis engages the relationship between an emergent category of literature and the world in which it is read. How is literature productive of the terms within which the world is understood? Who or what is excluded from this world, and how does the line between literacy and illiteracy sanction forms of participation in it? And the third axis considers the relationship between literature—as a discipline increasingly aligned with moral education—and debates around secularism and religion. How is literary reading indebted to and different from traditions of scriptural hermeneutics? In what ways is literature transformative of religious traditions? Is the world of world literature necessarily secular? What are the limits of this literary world?

In dialogue with debates in comparative literature and postcolonial studies, *In the Shadow of World Literature* questions the grounds of comparison across literary traditions.[7] We have grown accustomed to understanding the terrain of world literature as a conglomeration of national or linguistic traditions (relating French, German, Russian, and Kiswahili literature, for example), and we have grown accustomed to aesthetic categories as a basic unit in literary history (distinguishing between romanticism and modernism, for example). What I propose in the following pages gestures to a different type of analysis. If we link world literature to the sensibilities it presumes its readers to possess, then how do we trace these sensibilities across differing textual practices and traditions? This book ultimately claims that world literature is not the neutral meeting ground of a variety of textual practices, but rather assumes—and at times enforces—a particular place for literature in the world.

LITERARY MODERNITY IN COLONIAL EGYPT

Nineteenth-century Egypt is not only a meeting ground for the French, British, and Ottoman Empires, but also secures its place within a conventional narrative of modernization, including the consolidation of the modern state, increasing urbanization, and educational, legal, and religious reforms. Within modern Arab historiography, the nineteenth century is the period of the *nahḍah*—the moment when the Arab world undergoes a sort of renaissance and awakens from its supposed dormancy.[8] The *nahḍah* tends to be described as consisting of four historical moments, each of which underscores the broader phenomenon of modernization. First, Napoleon's invasion in 1798 is often understood to introduce the basis for a modern military, modern medicine, and the arts and sciences to Egypt. Second, the reign of Muhammad 'Ali (Muḥammad 'Alī Bāshā) (1805–48) coincides with a push for educational reform, which sees the emergence of a number of modern schools and a series of missions to France for training in the sciences, engineering, medicine, and languages. Third, toward the latter half of the nineteenth century, scholars Jamal al-Din al-Afghani (Jamāl al-Dīn al-Afghānī) and his disciple Muhammad 'Abduh (Muḥammad 'Abduh) are integral to an intellectual reformation of Arabic law and letters. During this same period, other scholars participate in expanding the Arabic language to accommodate new words based on Arabic grammatical principles, ultimately modernizing what had been taught as a traditionalist language. Last, the fourth moment entails the emergence of a national consciousness defined in terms of modern citizenship. As the conventional narrative of the *nahḍah* has it, this period of rebirth culminates in the uprising in 1919, the consolidation of the Wafdist movement, and the development of an Egyptian state.[9]

Although I deal with the dominant story of modernization, I am not working here as a literary historian, nor am I offering an account of how or why transformations occur. I am not trying to confirm or refute, empirically or otherwise, the terms in which the *nahḍah* is understood so much as I am pointing to its implications for the study of literature.[10] The once-common literary history of the Arab world points to the *nahḍah* as a sociocultural phenomenon inseparable from the rise of modern Arabic literature.[11] During the nineteenth century, Arab writers translate the works of authors such as Molière, Dumas, and Shakespeare into Arabic, and help forge the rise of the novel, as well as innovations in poetry, theater, and the short story. But this modernization story actually does more than merely recount the origins of modern Arabic literature—in effect, it produces a new understanding of literature aligned with the rise of the public sphere, the pedagogical reformulation of reading practices, and the institutionalization of literature as a field of study. In a rather explicit manner, the story of the *nahḍah*, which casts modernization as a passage from ignorance to enlightenment, becomes integral to the redefinition of literature and the semiotic ideology it comes to delimit.[12]

My argument is *not* that literature, known in Arabic as *adab*, is born with the colonial encounter, but rather that it is redefined through modernization, extending from Napoleon's arrival to Muhammad ʿAli's reforms and on through the period of British occupation. Where previously *adab* implied cultivated knowledge as well as character, conduct, and manners, with Egypt's modernization *adab* comes to refer to literature in a different sense, closely linked to the discourse of world literature and the emergence of transnational literary genres.[13] Within the context of Arabic letters, the term *adab* has a longer history, certainly predating the arrival of the French. During the Abbasid Caliphate in the ninth century, *adab* referred quite explicitly to norms of conduct with connotations of urbanity and being well-bred. On one hand, the term *adīb* (*udabāʾ* pl.) was used to describe one who was cultured, was educated, and had refined taste, and still tends to refer to someone with refined sensibilities. And on the other hand, *adab* was also understood as a genre of writing describing courtly conduct and proper behavior, often associated with figures such as al-Jahiz (al-Jāḥiẓ) in the ninth century and later al-Tawhidi (al-Tawḥīdī).[14]

Over the course of the nineteenth century, these connotations do not disappear, but *adab* acquires an additional meaning. The term comes to refer to new literary forms such as short stories and the novel, written in Arabic and circulated in printed form as books, journals, or newspapers. This new connotation of *adab* involves a transformation in print culture, education, and concepts of authorship. What emerges in this process is a model of the world republic of letters in which Goethe and Shakespeare stand alongside figures such as Hafiz Ibrahim (Ḥāfiẓ Ibrāhīm), Muhammad al-Muwaylihi (Muḥammad al-Muwayliḥī), and Tawfiq al-Hakim (Tawfīq al-Ḥakīm) in the pantheon of literary greats, all of them comparable across time, languages, and traditions in the universalizable idiom of literature. Not only is there a transformation in what comes to be recognized as literature, but there is also an emergent figure of the *Adīb*, whose conduct and manners relate to a cosmopolitanism and erudition geared for a modernizing world. Literature thus comes to envelop a host of textual practices and to delimit a particular set of manners and sensibilities.

Alongside an account in which modern Arabic literature secures its place in world literature, another story comes into play. In this march to modernization and the rise of literacy, we confront the emergence of an entire population deemed illiterate and a series of practices and institutions deemed traditional, rigid, and backward. The chapters that follow trace not only the narrative of modernization, the contours of this redefined domain linking literature, literacy, and print culture, but also the narrative against which the story of modernization is told. In order for nineteenth-century Egypt to be seen as moving forward, it reinvents those traditions from which it claims to develop. In this process, in the redefinition of literacy and competing demands for a different type of education geared for the modern world, there emerges an entire class deemed illiterate, ignorant, and lacking in education.

The story of Egypt's modernization is thus hardly the story of overcoming the past, but a matter of examining how this past comes to be refashioned, redefined, and ultimately integral to the ethical formation of the modern critical subject. The mutually constitutive relationship between the past and the future is ultimately inseparable from the emergence of the modern world. My book does not affirm the distinctions between the modern and the traditional, the secular and the religious, the educated and the ignorant, but investigates how these distinctions are secured in the story of modernization—and how, in turn, they become intrinsic to literary education.

Where world literature distinguishes between national, historical, and linguistic differences, *In the Shadow of World Literature* suggests that the domain of world literature shares in common a normative definition of literature linked to a particular semiotic ideology. By prying apart the historically contingent distinction between the literate and the illiterate, I am asking here for a consideration of world literature as a question of ethics, torn between the values and sensibilities of a new definition of the literary and those excluded from it. This is not a relativistic claim that we have different types of readers in the world republic of letters, nor is it a call to broaden definitions of literature to incorporate more textual traditions in its domain—it is, instead, an effort to map the normative force of world literature and the limits of the cosmopolitan sensibilities it implies.[15]

READING BEYOND REPRESENTATION

By engaging problems in world literature through a history of reading in nineteenth-century and early twentieth-century Egypt, I am implicitly arguing for a new set of questions with which to approach world literature. In addition to asking how literature plays out in a particular location at a particular point in time, I am asking about the reading practice necessary for a text to be recognized as an object of literary analysis. What is at stake, for example, in the recognition of scripture as literature? What is the difference between the memorization of the Qur'an and its analysis as a literary text? How is it that, in nineteenth-century Egypt, memorization ceases to be understood as literacy? What are the new attributes of literary reading? How might we understand the relationship between literary reading, critique, and the pedagogical reforms of the modern liberal state? These sorts of questions animate a shift from the analysis of literature as a product of national histories and authors to consider how the category of literature transforms and reconstitutes textual traditions.

Consider the ways and extent to which literary scholars relate to texts deemed literary under the rubric of representation. Within the field of postcolonial studies, for example, literature is commonly read as it both participates in and refutes the terms of colonialism. On the one hand, literature is the site of a colonial imaginary with characterizations of a despotic and spiritual East—in texts ranging from Percy Shelley's *The Revolt of Islam* to Gustave Flaubert's *Salammbô*.[16] We analyze these canonical literary texts for their repertoire of stereotypes and imperial fantasies, drawing either directly or indirectly from methods brought to light in Edward Said's *Orientalism* as a means of addressing the role of representation in the construction of the Orient. On the other hand, though, literature is also understood as the seemingly redemptive site through which colonial stereotypes can be mimicked, appropriated, and ultimately subverted.[17] The writings of a figure like 'Abdullah Nadim ('Abd Allāh al-Nadīm), for example, come to be read as enacting anticolonial resistance by recounting stories integral to the emergence of national consciousness at the time of the British occupation.[18] In either case, whether dealing with colonial stereotypes or anticolonial resistance, postcolonial studies tend to frame the colonial encounter in terms of conflicting and often-embattled representations, and time and again we turn to the literary text as the site through which to consider the problem of colonialism.

What I find striking is not so much the analysis of literary images, stereotypes, and caricatures, but that an exclusive focus on literary texts as representations tends to displace alternate understandings of literature—namely, literature as a disciplined reading practice or a cultivated sensibility linked to civil norms of what it means to be educated. Undoubtedly a corpus of canonical texts furnishes references and associations for those within the world republic of letters, but literature, in the nineteenth century, is not only the accumulation of canonical literary texts, but also an emergent discipline training how to read.[19] Inasmuch as literature is both a canon of texts and the practice by which to read them, it comes to delimit sensibilities and critical skills inseparable from what it means to be modern, cosmopolitan, and educated. This particular understanding plays out in accounts that relate the rise of modern literature to the developmental narrative of the *nahḍah*, and it also plays out when describing those deemed backward, intolerant, and provincial. Within this framework, what it means to be literate entails much more than learning to decode words written on a page or to recognize the caricatures of a colonized people—it comes to imply the cultivation of critical-thinking skills essential to informed participation in a modern state . . . or so the story goes.

If, though, we step back and consider how literature is constituted at a particular point in time, then we usher in the possibility of determining what it is defined against. Crucial to a narrative that sees literary education as an engine of modernization is not only a representation of literature's Other, but a moral argument about the apparent need to eliminate ignorance through education. Not only does literature come to demarcate new modes of being recognizably civilized, but it does so against those deemed products of religious zealotry and hidebound fanaticism. Where the literate mind is seen to be critical, detached, and unfettered by structures of authority, fanaticism tends to be explained in terms of causes—the product of an impoverished environment, inequitable social conditions, and lacking education. And inasmuch as the fanatic is understood according to causes, it delimits an almost indefensible position, for, in the end, to be recognized as a fanatic is to be understood as sociologically determined. In contrast to those who are understood to offer arguments, critical interventions, and strategies within modern politics, the fanatic is most commonly understood through the conditions that lead to a position—and here we might think of a common tendency to explain obedience to competing authority through sociologically derived explanations.

Focusing on the limits of world literature means focusing on the specter of the fanatic as the counterpart to the critical-thinking, cosmopolitan orientation at play in the world republic of letters. This is not a matter of representation in terms of depicting one subject versus another, but a matter of considering the disciplines necessary to being recognized as a critical subject. If the critical subject is considered freethinking insofar as she is not socially determined in her positions, then the fanatic is seen as uncritical and indelibly linked to religious structures of authority. This book is an argument that the world of world literature is not solely a matter of national and political boundaries, but a matter of the sensibilities embedded in the value attributed to literary reading and haunted by the specter of what gets deemed fanaticism. It is an effort to reorient literary study to consider how it is that literary reading informs rather particular sensibilities and how it is that textual practices are transformed in the process.

THE MORAL UNIVERSE OF A SECULAR WORLD

Not only does this book engage with colonial history and literary studies, it also attempts to assert a role for literature as a site within the contested terrain of secularism. On the one hand, there are those for whom secularism implies tolerance, critical detachment, and religious freedom; and on the other hand, there are those for whom the term implies the subordination of religious practice to belief and the redefinition of humanity in terms of political rights. I intervene in these discussions by investigating how literature relates to secularism, both as an instrument of moral instruction in secular schools and as a concept that informs modern understandings of time, subjectivity, knowledge, and imagination.[20] I draw from the work of scholars such as Talal Asad, Saba Mahmood, Charles Taylor, and Michael Warner, in suggesting that secularism actively defines religion, universalizes liberal notions of rights, and redefines the meaning of personhood.[21] In this framework, secularism is not the neutral detachment of religion from matters of the state, but the active involvement of the state in defining and delimiting what constitutes religion.[22] Secularism, in other words, demarcates the place of religion in the world.

It is by now a commonplace to point out that the conflation of secularism and modernization is more of a predominant myth than any empirical reality, and I share in questioning the presumptions that suggest secularism is a form of disenchantment or is linked to the decline of religion. In *A Secular Age*, Charles Taylor astutely points to the questionable subtraction theory of the secular, which sees modernization as the waning of religious belief in favor of the rise of science, and he points us in the direction of asking about the new conditions of belief in the modern age.[23] But secularism is not solely a matter of belief, and a scholar like Talal Asad richly models ways of looking at secularism as a practice with vast implications for the study of modern politics.[24] In Asad's work, secularism is the site from which to consider discourses on multiculturalism, governmentality, and human rights, and pertains not only to practices of the state, but to the affective dimensions of modern politics.

Drawing from these discussions, I am not proposing that secularization entails the waning of religion, nor am I arguing that secularism replaces religion, but instead I focus on what secularism does in redefining religion as part of modern life. With this understanding in mind, literature becomes a rich site not only as a pedagogical matter for cultivating a modern aesthetic sensibility, but also for the renegotiation of the terms through which reading, response, and representation play out. I see literary reading as a practice integral to secular education, but linking literature and the secular also animates my consideration of world literature in two additional ways: first, as relates to the world that grounds world literature, and second, as pertains to the aesthetic categories employed in literary history. Taking secularism as a point of departure entails rethinking some of the basic categories employed for literary analysis.

Where the vocabulary of national publics often grounds the study of world literature, secularism offers two competing conceptions of worldliness. On the one hand, secularism is often understood as it derives from the Latin term *saeculum*, which bears an etymological relationship to the current age or the world.[25] In Arabic, secularism tends to be commonly translated with the term *'almānīyah*, which, like *saeculum*, shares the root (*'a-l-m*) with the word for world (*'ālam*) and has connotations of both worldly and international (*'ālamī*).[26] In this understanding, we could say that the world of world literature is secular insofar as it pertains to the various national traditions that compose it—world literature, in other words, is the international meeting ground of national literature on a global scale. There are also scholars who link secularism to the term *'ilmānīyah*, the root of which (*'i-l-m*) relates to science and knowledge, which, one could say, would link secularism to discussions of the modern disciplines, science and reason.

On the other hand, though, there is another connotation to the term "secular." Where *'almānīyah* offers one possible translation for secularism, it does not necessarily evoke worldliness as it contrasts with the otherworldly. In Arabic, this understanding of the world is translated with the term *dunyā*, and the ensuing *nisbah* form, *dunyawī*, refers to being worldly, mundane, secular, earthly, or temporal. The distinction, then, between secularism as a matter of the world (in terms of internationalism) or as a matter of the worldly activities (as against otherworldliness) has profound implications for literature. Part of my goal here is to consider world literature as the negotiated terrain between these two understandings of the worldliness at stake in discussions of secularism. A question to be considered, then, is not only how literature is grounded in the world, but how it participates in the imagination of what this world is.

In addition to the geographical dimensions of world literature, secularism also complicates many of the aesthetic categories integral to literary history. A number of important studies link secularism and literature as part of a history of aesthetics in the West. Most frequently, literary scholars point to ways that romanticism negotiates secularism, religion, and aesthetics, offering the literary as the secularization of religious aesthetics. We might think here to the scholarship of Colin Jager and of Jean-Luc Nancy and Philippe Lacoue-Labarthe as two possible means of understanding the richness of this relationship between romanticism and literature as pertains to secularism.[27] Other studies point to developments within biblical hermeneutics as an indication of broader shifts in the history of knowledge and the rise of skepticism, noting, for example, the emergence of the Bible in the vernacular and in narrative form.[28] Many rich studies in this field take a history of reading and transformations in the scholarly relationship to scripture as the basis for an approach to thinking about secularism.

In either of these cases, whether secularism is considered as intrinsic to romanticism or as indebted to biblical hermeneutics, most of these stories offer an account that presumes the context of a supposedly Christian Europe and a reading public aligned with the national population under consideration. But nineteenth-century Egypt does not fit neatly within this broad story. My purpose here is not necessarily to refute the claims being made by these scholars, but to consider an alternate terrain within which the definition of literature is not a simply imported from modern European history.[29] The categories used for literary analysis are themselves presumed within a narrative that links the British, French, German, and Russian traditions through accounts of epic poetry, theater, realism, naturalism, romanticism, and beyond. Were Egypt and modern Arabic literature to be cast in these terms, it would always appear on some sort of aesthetic lag—as though catching up to the European model was the goal in a grand narrative of literary achievement. If we understand European literatures to have wrestled with romanticism during the eighteenth and early nineteenth centuries, then how do we account for the emergence of romantic poetry in the Arab world at the end of the nineteenth century and the beginning of the twentieth? Seeing literary history in these developmentalist terms only ever points to the challenge of comparative literary study, that is, the primary question of what grounds the terms of comparison. Why is it that this story of literary development so often marks Europe as the model?

If nineteenth-century Egypt allows us to question the basis of a model of literary development, it also leads us to question the historical inevitability of secularism. Many recent studies cast secularism as a phase or logical development out of Christian theology in Western Europe. The work of Marcel Gauchet, Jean-Luc Nancy, and, to a certain extent, Charles Taylor all tends to frame secularism as it pertains to a particular faith tradition, most often stemming from Protestant reformations within Western Christendom.[30] Looking at a colonial context, however, the boundedness of this tradition gets thrown into question. If secularism is the necessary outgrowth of Christianity, how do we understand the wave of theological reforms within Islam under figures such as Muhammad ʻAbduh to Jamal al-Din al-Afghani? In what ways does secularism play out within the colonial context of a predominantly non-Christian population?

This book does not take an examination of nineteenth- and early twentieth-century Egypt as an exception to secularism, nor as a case of secularism's imperial travel—instead, in what follows, I consider how the encounter between modern education and the conventions of Qur'anic schooling realigns the terms of literary study. The challenge and the provocation offered by literature is precisely its redefined role within the domain of secular governance—and this is a matter not solely of theology, nor of literary history, but of the transformative role of literary reading in cultivating the sensibilities deemed integral to critical engagement in the world.

A USER'S GUIDE

Focusing on transformations of literary culture in colonial Egypt, the following six chapters navigate a path between world literature understood as the transnational trafficking of texts, on the one hand, and the world-making function of texts, on the other. I draw inspiration from recent scholarship on the anthropology of the secular to think differently about literature—as both a category of text and a pedagogical practice. The general argument of the book posits an expansion of world literature beyond the analysis of texts in terms of cultural systems and meanings (the domain of both Saidian worldliness and Geertzian-inspired new historicism) in order to consider the ethics and disciplines of reading that emerge in the late nineteenth and twentieth centuries. I thus shift my attention from a focus on literary texts as objects to attend to the reading practices that constitute the contours of world literature, and I consider how world literature may be less an amalgamation of cultural traditions than the globalization of a way of reading. Doing so means not simply comparing across traditions, as though all are intrinsically equal, but considering the texture of the traditions and the arguments to which they give rise. The colonial encounter in nineteenth-century Egypt is one site crucial for considering the role of ethics and cultural difference, but it is also formative of generalizable concepts of the literary. Each of the six chapters traces the emergence of literary reading alongside colonial concerns with the methods of Qur'anic education and the extent of illiteracy in the colonized population.

When I first set out to write this book, I was compelled by an interest in exploring the place of Arabic literary traditions within discussions of world literature. I was lured initially to rehearse some of the classical tensions between the universal and the particular. There were those like Johann Gottfried Herder who address the particularities of specific literary traditions as reflective of distinct national characteristics; and there were those like Karl Marx and Friedrich Engels who provide a frame for thinking of world literature as the standardization of literary forms across territories, languages, and traditions.[31] These competing pathways were indeed appealing to me. The generic formulation of something called world literature, I was tempted to argue, does little to confront the particularities of the Arabic literary tradition. The place of Arabic within world literature, it seemed to me, should account for how Arabic literature anticipated many of the arguments currently in vogue—but did so in the eighth and ninth centuries. I was inclined to make a turn to history to emphasize contours of debates about literature during this period, noting how these arguments play out even in the period we call modern and how they impact the work of a writer like Taha Hussein.[32]

But this sort of argument—one that turns to history to insist on a linguistic or national exceptionality—both produces a linguistic or national tradition as something purified from foreign or presentist influence, on the one hand, and overlooks that the condition of particularity is already conceded in the generality of world literature, on the other. The question to be considered, then, is not how Arabic literary traditions either adhere to or are exceptional from other literary traditions, but instead, what it is that literature, as a category capable of having national and linguistic determination, comes to mean in the nineteenth and twentieth centuries. A central paradox of the term "literature" is that it refers both to a text (a novel, poem, or play) and to a discipline and manner of learning. It is a word whose meaning folds back upon itself, defined by a circularity in which a text is recognized as literary in part by how it is read. In the nineteenth century, comparative grammarians trace a philosophy of language across the world, and stories become narratives, grammar becomes systems, and forms become structures intelligible to inquiry outside an immediate context. In the early twentieth century, formalist critics refract literary texts through the lens of linguistic patterns, turns of phrase, and details that give rise to various narrational modes. In what follows, I take disciplines, practices, and sensibilities to be as inseparable from the understanding of literary form as the institutions (libraries, presses, or schools) that make the concept of literature itself thinkable.

Each of the six chapters takes a key term in the study of world literature as a framework for the analysis of a specific site of reading. You will notice in what follows that these chapters trace an arc that spans the borders of a literary world through to the development of literary institutions, the cultivation of readers, and ultimately the rise and limits of a modern literary public. Where the first few chapters deal broadly with the world in which we read, chapters 5 and 6 model ways of reading literary texts with attention to questions of literary formations. The book, then, can be read from start to finish as a narrative arc that progresses somewhat historically—or alternatively, as select chapters meant to sketch out specific debates in world literature.

The first chapter considers the *world* of world literature—understood as either the site at which a literary work is produced (for world systems theory) or the site disclosed in the literary work itself (through practices of close reading). The chapter links the scholarship of Franco Moretti, Pascale Casanova, and Edward Said in order to consider dominant frames for understanding world literature. These different frames are interwoven with selected scenes from modern Egypt: the first, the protests on the streets of Cairo of a Syrian novel deemed blasphemous, and the second, the awarding of the Nobel Prize to Naguib Mahfouz (Najīb Maḥfūẓ). In both cases, arguments about how to read properly delimit what literature is and how it ought to be understood. The chapter draws from Said's notion of secular criticism in order to claim that reading—and not solely textuality—should be understood as worldly activity with a normative force across interpretative communities.

If the first chapter presents a case for the site of reading in world literature, then the second considers translation in terms of how a particular relationship to language is born with the decoding of the Rosetta Stone. It tells the story of how an object, the Rosetta Stone, becomes a text to be deciphered, decoded, and analyzed by an international network of scholars. What is discovered with the Rosetta Stone, the chapter argues, is less an *object* than it is a particular *textuality* based on an understanding of language as a code. The chapter suggests that the translational ethic that points to the equivalence of Greek and hieroglyphics actually levels the political and theological distinctions between the three languages: Greek, the language of politics, demotic, and hieroglyphics, the language of the gods. This phenomenological leveling of languages is ultimately read in relation to the comparative gesture of world literature, which levels distinctions between literature and scripture under an emergent paradigm of modern literary reading.

The third chapter addresses the pedagogical instantiation of literature as a disciplined practice and looks at the role of education in the writings of Lord Cromer and Alfred Milner. For both of these colonial administrators, learning to read critically entails much more than learning to decipher words, sounds, and meanings; it comes to imply the cultivation of sensibilities necessary to the supposedly virtuous ends of liberal government. Drawing from distinctions between *taʿlīm* (instruction) and *tarbiyah* (cultivation), as well as opinions versus prejudice, the chapter charts the role of reading as part of a broader conceptualization of education, civic participation, and the colonial Egyptian state.

Building on discussions of education in the colonial state, the fourth chapter considers transformations in the connotation of the term "literature" in Arabic with the rise of literary study as a modern discipline. Moving between the institutional foundations of modern literary study in Egypt, a footnote from Jurji Zaydan's (Jurjī Zaydān) literary history of Arabic letters, and reflections on literature by the Orientalist H.A.R. Gibb, the chapter considers how definitions of the literary turn on assertions of how to read, respond, and relate to texts. This convergence of literature and *adab* ultimately enables an alternate genealogy of world literature—one based less on the accumulation of texts than on an emergent global discipline.

The second half of the project shifts from discussions of the literary field in order to address specific textual occasions in which reading, perceiving, and responding animate interpretative questions. The fifth chapter focuses on debates that highlight competing conceptions of critique as brought to light by discussions of Charles Darwin. I focus on a section of Naguib Mahfouz's novel, *Qaṣr al-shawq* (Palace of Desire), in which the youngest son, Kamal, publishes an article on Darwin in an Arabic-language journal. I cast this fictionalized incident alongside the Lewis Affair, in which a professor at the Syrian Protestant College, Edwin Lewis, resigns over a scandal involving his evocation of Darwin during a commencement address. Where Edwin Lewis emerges as a martyr for academic freedom in the Arab world, Kamal negotiates his relationship to his family's response to his work differently. In both cases, a literary sensibility comes into conflict with what it casts as its fanatical counterpart, and the argument for or against Darwin turns more upon conflicting understandings of what is appropriate than on any presumption about the validity of Darwin's propositions. The chapter examines the presumptions at play in critical response and its connection to modern education.

The sixth chapter also performs a reading of a literary text, but does so against the backdrop of André Gide's correspondence with Taha Hussein. The chapter begins by analyzing the transformation of theological questions into literature in a set of letters exchanged between the two authors, and it follows by asking about the world that literature makes thinkable. This discussion is followed by an imaginary correspondence staged in Hussein's novel that recounts the story of a friendship between two intellectuals from the same village. These two epistolary exchanges—between writers across national and linguistic boundaries, in the first instance, and between writers from the same village, in the second—lead to an argument about the inherent provincialism of the world republic of letters.

At a time when scholars face the waning of secular nationalist movements and the global rise of religion, it is worth approaching the field of world literature differently—doing so, however, means bracketing the presumptive autonomy of literature as a field of study and investigating its institutionalization in a new light. Drawing from the work of social scientists, who raise important questions regarding the relation between colonial institutions and knowledge production, and postcolonial literary scholars, who investigate how literature mediates the interactions between the colonizer and the colonized, *In the Shadow of World Literature* ultimately bridges political theory, religious studies, and anthropology toward an enriched understanding of the contours and limits of a literary world.

1

WORLD

The World of World Literature

Over the past few decades, literary scholarship has come to deal increasingly with the analysis of literature in a global framework. Issues such as globalization, migration, colonialism, and cosmopolitanism inflect how we think about our endeavor as literary scholars, and we often question the parameters offered by national languages and literatures as sites for the study of literary form. When, for example, Martin Seymour-Smith writes his introduction to *The New Guide to Modern World Literature*, he insists on the importance of broad definitions with which to account for the wide variety of national and textual traditions: "I have kept definitions as broad as possible: our understanding of literature does not benefit from attempts to narrow down the meaning of terms too precisely: the terms themselves lose their value."[1] Whatever distinctions are drawn between languages and nations, we are led to believe that literature is a universal category with which to understand a variety of narrative arts and textual practices. And world literature, in particular, provides the disciplinary terrain from which to analyze the full range of literary forms available—poetry, oral traditions, novels, short stories, theater, and film across a number of national literatures.

Beyond expanding definitions of literature, though, what is the world that grounds world literature? Does the world of world literature consist of the social conditions in which it is written—nineteenth-century England for Dickens or twentieth-century Japan for Mishima? Or is its world the imaginative domain of its stories—Combray in Proust's *À la recherche du temps perdu* (In Search of Lost Time) or Shahryar's palace in *Kitāb alf laylah wa-laylah* (One Thousand and One Nights)? For many of those offering responses, the apparent opposition implicit in these two questions is not quite as stark as it might seem initially—the world *of* literature and the world *in* literature are invariably entangled. When analyzing literary texts, we are often drawn to the interactions between political geography, which maps the social world, and aesthetic considerations, which map the particularities of literary form. And in turn, we are led to the intersection between area studies, including history, sociology, and anthropology, and literary studies, including language, linguistics, and aesthetics. Scholars ranging from Sarah Lawall to Franco Moretti and from Pascale Casanova to David Damrosch help to negotiate the implicit tension between locating texts geographically and aesthetically, and in a variety of ways, each ultimately enriches the contested domain of world literature.[2] At the intersection of numerous converging methods, world literature might appear as the logical outgrowth of discussions of transnationalism, postcolonialism, and cultural mobility, and as the opportunity to push literary studies into the twenty-first century.

Although it is tempting to see world literature as a domain beyond the boundaries of national literatures and languages, I want to suggest that the world of world literature has boundaries of a different sort. Even with its broadened definitions, world literature still presumes the centrality of an object understood as literature, capable of both traversing national differences and uniting a variety of textual forms. How, I wonder, might we consider the exclusions to this literary world? In what follows, I analyze texts not to suggest what they mean, but to ask about the conditions and terms in which they become meaningful as texts. This is less a matter of assessing how formal qualities determine meaning than of analyzing the contours of a world within which a text comes to be read as literature. What are the conditions for a text to be recognized as literature? In what ways does world literature define what literature is? How is a text included in the domain of world literature? Posing these questions also means asking about the normative limits of the literary: What falls outside, or on the margins, of world literature? How do presumptions about what literature is impact how a text is read? What practices are necessary to be recognized as a literary reader? And last, to return to the world in world literature, what world does literature make imaginable? Is there a force to the literary imagination that delimits how the world should be known? Is the world of world literature understood differently in history? This chapter is an effort to propose a different relationship between literature and the world. My argument is that the world of world literature is neither timeless nor universal, but contingent upon a series of practices, norms, and sensibilities integral to recognizing certain texts as literature and certain practices of response as reading.

In literature departments, when asked to situate a literary text, we tend to turn to the language or national tradition from which it stems—English departments tend to deal with the Anglophone world, French departments with the Francophone world, and even departments of comparative literature reaffirm, to some extent, the analysis of texts within national or linguistic canons. Rather than see the language or national tradition in which a text is written as the determinant of its meaning, I am arguing here for an analysis of the category of literature as it plays out in the world of readers. In doing so, I focus less on a text than on the practices that consecrate it as a literary object, and I thus consider the contingency of literature within the world in which it is read. A history of the category is ultimately a call for a more robust and embedded literary history—one that entangles literature and the world by considering the transformation of publics, reading practices, and institutions as they are situated over time. This embedded history situates literature within and among the competing traditions and sensibilities inflecting how the category comes to matter in the world, and it considers world literature as the negotiated site between those deemed readers and those unrecognizable as such.

Against any metaphysical postulation of what literature is, this chapter traces predominant paradigms in the field of world literature, all in an effort to investigate the relationship between worldliness, secularism, and the conditions of belonging in the world republic of letters. In the first half of the chapter, I address world literature as pertains to recognition—initially in the Nobel Prize speech for the Egyptian novelist, Naguib Mahfouz, and then in Pascale Casanova's conception of world literary space. And in the second half of the chapter, I consider the world implicit in Edward Said's notion of worldliness and secular criticism. I frame each of these two poles, world literary space and secular criticism, in the context of the controversy surrounding a novel by the Syrian writer Haydar Haydar. Looking closely at responses to this literary scandal, I ask about who or what speaks on behalf of literature and who is excluded from its domain. By framing literature as a contested category between interpretative communities, I move here from a world understood in terms of nation-states and languages to a world understood in terms of sensibilities delimited and cultivated through literature. And I move from a world of literary works and celebrated authors to a world of those impacted by the social life of a text. At its most ambitious, this first chapter is an argument that the world of world literature may not be as universal and timeless as we are often led to believe.

THE CONSTRAINTS OF DEMOCRATIC CRITICISM

In September 2000, writing in the *New Left Review*, Sabry Hafez described the controversial Egyptian publication of *Walīmah li-aʿshāb al-baḥr* (A Banquet for Seaweed) by the Syrian writer Haydar Haydar (Ḥaydar Ḥaydar).[3] The novel recounts the story of two leftist Iraqi intellectuals, both of whom flee Saddam Hussein's regime to Algeria, where they find themselves equally disillusioned with Boumédienne. Through the grim daily life of these two disaffected intellectuals, Haydar imagines the plight of the Iraqi Communist

Party framed within a tale of parallel revolutions—the first, the failed liberation of Iraq under the ICP, and the second, the liberation of Algeria under the FLN. As literary critics in the Middle East and abroad have remarked, Haydar's novel is an occasion to reflect on the waning of the secular left, the rise of Islamic social movements, and the emergence of autocratic dictators across the Middle East. For its admiring readers, the novel lends texture to the political, social, and imaginative landscape of pan-Arabism and the visceral challenges faced by the intellectual in the modern Middle East.

At first glance, the world quite explicitly described in the novel would appear to align with the world in which the novel is received. As it tends to be understood, the novel bespeaks intellectuals' discontent with postcolonial states in the Middle East and with the increasing visibility of Islamic movements as a force in the public sphere. The founding of the Islamic Republic in Iran, the rise of the FIS in Algeria, and the war against the Soviets in Afghanistan all tend to be seen as the basis for the rise of religion across the region. Both Haydar's novel and Hafez's article share in their apparent embrace of this conventional account and the world it describes—a world torn between the secular left and the rise of religion.

When Hafez writes his passionate article on the pages of the *New Left Review*, he is notably less concerned with the story in the novel than with the story of the novel's reception—and in particular its reception in Egypt, years after the initial publication, by an audience less than admiring of Haydar's work. *Walīmah li-aʿshāb al-baḥr* was first published in Cyprus in 1983 to immediate critical acclaim. Subsequent editions appeared in Damascus and Beirut, and in 2000 the Egyptian Ministry of Culture reprinted the novel in a series dedicated to modern Arabic literature. As Hafez's account has it, Muhammad ʿAbbas, working for the Egyptian newspaper, *al-Shaʿb* (The People), published scathing condemnations of the novel that claimed it was, in effect, blasphemous. The accusations were especially pointed—according to those incensed by the novel, Haydar juxtaposed a reference to the Qur'an with an expletive.[4] Contentious as the accusations were, they revolved around what many in the literary community understood to be the decontextualization of select passages. Nonetheless, the reviews and articles escalated over a few weeks, and bowing to rising pressures, the Egyptian government eventually discussed withdrawing the novel from circulation. Meanwhile, with tensions rising, a number of students protested the novel at the Islamic university al-Azhar. On the streets surrounding the university, rallying around a novel that moved them to action, they were met and fired upon by the Egyptian police. In the end, one hundred fifty protesters were hospitalized from wounds suffered during the attacks.

For a critic like Hafez, the story surrounding Haydar's novel reads as a tragedy—the defeat of free speech, and more broadly, of "secular and rationalist culture" on account of a most curious misreading.[5] Hafez laments the fact that Haydar's work fell victim to calls for censorship, and worse yet, that many of the students protesting had not so much as read the book before taking to the street. "Ironically," he writes, "given that the first word of the Qur'an is the imperative *iqra'* (read!), students of the Azhar do not need to perform this deed before they demonstrate."[6] His comments echo responses to protests surrounding Salman Rushdie's *The Satanic Verses*, in which critics commonly suggest that angry readers either misread the literary complexity of crucial passages or misunderstand the artistic play of a literary text.[7] A critical reader understands not only the language of a text, but the appropriate manner of responding to and analyzing the subtleties of a literary work. What it means to be literate, in such discussions, far exceeds the bounds of linguistic comprehension—being a good reader, it seems, comes to entail a number of presumptions about the appropriate place of literature, aesthetics, and criticism. For the protesting students, literature is hardly the disinterested domain of poetic playfulness, formal innovation, and the infinite unraveling of an eternally complex text. Instead, literature delineates a field of representation, a semiotic ideology, whose apparent importance is enforced by the gunfire of Egyptian police.[8]

The conflict over Haydar's novel reveals not only how certain stories matter differently to different audiences, but also passionate attachments to the category of literature. In this instance, many intellectuals perceived literature and the freedom of speech to be under attack. The debates following the events subordinated the violence against the protesting students to the violence that the protests were seen to have enacted on literature. The literary community tended to focus on the protesters as fanatical, uneducated zealots, whose grievances not only were misguided, but also resulted from religious indoctrination. When, weeks later, newspapers covered the fight against legal proceedings to withdraw the novel, they emphasized the intellectuals' solidarity with the editors of the novel.[9] In a curious twist of logic, the issue was framed as freedom of speech, but the speech to be defended was the literary text and *not* the students' protest. What was at stake was ultimately a defense of a book from its public—in a word, a defense through which the literary establishment purged supposedly fanatical reading from its domain. In this process, not only did the logic of rights shift from protesting students to the rights of literature, but the students' activism was itself relegated to the domain of the irrational. It was only by seeing the students as misguided and ignorant that they were understood to have suffered in the attacks. And even then, their suffering was seen to derive from the unfortunate conditions of their apparent indoctrination.

My point is not to argue that the students ought to be understood as having properly read the text, but to consider how it is that the category of literature is secured in the contention between publics. More than a matter of misrecognition, the story surrounding Haydar's novel offers an account of who polices the proper interpretation of a literary text. From the pages of the newspaper to the orders of the state courts, the actions on the street quite palpably unfurl conflicting interpretations in the world of literature. Interpretation here implies not only a hermeneutic question of what a passage means or how to appreciate its aesthetic properties, but the dictate of how properly to respond to a text deemed literary. And what is at stake in this situation is not solely the physical attack on one hundred and fifty protesters, but also a symptomatic transformation of the students' activism into the domain of the irrational. These students were not seen to be critical readers in the proper way—once positioned outside a literacy integral to making a recognizable interpretative move, they are outside the domain of the public sphere, free speech, and the logic of rights and freedom. Unwilling to respond as addressees of the literary text, they remain unrecognizable as readers at all—and as a result, drawing from Hafez's terms, they are deemed outside the parameters of "secular and rationalist culture."

For the students, the text matters neither because it participates in a broad conversation about Arab nationalism, nor because it demarcates a formal innovation in the modern Arabic novel, but because it is deemed blasphemous. And ascertaining its blasphemy is not necessarily a matter of reading carefully or closely accounting for the grammatical distinctions between terms—in fact, in the end, it might have little to do with the text itself. It is rather a question of asking how it is that a text has come to mean what it does for the protesting students. Correcting the apparent misreading by asserting literary knowledge ends up doing little except prescribing a particular understanding of the text. We could gloss over the situation, as Hafez does, by bemoaning the terms in which the text is understood; or we could suspend the judgment of what constitutes right and wrong, and ask how the response to the text comes to be negotiated socially. The goal in this clarification is not to broaden what we mean by reading or even to include the students' protest as a form of reading, but to ask about the world in which texts acquire meaning—in this case, both the world that bestows literary value upon Haydar's novel and sees the students' protests as a threat to literature and the world in which the novel is understood as blasphemy.

If we view the controversy as a conflict over the category of literature, then we map a rather different understanding of what constitutes the world of world literature. The protesting students, moved to protest by the novel, are understood not to value literature in the proper way. They do not necessarily read the novel, nor are they necessarily engaging any questions at all pertinent to its literary value. But I begin with this story not to argue that world literature cannot account for these students, but to suggest that it prompts a consideration of the normative force of the literary.[10] Critics commonly consider world literature as the accumulation of literary texts from across the world—it is the site at which Shakespeare, Goethe, and al-Mutanabbi (al-Mutanabbī) all come together in spite of stemming from different literary traditions; and it is a world, in most accounts, that has very little to do with the readers of these texts. But there is another dimension that this opening story makes thinkable. The world is to be understood in a distinction between two means of engaging with the novel, divided, in large part, by the rhetoric of religion. The protesting students pose a challenge to the literary public for being deemed irrational and ultimately outside the parameters of informed critique. For the protesting students, literature matters differently—not as an abstracted textual problem to be analyzed and studied in the context of an author's work, but as a matter of moral injury.[11] In this context, the world of world literature delineates not only a world in which to recognize texts as literature, but a semiotic ideology delineating the terms in which to read.

There is more to the analysis of this situation than merely pointing to the violence enacted against the protesting students. What is at stake is both the violence itself and also the way it animates reflections on the incident, framed, most often, in terms of the students' apparent religiosity. It is not simply that the students protested the novel, but that, by implication, they are cast under the cryptic language of fanaticism, as though coerced into action by religion. Hafez's article reads the controversy as emblematic of broader struggles over the authority of the intellectual in the Arab world at odds with the traditional religious establishment and reaffirms a conventional narrative of modernization in the Middle East. The first few sections of Hafez's essay, "Power and Learning" and "Modernity on the Nile," tell of a shift from education under the oversight of religious authority to the reforms of Muhammad 'Ali in nineteenth-century Egypt, "when the symbolic capital of traditional elites began to erode."[12] Recounting this well-known story, Hafez continues, "By the time Muhammad Ali's grandson, Khedive Isma'il—educated in Paris, and determined to 'make Egypt a part of Europe'—was deposed by British intervention in 1879, the modern educational system had established complete ascendancy over its religious rival, its products outnumbering their counterparts from the traditional schools by ten to one. The latter, however, were marginalized rather than uprooted—an error for which Egypt would later pay dearly."[13] Not only does the conventional account frame two educational worlds, one that "was marginalized rather than uprooted," but it also describes two types of subjects that ultimately emerge—those who learn to read critically and those who learn through memorization. The traditional structures of education tend not toward the production of critical-thinking students, but are seen to "transmit the concepts and rules of Muslim tradition."[14]

Rather unsurprisingly, the controversy surrounding Haydar Haydar comes to be read within the context of this rivalry Hafez constructs—modern intellectuals, as his argument has it, are under siege from the dictates of al-Azhar. When Hafez describes the students, he goes on to note, "It was also reported that students who were asked 'Did you read the novel?' invariably replied 'No, but our teachers told us it was blasphemous.'"[15] What he offers is the sense that these protesting students cannot and do not think for themselves, but blindly follow the dictates of authority. Never mind the disciplines and constraints necessary to being recognized as a critical thinker—in this understanding, detaching oneself from religious authority is ultimately seen as what it means to be modern, free, and educated. Reaffirming the forces of good and evil integral to the modernization story, Hafez suggests, "The affair now divided into two different fronts: on the one hand, the right of the Islamicists to express their views; on the other, the character of their crusade against secular and rationalist culture."[16] The stark contrasts set up in this account pit critical thinking, modernization, and literature against tradition, fanaticism, and obedience.

When we step back from the situation and consider how the story is told, the binarism separating the world of the protesting students from the world of literary readers is quite logically seductive. It draws together a world in which civilized readers from all corners of the globe recognize themselves engaged in a common struggle—and it produces a group, in this case the protesting students and what Hafez describes as a religious authority, threatening free speech and literary culture. We have constructed before us a world in which literature is under siege by perceived cultural conservatives. In the convoluted narrative of education in Egypt, the protesting students come to be understood as the victims of an outdated pedagogy, and they are seen pitted against the world of readers, writers, and critics, who become visible as a community at the moment their literary world is threatened. And it is telling that this story is not limited to the streets of Cairo on which it transpires—as it is told, the story bespeaks an almost allegorical struggle in which Hafez rallies his readers to defend "secular and rationalist culture" from attacks. But, in this rhetorical game, what precisely is being supported in the defense of Haydar? Is it literature as such? And if not through a binarism of modernization and traditionalism, criticism and fanaticism, literature and its other, then how else might the controversy be understood?

To answer this question, we might consider Talal Asad's response to the protests surrounding Salman Rushdie's *The Satanic Verses*. "In what sense, precisely," Asad asks, "can Western readers who have little familiarity with these multiple references be said to have read the book?"[17] As he continues, Asad notes in the context of the Rushdie affair, "Oddly enough, the 'fundamentalist' position—according to which the text is self-sufficient for arriving at its meaning—is being taken here not by religious fanatics but by liberal critics."[18] Even though with the protests surrounding Haydar Haydar's novel, we are not dealing with a schism between the West and the non-West, we are dealing, in the end, with an account of what it means to read properly. The debates over the novel turn, in both instances, on the literary community's efforts to clarify how and in what sense the text comes to mean. When Hafez himself notes, "It is striking how little attention the controversy has paid to the subsequent work of Haydar himself, who has continued to produce writing of notable imaginative power and uncompromisingly radical intent," he presumes the importance of a certain understanding of literature. Could it be that for those protesting the novel, it was not a matter of valuing an author's literary work for its "imaginative power and uncompromisingly radical intent"? What alternate axis for thinking about textual meaning does the controversy make thinkable?

Asad's analysis is compelling both because it questions what is meant by reading and also because it refuses the conventional binarism of the secularist versus the fundamentalist. The questions that Asad poses guide us to consider how secularism delimits and defines the category of the literary—and in turn, the category of the religious. Even as he offers us an anthropology of the secular, Asad is notably not interested in countering secularism through a simple inversion of its categories. What he asks of us is weightier. Literature does not inhere in the intrinsic attributes of the text, but relies upon the world that gives the text its contingent meaning. By pointing to the specificity of how texts come to be read and how they come to acquire meaning, Asad links literature to practices, sensibilities, and ethics that constitute its value in the humanist discourse of secular liberalism. What is at stake for Asad is not a matter of claiming that the protesting students had not properly read the text, but of asking about how the text comes to matter in the world. It is this terrain of world literature that I ultimately explore in what follows—less the story of a given text than the story of how it comes to matter and for whom.

INTERNATIONAL STANDARDS OF EXCELLENCE?

While the story of the controversy surrounding Haydar Haydar offers one means of thinking about the world of world literature, there is another force at play in the negotiation of what literature is. In this section, I focus on the terms of inclusion in world literature by looking at how the Egyptian novelist Naguib Mahfouz comes to be recognized by the Nobel Prize committee. This is both an account of the constraints of world literature as well as an inquiry into the conditions of recognition in the world republic of letters. Against the apparent provincialism of language-based or nation-based inquiry, world literature, it might seem, offers us the occasion to study texts without the demands of national canons. But far from being an open-ended, all-inclusive domain for writers, world literature has its own constraints—and these constraints are implicit in what is recognized as a work of literature. My argument here is *not* that world literature fails to account for the richness of the distinct textual practices and traditions that it subsumes in its domain, but rather that it constructs and redefines what literature is in the process of recognizing excellence.

When, in October 1988, Mahfouz was awarded the Nobel Prize for literature, not only was he the first modern Arabic writer to receive this unique form of international recognition, he became, in many ways, paradigmatic of modern Arabic literature for readers across the world. In a speech delivered on Mahfouz's behalf, Sture Allén of the Swedish Academy emphasized many key literary traits, locating in Mahfouz what he described as "international standards of excellence": "Naguib Mahfouz has an unrivalled position as a spokesman for Arabic prose. Through him, in the cultural sphere to which he belongs, the art of the novel and the short story has attained international standards of excellence, the result of a synthesis of classical Arabic tradition, European inspiration and personal artistry."[19] In a manner by no means foreign to discussions of world literature, Allén's remarks perform a most intriguing celebration of Mahfouz, noting his participation in a cultural sphere ambiguously situated between the world of letters and the urban life of modern Cairo. Beyond locating in Mahfouz a "synthesis of classical Arabic tradition, European inspiration and personal artistry," the award acclaims his role as a master storyteller, who weaves together rich plots and characters, and as a socially perceptive observer, who functions as a critic of the world around him. For the global audience to whom the Nobel Prize committee speaks and for whom Mahfouz's literary work is supposedly so powerful, the merits of this world-class author speak to both his exemplarity within the world of letters and his affirmation of the "international standards of excellence" by which his work is understood.

While a seeming detail from the nearly countless volumes of critical material written on this "spokesman for Arabic prose," Allén's comments highlight a certain tension implicit in discussions of world literature, torn between a seemingly universal form, literature, and its particular manifestation, often linked to the place in which it is written. Mahfouz himself draws from this tension in his acceptance speech delivered by his daughters on his behalf. In this speech, he situates himself as an Egyptian writer, weaving together his professed relation to pharaonic and Islamic influences: "I am the son of two civilizations that at a certain age in history have formed a happy marriage. The first of these, seven thousand years old, is the Pharaonic civilization; the second, one thousand four hundred years old, is the Islamic one."[20] With these words, Mahfouz invokes the seemingly classic tropes of modern Egyptian nationalism. These two civilizational motifs emerge in the 1920s and 1930s, at a time when many Egyptian writers and intellectuals were forging the terms of *adab qawmī*, roughly understood as a national literature. In the mid-1920s, the weekly magazine *al-Siyāsah al-usbūʿīyah*, advocated invoking a pharaonic past for Egyptian literature, most especially in a 1928 article by Muhammad Husayn Haykal (Muḥammad Ḥusayn Haykal).[21] By 1935, Haykal, like the journal itself, had moved in an alternate direction, transitioning to Islamic motifs, publishing *Ḥayāt Muḥammad*, a biography of the prophet initially based on a translation of Émile Dermenghem's *La Vie de Mahomet*. Other writers of the period, such as Salama Musa (Salāmah Mūsā), in whose journal Mahfouz first published, Muhammad Taymur (Muḥammad Taymūr), affiliated with the journal *al-Sufūr*, and Yahia Haqqi (Yaḥyā Haqqī), affiliated with *al-Fajr*, were also instrumental in laying the terms through which modern Egyptian literature would be understood, pulled between an Arab and Islamic literary tradition and a pharaonic Egyptian past in fusion with European letters.[22]

But the intertextual resonance implicit in how Mahfouz situates his work likely falls deaf on the ears of an audience of world literature.[23] In the pantheon of global authors, there are different references by which to map Mahfouz's significance, and Mahfouz also weaves these into his talk, speaking of civilization less as the domain of one national tradition than as the collective labor of humanity: "Today, the greatness of a civilized leader ought to be measured by the universality of his vision and his sense of responsibility towards all humankind."[24] At the same time as citing the competing influences in his work, Mahfouz diplomatically embraces the honor afforded him by the Nobel Prize, acknowledging, somewhat humbly, what he sees to be rare international attention for his works. In receiving the award, like many writers before him, Mahfouz acknowledges the international scope and thanks the committee for bolstering the presence of his tradition within the world literary scene. "I have great hopes," Mahfouz states, "that literary writers of my nation will have the pleasure to sit with full merit amongst your international writers who have spread the fragrance of joy and wisdom in this grief-ridden world of ours."[25] His remarks, much like those of the Nobel committee framing his presentation, bespeak a broad vision of world literature, one that not only unites texts from a number of differing languages and traditions, but also assumes the apparent ubiquity of literary readers. There is a careful shift from the terrain of the national reader, for whom the intertextual resonance of Mahfouz's work is woven into a constellation of debates in Arabic literature, to the terrain of the world literary public, for whom the national tradition comes to be legible analogically and for whom Mahfouz is on the order of Dickens and Balzac.

The speech does more, though, than simply read Mahfouz as emblematic of literary production in Arabic and as a representative of Egypt—it also points to his recognition as a member of a certain cultural sphere as a world-class writer. What is the status of this recognition? Had Mahfouz not written novels, would he be recognizably literary in a manner to be appreciated by the Nobel Prize committee? While arguments are made that world literature ought to include more traditions under its domain, it is worth considering how world literature produces the conditions through which traditions come to be recognized. Whether explicit or implicit, the "international standards of excellence" tend to assume an aesthetic trajectory within which the novel and the short story are deemed more modern if certain narratological forms are adopted—Mahfouz is valued for some of the innovations he is seen to provide in the modern Arabic novel, ranging from the mature realism of the *Cairo Trilogy* to the modernist innovations of *Mīrāmār* (Miramar). The counterpoint to this claim is not to argue for indigenous literary categories—to assume, in other words, that the Arabic novel has its own structuring principles—but to consider the force of categories on the production of readers, codes, and stylistic features recognizable within the expansive literary world arguably consolidated through the institutionalization of literature, printing, and reading practices. This world literary system makes possible the recognition of texts as literary and makes possible qualitative assessments, on some level, comparing texts across traditions.

Both the presentation speech and Mahfouz's acceptance allude to an international space uniting readers across nations and literary traditions, but both remarks are also haunted by the inadvertent question of quality: for the committee, what constitutes "international standards of excellence," and for Mahfouz, what it means to be "sitting with *full merit* amongst your international writers." Literature here is not so much an intrinsic given, but is instead underwritten by a subtle bracketing of—yet explicit allusion to—those standards by which to make qualitative assessments of texts deemed literary across traditions. In the effort to situate the writer and the literary work, the speeches assume both an axis of world literature based on the geographic spread of literary production and an alternate axis that draws together a range of literary forms, many of which are based in alternate cultural traditions and all of which fall under the seemingly universal rubric of literature. This is not to say literature is understood relative to the context within which it is read: on the contrary, for the Nobel Prize committee, the horizon of readership only ever reaffirms the "international standards of excellence" that Mahfouz helps the short story and the novel to achieve. The Nobel Prize committee, in other words, bespeaks those standards from which to make qualitative evaluations across a range of traditions—the space of world literature would seem to have as much to do with the "international standards of excellence" as with the specific locations in which texts are written.[26]

When it comes to world literature, it is quite common to emphasize location and authorship—to see, in other words, Mahfouz as an Egyptian novelist. It is, though, far less common to step back and question what constitutes the authoritative basis of a standard in the terrain of world literature. Language, as is often noted, unravels its own rules and possibilities for free play, genre furnishes a horizon of constraint for the writer, and national literary traditions also provide a certain framework with which to understand the operations of a literary text. With world literature, however, and especially an award like the Nobel Prize, who or what grounds the standards by which literature, notably across languages, genres and national traditions, is to be qualitatively assessed?

More often than not, literature is understood as it is in Allén's remarks, as though its "international standards of excellence" are uniquely negotiated in each specific literary text. The mark of literary excellence, in other words, is seen as intrinsic to the given form and style of a particular work, something that the critic is given to unravel. These standards—as much international as universal—are reaffirmed in Allén's speech, which is meant as both an exposition and a celebration of Mahfouz's contributions to world literature. Although it claims to celebrate Mahfouz, in effect it functions as a consecration of what constitutes his literary value, delineating the terms through which Mahfouz is to be appreciated. The award, then, is as much an affirmation of the supposed universality of literature, which is shown to traverse language, nations, and traditions, as it is the universalization of literary reading, which it professes by articulating what to appreciate in Mahfouz's literary work.

In its recognition of the first Arabic-language Nobel Prize award, the Swedish Academy both broadens the terrain of world literature, incorporating another tradition within its domain, and reasserts the terms through which a literature can be appreciated: in this instance, to appreciate the subtleties of Mahfouz's writing—its command of style, visuality, theme, and genre—is to be acculturated to this appropriately literary way of reading. In this act of international recognition, Mahfouz is, at the same time, read as an embodiment of the local particularity of a place, in this instance Cairo, and as a practitioner of a universal discourse, invoking themes applicable, as we learn, "to all mankind."[27] The universality of Mahfouz's excellence thus comes to rest on his implicit affirmation of a field of literary norms, which not only make his work exemplary, but also make the particularity of the places it describes legible to the world at large. The story of literary excellence is far from universal—it is instead the story of how literature becomes, through forces of globalized literacy, the universalization of a mediated practice of reading in which rather particular conceptions of difference, experience, and subjectivity are made thinkable.

WORLD LITERARY SPACE

In her consideration of the transnational dimension of the world of letters, Pascale Casanova also takes the Nobel Prize as a key site within world literature. She notes the year 1913, when, ten years following the inception of the Nobel Prize, the Nobel committee of the Swedish Academy recognized the Bengali poet Rabindranath Tagore. This moment, in the words of Casanova, marked a "first attempt to move beyond Europe," and functioned in critical ways as a broadening of the world republic of letters, simultaneously affirming the prestige of a literary capital and recognizing the conflicting struggles of authors on the periphery.[28] Curiously enough, the award speech from 1913, like the speech from 1988, alludes to Tagore's poetry in terms of its approaching the "prescribed standard."[29] Although in 1913 the committee was shy, even reserved, about alluding to Tagore's nationality, it does, in quite a pronounced manner, return to the supposed universality of literature, suggesting that Tagore's work is "by no means exotic but truly universally human in character."[30] While this "attempt to move beyond Europe" highlights the tension between literature and its place in the world, it functions, in less than subtle ways, as a universalization of the terms of literature, assuming, in the process, the stability of its existence as a conceptual category and the standards it necessarily presumes.

By the time of Mahfouz's recognition in 1988, a number of writers from the Global South had been recognized, and quite often, with explicit reference to their national traditions: in 1945 the Chilean poet Gabriela Mistral, in 1967 the Guatemalan Miguel Ángel Asturias, in 1971 the Chilean Pablo Neruda, and in 1986 the Nigerian Wole Soyinka. Such a listing of writers demonstrates, for a critic like Casanova, the emergence of what she calls "world literary space," one whose terms of participation are closely linked not to any professed universal humanism, but more critically to an intricate system of cultural capital and linguistic value:

> It is the global configuration, or composition, of the carpet—that is, the domain of letters, the totality of what I will call world literary space—that alone is capable of giving meaning and coherence to the very form of individual texts. This space is not an abstract and theoretical construction, but an actual—albeit unseen—world made up by lands of literature; a world in which what is judged worthy of being considered literature is brought into existence; a world in which the ways and means of literary art are argued over and decided.[31]

Within this world literary space, the Nobel Prize serves as "the highest honor the world republic of letters has to give," and it plays, in a crucial sense, a role in the attribution of value to literature. Casanova's argument focuses on a dynamic of *littéralisation*, a process by which writers and texts gain in literary capital, and she is interested in the movement between literary capitals and the periphery, tracing, at one point, the role of Paris for writers such as Cioran and Beckett.[32] The model of the republic she espouses, while tinged with an underlying structuralism, actually leads her to privilege the sort of intuitions of those writers from the periphery. As Casanova discusses Octavio Paz, who received the Nobel Prize in 1990, she invokes him almost paradigmatically of "those writers on the peripheries of the world of letters who, in their openness to international experience, seek to end what they see as their exile from literature."[33]

What is telling, and perhaps symptomatic, is that the scholarly emphasis on world literary space tends to bracket literature as it is understood differently for different communities of readers over time. The story Casanova offers, in other words, centered on Paris as a key literary capital, tends to assume a certain historical continuity in readership, both historically and geographically. Participation in the world republic of letters certainly entails a dynamic of literary value, as Casanova points out, but it also entails the production of a world of literate readers, attuned to its supposedly "international standards of excellence." Whether one looks globally or within the nation for such a story, the acculturation into the world of letters—that is, the process of becoming literate—is unlike citizenship. It is, after all, not a matter of blood or birthright, but instead a disciplined practice and an education of the terms within which to respond and react.

It is worth noting that Casanova's world literary space cuts against a predominant logic of native intelligence in reading practices. By aligning writers such as Pablo Neruda and Stéphane Mallarmé, she abstracts the literary text from the problem of address—appreciating Neruda, for example, has less to do with the proximity of his address to a known situation in the lifeworld of the reader than it does with his mastery of forms. And for years, it has been common to assume that a reader familiar with the lifeworld of a text is better able to grasp its subtleties, both linguistic and cultural. Within this predominant logic, the novel is read as a window onto the lifeworld from which it emerges, helping to unravel the complexities of lived experience for the reader and ultimately making possible a sort of transcultural empathy. For Casanova, the process of *littéralisation* is not so much one that binds a writer to an imagined national public as it is the process that links writers to one another in an international commerce of literary texts.

In the case of Naguib Mahfouz, we might recall how the Nobel Prize speech refers to his participation both in a world republic of letters and in his "committed, perceptive, almost prophetic commentary on the world around him."[34] And we might be led to believe that a reader familiar with this world, in responding to the world around him, has a richer insight into the complexities of his writing. Common though this argument may be, it has two critical shortcomings: first, to assume that a reader from Mahfouz's lifeworld would better understand the text is to assume that the form of the text's execution (that is, the very material characteristics of its literariness) is parenthetical to the world presented; and second, a reader familiar with the novelistic form with which Mahfouz engages (its rules and formal characteristics) could be seen to have a supposedly better understanding of the text, even if the content is itself entirely in the realm of the imagination. We return here, then, to the question with which I began—the apparent opposition between the world *of* literature and the world *in* literature. Casanova highlights how the world *of* literature is related to the world *in* literature, divorced of questions of how a text might be situated differently over time. World literary space, in other words, makes the institutions intrinsic to world literature the domain in which works deemed literary come to be understood.

Discussions of world literary space and the institutional dynamics of the Nobel Prize committee offer us accounts that complicate how to situate texts of world literature. The Nobel Prize speech and its allusions to international standards of excellence and Casanova's discussion of *littéralisation* allow us to consider that there are in fact rules and norms that constrain how texts come to be recognized as works of literature. The path to recognition entails working within genres, categories, and motifs that can be understood within an intertextual field, and as such can be intelligible to readers as reaffirming and working within debates of this literary world. Drawn into a set of associations mapped by the likes of Balzac, Dickens, Beckett, Goethe, Shakespeare, and Proust, this world of world literature helps to constitute a metalanguage integral to being recognized as highly literate. Being a good reader of world literature does not necessarily imply mastering the languages of all of the texts, but mastering the comparative categories integral to appreciating what Casanova describes as "lands of literature."[35] But this level of abstraction, drawing from the role of literature in the world to the world of literature, leaves a number of remaining questions, and other critics, dissatisfied with an emphasis on textual systems, provide a different set of answers.

THE SAIDIAN GROUNDS OF WORLDLINESS

When it comes to a figure like Edward Said, there is more to the world of world literature than an account of the rules and institutions that arbitrate the recognition of literary excellence. While these rules help to affirm the terms within which literature is valued, they have little to say about the ways in which literature relates to and inflects the political world in which it is written. If Casanova's discussion of world literary space charts the supposed autonomy of literature and its break from national politics, then in Said's work we find a different understanding of what it means for a text to be situated. The world of world literature comes together with a caveat in his writings—he is attentive to the literary text, but he refuses the binarism implicit in Casanova's distinction between internal and external criticism, between literary form and social history. He engages literature as it relates to the political world from which it stems, and he is critical, in large part, of how it is institutionalized in the academy and placed in the hands of self-appointed experts.

In his collection of essays, *The World, the Text, and the Critic*, Said invokes secular criticism as a means of situating literature, reading, and criticism in the world. He begins his opening essay, titled "Secular Criticism," by outlining four forms of literary criticism, including practical criticism, academic literary criticism, literary appreciation, and literary theory. Doing so, the essay appears, at least tentatively, to bracket what is meant by the secular in favor of describing "the prevailing situation of criticism."[36] And in tackling this prevailing situation, Said expresses outright his dissatisfaction with professional humanists for supposing that "the approved practice of high culture is marginal to the serious political concerns of society."[37] Said writes, "We tell our students and our general constituency that we defend the classics, the virtues of liberal education, and the precious pleasures of literature even as we show ourselves to be silent (perhaps incompetent) about the historical and social world in which all these things take place."[38] He then couches this criticism in his underlying frustration with the relegation of literature to a limited cadre of self-perceived experts—this increasing specialization, he tells us, has "given rise to a cult of professional expertise whose effect in general is pernicious."[39] Against those who write "to join up with a priestly caste of acolytes and dogmatic metaphysicians," Said and each of the essays in his book "affirms the connection between texts and the existential actualities of human life, politics, societies, and events."[40]

Positioned against the mystifying abstractions offered by a cadre of experts and geared to address "serious political concerns of society," Said's remarks offer both what constitutes the "existential actualities of human life, politics, societies, and events" and what constitutes criticism and the critical consciousness—ultimately the world, as he sees it, and the ways literature mediates our understanding of it. And in this process, Said escapes abstraction largely by working through anecdotes and descriptions of the activities of self-perceived experts in the field of literary study. In the first few pages of this opening essay, for example, he considers "[t]he degree to which the cultural realm and its expertise are institutionally divorced from their real connections with power," and he does so by drawing relations between expertise in literary studies and expertise in foreign policy, which, he tells us, "has usually meant the legitimization of the conduct of foreign policy and, what is more to the point, a sustained investment in revalidating the role of experts in foreign affairs."[41] Not only do literature and foreign affairs come together around the figure of the expert, but they lead him to a narrative moment in these seemingly theoretical reflections.

Having presented the contours of the basic argument, Said recalls a conversation with a friend at the height of the Vietnam war, who claims that the secretary of the Department of Defense was not a "cold-blooded imperialist murderer" and points to the fact that he had a copy of Durrell's *Alexandria Quartet* in his office.[42] The anecdote is itself quite remarkable, but so too is the lesson that Said draws from this incident: "What the anecdote illustrates is the approved separation of high-level bureaucrat from the reader of novels of questionable worth and definite status."[43] In a richly suggestive line of associations, the initial caveat of literary expertise being similar to expertise in foreign affairs takes on the weight of argumentative explanation—it functions here as a story that explains and charts some of the relationships of direct interest to Said. It is worth noting that he wants to wrest literary reading from the bastion of experts, whom he likens to the intellectuals so critiqued in Julien Benda's famous text, and that he does so by invoking those, such as the secretary, for whom reading is a sign of status. But Said offers us more—he moves from this anecdote to focus on those who take literature away from the reader and abstract what it means to read under the rhetoric of textuality.

In delineating a relationship between the text and the world, Said celebrates the intellectual origins of literary theory in Europe, which he describes as "insurrectionary."[44] He points to figures such as Saussure, Lukács, Bataille, Lévi-Strauss, Freud, Nietzsche, and Marx, and notes that these "influential progenitors" allow us to consider how "the domains of human activity could be seen, and lived, as a unity."[45] And yet his account takes on a more somber tone when describing problems in contemporary methods. He specifically laments a shift from the insurrectionary origins of literary theory in Europe to the retreat, during the late seventies, into "the labyrinth of 'textuality,'" which he glosses as "the somewhat mystical and disinfected subject matter of literary theory."[46] "Textuality," he writes, "is considered to take place, yes, but it does not take place anywhere or anytime in particular."[47] His seeming frustration with the situation of literary theory culminates in this statement: "As it is practiced in the American academy today, literary theory has for the most part isolated textuality from the circumstances, the events, the physical senses that make it possible and render it intelligible as the result of human work."[48]

Fearful of the ways that a "precious jargon has grown up and its formidable complexities obscure social realities," Said does not entirely despair, but finally arrives on the virtues of secular criticism. As he defines it, secular criticism is not the obscurity of textuality of an anywhere at anytime, but is instead situated historically in the world. His argument, as he states it, "is that texts are worldly, to some degree they are events, and, even when they appear to deny it, they are nevertheless part of the social world, human life, and of course the historical moments in which they are located and interpreted."[49] In the oppositions set forth, textuality detaches the text from the social world and places literature in the hands of experts—and secular criticism makes possible a means of reintegrating, as the title has it, the world, the text, and the critic. With these issues in mind, Said offers us neither the literary world of the Nobel Prize nor the dynamics of literary value in Pascale Casanova's world literary space, but a world whose terms are to be grounded in the "social world, human life, and of course the historical moments in which [texts] are located and interpreted." Is this, we might ask, the world of world literature?

If Said proclaims this way of being situated as secular criticism, then he also delimits a particular understanding of the world in which to historicize texts. He willfully aligns textuality with the political forces to which he sees it linked, notably the rise of Reagan, and he refuses any gesture to study literary form divorced from implicit connections to the world—that is to say, being situated for Said is less a matter of questioning how texts come to be understood as literary than a matter of situating a text in the world from which it stems. This understanding, which sees worldliness in terms of history, politics, and social situations, has rather deep implications for how Said subsequently understands criticism, or as he, like Foucault, calls it, "a critical attitude."[50] He thus draws together considerations about not only how to approach a text, but also the role of the critic in the world.

As the essay develops, Said's functional opposition between a mystifying textuality and grounded secular criticism comes to affirm this broader investment in a "critical consciousness." The subsequent connection drawn between secularism and critique leads him to the following question: "What does it mean to have a critical consciousness if, as I have been trying to suggest, the intellectual's situation is a worldly one and yet, by virtue of that worldliness itself, the intellectual's social identity should involve something more than strengthening those aspects of the culture that require mere affirmation and compliancy from its members?"[51] This passage is striking not only for its ambitions to address the question of what constitutes critique, but also for how it situates critique in the world. The stakes are articulated most explicitly: for a text to be worldly, it is to be "part of the social world, human life, and of course the historical moments in which they are located and interpreted"; and yet when it comes to the critic, "the intellectual's social identity should involve something more than strengthening those aspects of the culture that require mere affirmation and compliancy from its members." It would seem, then, that Said privileges a critical stance not determined by social positioning. In a sense, being critical for Said entails the capacity to break from "compliancy."

The relation between the noncompliant critic and the question of interpretation leads to a further exploration of yet another aspect of critical consciousness:

> Criticism in short is always situated; it is skeptical, secular, reflectively open to its own failings. This is by no means to say that it is value-free. Quite the contrary, for the inevitable trajectory of critical consciousness is to arrive at some acute sense of what political, social and human values are entailed in the reading, production and transmission of every text. To stand between culture and system is therefore to stand *close to*—closeness itself having a particular value for me—a concrete reality about which political, moral, and social judgments have to be made and, if not only made, then exposed and demystified.[52]

The assertion that criticism is "skeptical, secular, reflectively open to its own failings" provides a glimpse into what it is that Said might mean by this most loaded term: "secular." It would seem, for example, that the "closeness" to which he attributes value is one understood in its relation to "a concrete reality." This "concrete reality" presupposes a set definition of values, which Said suggests are "political, social and human," and "entailed in the reading, production and transmission of every text." And at the same time, criticism is, for Said, opposed to any particular allegiances: "If criticism is reducible neither to a doctrine nor to a political position on a particular question, and if it is to be in the world and self-aware simultaneously, then its identity is its difference from other cultural activities and from systems of thought or of method."[53] By the essay's conclusion, Said grows even more explicit with what is at stake in this critical consciousness. He tells us, "criticism must think of itself as life-enhancing and constitutively opposed to every form of tyranny, domination, and abuse; its social goals are noncoercive knowledge produced in the interest of human freedom."[54] Not only does Said switch here from describing the role of the critic, but he attributes to criticism a capacity to "think of itself" and to carry certain "social goals" "in the interest of human freedom." We have moved, then, from postulations about the world within which a text is to be read to the imperative consciousness necessary to be recognizably critical. Secular criticism ultimately seems to take shape around this presumption about what constitutes the worldliness of texts and the tension of a critical consciousness between being "in the world and self-aware simultaneously."

It is revealing, though, that Said's definition of secular criticism emerges most pointedly when he describes its opposite in the concluding essay of the volume, titled "Religious Criticism." In these concluding remarks, Said likens the terms "Orientalism," "religion," and "culture" one unto the other by proclaiming each "an agent of closure, shutting off human investigation, criticism, and effort in deference to authority of the more-than-human, the supernatural, the other-worldy."[55] He writes, "Like culture, religion therefore furnishes us with systems of authority and with canons of order whose regular effect is either to compel subservience or to gain adherents."[56] Curiously here, at the moment of proclaiming the value of secular criticism, the category of religion comes to rest for Said devoid of any particular situation—he at once flirts with reference to practices in the world and abstracts them into the conventional binarism of secularity and religiosity. If we read with Said and allow the abstract category of religion to function as he wishes, then even still, the practices delineated ultimately fall outside of the historical analysis Said earlier lends to texts as he proclaims the virtues of worldliness.

Said of course writes at a moment in which he saw the specter of expertise and the rise of religion haunting the critical consciousness, and so he ends his book by proclaiming, "Once an intellectual, the modern critic has become a cleric in the worst sense of the word. How their discourse can once again collectively become a truly secular enterprise is, it seems to me, the most serious question critics can be asking one another."[57] The call for a "truly secular enterprise" is cast against "the cost of this shift to religion," whose effects are "unpleasant to contemplate." It is telling that for Said secular criticism is necessarily grounded in human activity and that, in the end, it is indelibly linked to a fundamentally humanist project. It is also telling that Said's secularism curiously brackets its own situatedness in a world whose terms would eventually be echoed in foreign policy along this fantasy of the secular and religious divide. In the end, what I am asking for here is that we push Said's secular criticism one step further to ask how the methods, reading practices, and supposed virtues of worldliness—and ultimately humanism—are situated in time and place. Doing so returns us to the scandal surrounding Haydar Haydar's novel.

THE FORCE OF A SECULAR WORLD

Since the publication of *The World, the Text, and the Critic*, Said's secular criticism has had a resounding impact on literary and cultural scholarship, providing what David Damrosch celebrates as "a sort of manifesto for the social role of literature—and for the crucial role of the critical intellectual in assessing literature and society alike."[58] And yet, as much as scholars have been inspired by Said and his legacy, his professed secularism leaves lingering questions for those of us questioning the world of world literature—especially those of us confronted with worlds that trouble the presumptions of the secular critic. What is the world of world literature? Is it necessarily secular? How, as scholars, do we come to terms with the differences between reading texts deemed literary by some and sacred by others? Robust as Said's views of secular criticism are, they tend to level out the variety of worlds confronted in the study of world literature. As we shall see in subsequent chapters, not only do various texts complicate the simple opposition between the secular and the religious, but they lead us, on some level, to question the secular with the sort of skeptical distance that Said himself asks of the critic. Being critical, in the end, means considering some of the constraints of the secular as the terrain upon which to analyze literature.

In a broad sense, we might ask how Said's secular criticism resonates for those of us working at a time when the discourse of religion has come to bear quite directly on foreign policy. When faced with student protests of Haydar Haydar, do we as scholars retreat, as Hafez does, behind the rallying cry secularism? Or do we embrace a critical consciousness to question the terms of what it means to be secular and what attachments this might entail? Is it not our responsibility as critics to question the parameters within which this secular world is made known? Doing so is not a matter of celebrating or dismantling secularism, but rather of asking about its mediating force. In the context of the Haydar Haydar scandal, the story I have told here veers dangerously close to delineating two different interpretative worlds. To succumb to the temptation of this two worlds theory—distinguishing the literate and the illiterate, the modern and the traditional, the secular and the fanatic—not only would be reductive, but would entrench the terms with which Sabry Hafez frames his account. What is needed is not a comparison between worlds, but an analysis of how the distinctions themselves emerge—the grounds of comparison.

The world that supposedly grounds our readings of texts is a world whose terms are, in fact, contested. When we describe and justify the supposed value of literature, we inevitably articulate a particular vision of what constitutes knowledge and the peculiarity by which moral education detaches from scriptural authority. Part of interrogating the limits of the secular lies in considering the authority that secular humanism grants to an observable world over and above the cosmological vision of a religious tradition. It is the secular world that tends to ground comparative work, be it in the guise of area studies, comparative grammar, or comparative religion, and it is a secular world that tends to level out phenomenological differences between interpretative lifeworlds. For the students protesting Haydar Haydar, literature is hardly the domain of aesthetic and formal innovation—it is, instead, not only an assertion of the proper way to perceive, but the simultaneous justification for the violent policing of those who supposedly misunderstand.

If this opening chapter has sketched broad considerations spanning world literature, literary publics and secular criticism, then the remaining chapters are meant to model ways of engaging, questioning, and ultimately rethinking the force of the secular. What are the conditions of the world that grounds the analysis of literature? How does a critic account for how texts might matter differently across traditions? Where this chapter posed these questions by pairing Haydar Haydar and Edward Said, the next chapter moves us to the site of reading an object as a text. It is meant to model the rise of a particular literary hermeneutic anchored in an analysis of an event of a particular sort. With this in mind, let us move from the discussion of criticism and textual systems to a discussion of the emergence of the object or artifact as a text to be read, decoded, and analyzed as the reflection of its textual world—the story, in other words, of the Rosetta Stone.

2

TRANSLATION

The Rosetta Stone from Object to Text

1799. A rock is unearthed during the building of a fort in Rashid, Egypt. In the years that follow, this rock comes to matter in particular ways: first, as part of the story of colonial encounter, involving debates over ownership between the French General Jacques-François Menou and the British General John Hely-Hutchinson; second, as part of the story of comparative grammar, in which the stone was understood as the key to hieroglyphics in the scholarly labors of Thomas Young and Jean-François Champollion; and ultimately, as I will suggest, as part of a discourse on world literature. Now housed in the British Museum, the rock is known as the Rosetta Stone. It is an object given over to broader reflections on language, textuality, and reading. Its three inscriptions in Greek, demotic, and hieroglyphics lay guarded behind a plate of Plexiglas, protected from hands eager to trace the contours of the ancient script. A whiteness to enhance the readability of the stone's surface lingers in the grooves of its letters, and on the edges, inscriptions added by the English attribute the stone to the British army and King George III. This is a rock that comes to matter both as an index of a colonial past and a key to a lost language—as an object and as a text.

For those of us engaged in transnational literary scholarship, there is a tendency to discuss literature, translation, and the intercultural trafficking of texts in terms that demand contextualist readings. We are trained to take seriously the particularities of language and history that impact how a text is situated in the world. It might appear that contextualization turns us, as literary scholars, into historians and archaeologists and our objects into artifacts, but we aspire for a balance. When discussing translation in the context of world literature, for example, we tend to trace how a text travels from one location to another and from one language to the next, but we still emphasize

FIGURE 1. The Rosetta Stone.
Source: http://commons.wikimedia.org/wiki/File:Rosetta_Stone_BW.jpeg.

the material words of the text. In the end, we have been trained to focus our eyes as readers on linguistic subtleties and details, even if doing so means attending to the world in which the text is produced. Being a good reader, we have been led to believe, means anchoring our claims in textual observation as much as in the relation of a text to its context.

But what if the text and the language of its writing are actually less consequential than the manner in which we come to read? What if, in other words, the materiality of the object is inseparable from the disciplined practice through which it is understood? How might we understand intercultural translation if we consider the terms that anchor the recognition of an object as a text? These sorts of questions gesture to a crucial shift away from the primacy of the textual object and toward the disciplines and practices through which an object becomes a text. This shift is less a bracketing of materiality than an effort to locate the grounds of a disciplined practice of reading. I aim in what follows here to address the implications of an emergent textual culture in the nineteenth century, one that redefines relationships to objects and comes to inflect how language matters. It is a textual culture that cuts across national traditions and produces unto itself an interpretative community of a unique sort.

Common though it may be to anchor readings geographically in this contextualist age, the significance of the Rosetta Stone explodes frameworks of history, literature, archaeology, semiotics, and aesthetics. Understood as an object, is the Rosetta Stone ancient Egyptian, French, Ottoman, or British? As a textual artifact, where does it take place—in the initial context of its production, the site of its discovery in Egypt, or the site of its decoding in a transnational network of scholarly articles? What interests me here is *how* this object comes to matter—that is, how the rock comes to speak, to whom, and toward what ends. I thus read the Rosetta Stone as an interpretative moment in the framework of world literature, and I see the event of its discovery as part of a broader transformation of an object into a text and as part of an emergent literary culture. In this chapter as in the book itself, I focus on world literature less as an accumulation of texts from across different literary traditions than as the globalization of literary hermeneutics.

What is lost when all languages, texts, and traditions are subsumed under the disciplinary scrutiny of literature? What is leveled out when summoning objects from a variety of contexts and traditions as specifically literary texts? My argument is the following: What is discovered with the Rosetta Stone is less a prized object than a scholarly frame in which the object is understood as a key to translation, as a set of codes and an invitation to decipher. As this object becomes text, it is fractured into signs, copied, and read, disseminated across a scholarly world as the puzzle of its age. And to be understood as a puzzle, each of the three languages on the stone's surface must be read as the equivalent of the other. This notion of linguistic equivalence, integral as it is to theories of translation, levels out the phenomenological distinctions of languages, bracketing the critical differences between them. The philological impulse, in other words, trumps the theological, political, and vernacular distinctions between hieroglyphics, Greek, and demotic. And this leveling of the phenomenological differences makes of the object a text of a particular sort.

If the last chapter considered the world of reading and the place of interpretative communities, then this chapter excavates an object to consider the frames of its analysis and the philosophy of language that informs its recognition as a text in need of decoding. At issue is not only the material basis of reading, but the founding of a discipline linked to comparative grammar, archaeology, and the broader colonial mapping of Egypt. I point to a triangulation that haunts literary analysis more generally: first, the treatment of the Rosetta Stone as an *object* with a specific history of its own; second, its treatment as a *text*, a linguistic puzzle or set of words to be analyzed and decoded; and third, its emergence as a sort of blueprint for what comes to be actualized in the mind of the *reader* properly trained to make sense of it. As you will see toward the end of this chapter, the Rosetta Stone comes to articulate an interchangeability in a linguistic system that itself echoes the organizational logic of world literature. I thus extend my reading of this object as part of an interpretative community for which it comes to matter in particular ways.

As I recount the story through which an object becomes a text, I want to extend outward from the first chapter. Linking objects to texts to entextualization, I will ultimately be addressing world literature as a framework that understands objects as texts—an approach that excavates, discovers, unearths, and decodes, and an approach that deciphers, entextualizes, and reads.[1] At the intersection of colonialism, translation, and philology, the Rosetta Stone is a world literary text of a very particular sort and one whose significance derives from the frame within which it is seen as meaningful.[2] Telling its story is a matter of both narrating the object, but also narrating how and for whom it comes to matter as an artifact, a text, and a scene of translation. We could say that my story here is an account of how this rock comes to matter and where its matter rests: between object and text, between text and reader, between beholder and the regime through which this object comes to speak.

MAKING STONES SPEAK

In July 1799, a letter read aloud at the Institut d'Égypte in Cairo, Egypt, announced the discovery of the Rosetta Stone.[3] The letter was authored by the French engineer Michelange Lancret and sent from the port city Rosetta directly to the institute, where it was heard by an audience of scientists and scholars, all part of Napoleon's expedition and its scientific mission in Egypt. The French scientists gathered regularly in the palace of Hassan Kashef in downtown Cairo to share their research in fields ranging from botany and geology to literature, archaeology, and the arts. The discussions that afternoon spanned a number of topics: the discovery of an ancient fish, the tetrodon, by Geoffroy Saint-Hilaire, the ruins of a circus in Alexandria by the architect Charles Louis Balzac, a poetic recitation by Parseval Grandmaison, the botantist Alire Raffeneau Delile's report on names of Egyptian plants, as well as the announcement in Lancret's note.[4]

During this thirty-first session, Sheikh al-Mahdi, the Divan's secretary, was present as a guest of honor, joining the scientists for the series of announcements. As each scientist presented, an interpreter provided a gist translation in Arabic for the sheikh. In addition to this moment of vocal translation, the announcements were subsequently glossed and published in various stories in journals sponsored by the Institut d'Égypte. There were publications such as *Courier d'Égypte*, printed every ten days for the French soldiers, and the literary and scientific journal *La Décade Égyptienne.* Even more famously, though, much of what was undertaken by this group of French scholars eventually appeared in *La Description de l'Égypte*, published serially between 1809 and 1829 for readers across the world. Its twenty volumes were destined for a cosmopolitan literary elite and printed in limited editions with large plates and refined graphics. Reproductions of the face of the Rosetta Stone appeared in the fifth volume on antiquity with pages dedicated separately to the upper, middle, and bottom scripts from the face of the stone.[5]

Of all of the materials reported at the institute, the announcement of the Rosetta Stone helped to escalate further a general interest in Egypt as a scholarly domain, culminating in Champollion's claim to have deciphered hieroglyphics in 1822 (the same year as the founding of Egyptology as a formal discipline at the Collège de France and notably the same year as the death of the Egyptian chronicler 'Abd al-Rahman al-Jabarti ('Abd al-Raḥmān al-Jabartī). Much depended on the significance attributed to the Rosetta Stone as the key to a lost language, something Lancret's letter already framed in a particular way.[6] The letter reported that an officer of the engineering corps, Citizen Bouchard, encountered a large black stone with inscriptions in three different languages. The stone had been accidentally discovered during reconstruction of the walls at Fort Rashid, renamed Fort Julien, in the Nile Delta. Once discovered, the Rosetta Stone passed almost immediately from Citizen Bouchard to the hands of the commanding general, Jacques-François Menou, who in turn had it cleaned and stored in his tent, recognizing its significance for the French archaeological mission.

Moving from the description of the object to the text inscribed on its surface, the letter then distinguished the existence of three scripts contained on the stone's face. It went so far as to recognize the bottom register of the stone as a proclamation in Greek from the reign of Ptolemy Philopator. Citizen du Theil of the French expedition was commissioned to provide an initial and nearly immediate translation of the Greek. And already in Lancret's initial announcement, the significance of the stone was framed in terms of the equivalence between the three languages, which allowed the stone to stand as a potential key to unlocking hieroglyphics. The letter marked but the beginning of a much longer story of how this stone came to be understood as the key to a lost language and a more robust understanding of an ancient Egyptian world. It would be followed in the coming years by announcements in the *Courier d'Égypte*, *La Décade Égyptienne*, and a proliferation of letters and articles in journals destined to unlock the hieroglyphic code.

Not all in the room on that day in July 1799 were equally impressed. The Rosetta Stone would soon take on a life of its own when reproduced in scholarly journals disseminated across the world; and yet a few of those in the audience that afternoon saw the object differently. Quite famously, 'Abd al-Rahman al-Jabarti is known to have responded with outright indifference. And even the Sheikh al-Mahdi, who was the guest of honor at this thirty-first session, is known to have been unimpressed, reserving his most critical comments for the presentation of the tetrodon by Saint-Hilaire: "What!" he is said to have remarked, "So many words for a single fish? I am truly sorry for the author if he is obliged to say as much about each species that live in the water."[7] If the Rosetta Stone served as a monumental discovery, not all shared in the terms of its apparent value.

For those who looked at the object differently than as a linguistic puzzle, the Rosetta Stone was a testament to the passing of time rather than an artifact testifying to a scientific problem of origins. In his book *Conflicted Antiquities*, Elliott Colla contrasts the perspective of the French with that of the Arab scholars for whom "the meaning of the monuments in these accounts is not the positive knowledge they offer about the past, but rather the lessons they offer about the passing of time. Like ruins in classical odes, Pharaonic monuments figure as physical markers by which time itself might be grasped, its lessons heeded, and its contemplators humbled in the process."[8] In a different light, the scholar Okasha El Daly points out that the key to hieroglyphics may stem less from the Oriental sciences of the nineteenth-century empires than the labors of medieval Arab scholars. He points to the writings of Ibn Wahshiyya (Ibn Waḥshīyah) and an extensive tradition of Muslim scholars reflecting on Egyptian antiquities.[9]

If we analyze the scene of the Rosetta Stone's announcement, then we are led to believe that the object was not significant in the same way for all of the audience—it was, we could say, subject to competing frames of understanding. Here, as the story of the Rosetta Stone is told, we see the object referred to as a sort of relic testifying to a particular past and trafficked between two colonial powers. The initial announcement recounts the significance of the languages inscribed on the face of the stone, but it also proclaims the find to an audience dedicated to documenting artifacts, observations, and discoveries. This scholarly frame has as much to do with the occasion and mode of address as with the object being described. The terms that delimit its significance already produce the object itself. At base, then, we deal less with the object than with the frame in which it is valued and through which it is recognized as a discovery at all.

It is worth noting that the literary culture described does not split neatly along a native and nonnative divide. In this story of the French savants, we do encounter the indifference of the Egyptian visitors to the announcement of the Rosetta Stone, but it would be far too convenient to assume that the broader contours of literary and scientific culture divide along national lines. For one, there are literary and scientific institutions that predate the arrival of the French and flourish under the Ottoman Empire; and second, various models of schooling exist within the emergent state. As the story of the Rosetta Stone plays out, we confront not so much imperial discourse on language as the emergence of a scholarly curiosity that traverses national borders. The journals that proclaim the object do so already to a literary and scientific network of interested parties. And in this process, we see mirrored a sort of republic of letters that produces the terms of participation, something to which

I will return in the coming chapters. Bracketing the convenient language of colonizer and colonized, the celebration of the Rosetta Stone demarcates distinctions between interpretative communities within and among national and cultural boundaries.

For now, though, I want to push a bit further and suggest that the scene announcing the Rosetta Stone (to the room of the French savants) mirrors processes implicit in world literature. When scholars approach a text deemed a work of world literature, the text takes on life as an object, and is described from a point of origin to its point of dissemination. In this way, it functions as an artifact, an index of the world from which it is seen to stem, and meaningful on account of how it fits within a world literary system. With a concern for the framework within which world literature is valued, we move away from David Damrosch's model of world literary works (that travel beyond their place of origin) to Pascale Casanova's or even Franco Moretti's mappings of a world literary system (within which objects become meaningful).[10] We move, in other words, from thinking of Naguib Mahfouz as a window onto Egypt or Yasunari Kawabata as an index of life in Japan toward an analysis of how they come to be recognized as literary and how literature matters across cultures and time.

LEVELING LANGUAGES, OR THE CONDITIONS OF EQUIVALENCE

From the reading of the letter at the Institut d'Égypte, the Rosetta Stone quickly found its way into textual form. On September 15, 1799, a few months following Lancret's letter, the *Courier d'Égypte* announced the discovery of "a stone of fine black granite" at the mouth of the Rosetta branch of the Nile River. The British *Gentlemen's Magazine* in 1802 also described the acquisition of the stone: "Col. Turner has brought home in his Majesty's ship Égyptienne, a very large block of black granite, found by Menou, at Rosetta, and intended to be sent by that General, the first convenient opportunity to France."[11] And figures such as the English traveler Edward Daniel Clarke offered accounts of the stone in their writings and travelogues.[12] The archaeological discovery was a newsworthy event of its own, and stories of its significance nearly all linked the object to the three languages on its surface and the imagination of the lost world described in hieroglyphics.

Of the many accounts offered, it is worth noting in particular the labors of Jean-Joseph Marcel, a young Orientalist, translator, author, printer, and member of Napoleon's expedition. The godson of the former French consul in the Levant, Marcel was tapped at a young age to join Napoleon's invasion of Egypt. Both Marcel and Marc Aurel helped to establish printing presses in Egypt. The first of these presses was established on the ship *The Orient* just off the shores of Alexandria, where it printed the now notorious declaration of Napoleon's loyalties to the prophet Muhammad. Once the expedition was set up, Marcel ran the press out of Alexandria and then eventually directed its operations in Cairo. Following initial missteps by Marc Aurel, Marcel became primarily responsible for publishing the literary scientific journal *La Décade Égyptienne* in which his own remarks on the Rosetta Stone were printed. This journal in particular was dedicated to the findings of the Napoleonic Institut d'Égypte, spanning geography, biology, archaeology, literature, and religion.

Marcel's brief comments on the Rosetta Stone appeared in the third volume of *La Décade Égyptienne*. He referred explicitly to the initial arrival of Lancret's letter and to the significance of the discovery it announced:

> Dans la séance du 1.er thermidor, on a donné lecture d'une lettre dans laquelle le citoyen *Lancret*, membre de l'institut, informe que le citoyen *Bouchard*, officier du génie, a découvert dans la ville de Rosette, des inscriptions dont l'examen peut offrir beaucoup d'intérêt.[13]

> In the session of the 1st Thermidor, a letter was read aloud in which Citizen Lancret, a member of the Institut, reported that Citizen Bouchard, an officer of civil engineering, discovered in the town of Rosetta some inscriptions which upon closer examination could be of great interest.

In his entry, Marcel corrected some of the inaccuracies previously reported in *Courier de l'Égypte*—and also generated some of his own, misciting the king's name (as Ptolemy V Epiphanes) and the date of the proclamation (March 27, 196 BCE). He was one of the first to recognize the intermediary characters as demotic. Like those who would follow, Marcel explored the technicalities of the translation itself, going so far as to isolate the proper names in Greek, all as part of an effort to engage both formally and linguistically with what was written. In the end, he offered yet another incarnation of the object in a textual world, and he framed the object, as the entries before it, as a potential key to languages.

Marcel's involvement with the Rosetta Stone would be exemplary of entextualization not only for his writing about the announcement at the Institut d'Égypte, but also for his unique positioning as the director of printing and a key figure in the emergence of print culture in Napoleonic Egypt. On January 24, 1800, Marcel employed a process known as autography to produce several prints of the stone's surface. His efforts marked a preliminary step in extracting the text from the object. He was assisted in this process by Antoine Galland—a publisher, printer, and esteemed savant who shared a name with the famous translator of *One Thousand and One Nights*. In their initial reproduction of the stone, water was poured into the crevices of the stone's surface so that a print could be made off of the relief. In this way, the surface of the Rosetta Stone became a printing block from which the various reproductions would be crafted.

Marcel and Galland were not alone in their efforts. In the spring of 1800, Nicolas-Jacques Conté treated the surface of the stone with rubber and nitric acid to produce the effect of an engraved copper plate. He passed the proof sheets to General Dugua, who in turn delivered them to the National Institute in Paris. And the third method, employed by Adrien Raffenau-Delil, used casting with sulfur to reproduce the text and years later was included as the authoritative version in the *Description de l'Égypte.*

The reproduction of the text both sacralized and desacralized the authenticity of the original object—and entextualized it for the analysis of scholars across the world. There had been many efforts to decode hieroglyphics, but the dissemination of the text of the Rosetta Stone invited global efforts to read it, decipher it, and master a secret alphabet, as though part of a larger inquiry into codes. With the ever-proliferating copies, the Rosetta Stone became a text of world literature in the Damroschian sense, traveling beyond the borders of its production, both historically and culturally displaced. In this form, it was given over to a worldwide network of readers eager to crack its code.

Once the object was multiplied, it became text and was treated as a series of signifiers without a particular link to the stone upon which they were initially printed. And in this global dissemination, the text was opened up further for translation. Initially, even prior to Lancret's letter, Citizen Du Theil furnished a French gloss translation of the Greek inscription on the stone, and in 1801, Citizen Ameilhon provided a Latin translation. The year 1802 saw Reverend Stephen Weston's translation of the Greek into English, and Silvestre de Sacy and Johan David Åkerblad both worked at the demotic text—de Sacy furnished translation of the equivalences between Greek and demotic, and Åkerblad translated the proper names in the demotic. In fact, it was initially the proper names that would serve as points for the translation of the hieroglyphics, leading Thomas Young to note in 1814 that the two scripts, demotic and hieroglyphics, were closely related, an observation that eventually assisted Champollion in his decipherment.

In this common story of decoding, we move from a discussion of the Rosetta Stone as an object, described as something that can be trafficked between countries, to the Rosetta Stone as the occasion for a certain way of reading. As the story has been received, the Rosetta Stone, the object of competing claims for ownership between the French and the British, was eventually decoded by the labors of figures like Young and Champollion, not only allowing for the comprehension of hieroglyphics, but also enabling the emergence of the field of Egyptology. The Rosetta Stone transformed archaeology into literature, shifted the terrain of reading from deciphering to analysis, and enabled the careful reimagination of a past world. That is to say, the Rosetta Stone becomes meaningful not on account of what the object is, but on account of how it is read. And in being read, the object becomes the grounds for its own reproduction as text, serving as the printing press from which its signifiers imprint pages to be disseminated to scholars across the globe.

Let me summarize briefly the processes of entextualization thus far. We have gone from the reading of the letter at the Institut d'Égypte to Marcel's entry in *La Décade Égyptienne* to Marcel's reproduction of it through printing, and finally to the proliferation of translations and debates in scholarly journals. I want now to emphasize one crucial aspect that occurs in this process. Historically speaking, each of the three scripts on the Rosetta Stone functioned differently—hieroglyphics as the language of the gods and Greek as the language of politics. The fact that in the latter part of the eighteenth century language becomes intelligible as a code is especially revealing. Comparative grammar gives rise to a study of language, and the labors of figures such as Silvestre de Sacy help establish the place for comparative philology as part of the modern disciplines. This discipline, this understanding of language, and this relation to the historical past all help to frame the Rosetta Stone as a site of discovery. As a monument of world literature, we could go so far as to say that the Rosetta Stone makes available to us a way of rendering linguistic and textual traditions equivalent in spite of phenomenological distinctions between them. This is a world in which scripture and literature fold together, and a world in which culture, language, and society become the leveling logic of comparison.

ENTEXTUALIZATION AND THE PURELY LITERARY

If thus far I have discussed the movement from object to text and text to translation, then I want here to consider quite squarely the implications of entextualization for the rise of world literature. We already saw that the recognition of the Rosetta Stone as equivalent languages relies upon the disavowal of the qualitative and phenomenological distinctions between sacred and worldly languages, but the implications for world literature play out even further. As I hope to suggest, they lead us to consider the provincialism of the literary world within which these texts are read. But let's continue with our story.

Jean-Joseph Marcel was not solely a printer, a scholar, and a reporter of events at the Institut d'Égypte, he was also a translator and literary scholar. In 1799, soon after his arrival in Egypt, he published *Les Fables de Loqman*, a sort of Arabic version of Aesop's fables that he published in French.[14] After returning to France, in 1829, he published a longer translation, *Les dix soirées malheureuses d'Abdelrahman al-Iskandri*.[15] In addition to these book-length literary translations—and more immediately related to the Rosetta Stone—Marcel published a translation of an Arabic poem in the first issue of the journal *La Décade Égyptienne*. His entry, "Ode arabe sur la Conquête de l'Égypte," lists his own name in the title line, subordinating the name of the poet, Niqula al-Turq ibn Yusuf Istanbuli, to the body of the article. And as though echoing

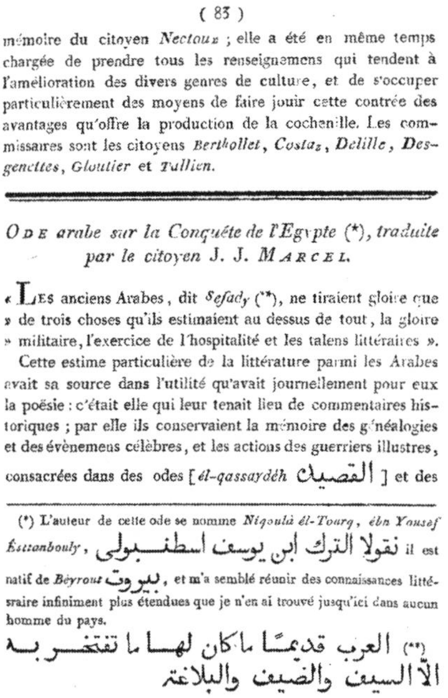

(83)

mémoire du citoyen *Nectoux* ; elle a été en même temps chargée de prendre tous les renseignemens qui tendent à l'amélioration des divers genres de culture, et de s'occuper particulièrement des moyens de faire jouir cette contrée des avantages qu'offre la production de la cochenille. Les commissaires sont les citoyens *Berthollet*, *Costaz*, *Delille*, *Desgenettes*, *Gloutier* et *Tullien*.

Ode arabe sur la Conquête de l'Egypte (*), traduite par le citoyen J. J. Marcel.

« Les anciens Arabes, dit *Sefady* (**), ne tiraient gloire que » de trois choses qu'ils estimaient au dessus de tout, la gloire » militaire, l'exercice de l'hospitalité et les talens littéraires ».

Cette estime particulière de la littérature parmi les Arabes avait sa source dans l'utilité qu'avait journellement pour eux la poësie : c'était elle qui leur tenait lieu de commentaires historiques ; par elle ils conservaient la mémoire des généalogies et des évènemens célèbres, et les actions des guerriers illustres, consacrées dans des odes [*él-qassaydéh* القصيدة] et des

(*) L'auteur de cette ode se nomme *Niqoulà él-Tourq, ébn Yousef Éstanbouly*, نقولا الترك ابن يوسف اسطنبولي il est natif de *Béyrout* بيروت, et m'a semblé réunir des connaissances littéraire infiniment plus étendues que je n'en ai trouvé jusqu'ici dans aucun homme du pays.

(**) العرب قديما ما كان لها ما تفتخر به الا السيف والضيف والبلاغة

FIGURE 2. Marcel's preface to the translation of an Arabic ode published in the first volume of *La Décade Égyptienne*.
Source: La Décade Égyptienne, vol. 1 (Cairo, 1798–1799), 83.

some of the terms of the initial proclamation he helped to author on board *The Orient*, the poem celebrates the arrival of the French, casting Napoleon as a sort of liberator of Egypt.

But the translation of the poem is merely one part of the article, and Marcel's entry has as much to do with delineating the role of poetry in Arabic literature as with the translation itself. He notes, for example, the particular role that poetry has in daily life and in historical commentary among the Arab people:

> Cette estime particulière de la littérature parmi les Arabes avait sa source dans l'utilité qu'avait journellement pour eux la poésie: c'était elle qui leur tenait lieu de commentaires historiques; par elle ils conservaient la mémoire des généalogies et des évènements célèbres, et les actions des guerriers illustres, consacrées dans des odes [*él-qassaydéh*] et des poèmes [*él-hhamâséh*], que chacun s'empressait d'apprendre par cœur, se transmettaient de bouche en bouche et d'âge en âge.[16]

> This particular regard for literature among the Arabs has its root in the daily utility they found in poetry. This poetry grounded their historical commentary; through it they preserved genealogical memory and great events, and actions of decorated warriors, consecrated in odes and poems, that each was encouraged to learn by heart, passed on from mouth to mouth and from age to age.

Intriguingly, the remarks about poetry come prior to the translation itself, and much like the articles announcing the terms of the Rosetta Stone, they frame how this poem is to matter—as an index of Arabic poetry generally and as an exemplar of the Arabic ode. And perhaps tellingly, Marcel describes it as part of a larger literary empire:

> Peut-être partagera-t-on mes sentimens; peut-être en y reconnaissant étincelles de ce feu électrique qui caractérise la veritable poésie, pensera-t-on que la muse arabe n'est pas tout à fait indigne d'occuper une petite place dans cet empire littéraire où jusqu'ici ont régné presqu'exclusivement les muses européennes.[17]

> Perhaps one will share my sentiments; perhaps recognizing there an electric spark that characterizes true poetry, we will think that the Arab muse was not altogether unworthy of occupying a small place in the literary empire, where until now almost exclusively European muses have reigned.

As the entry continues, Marcel moves to his translation of the poem, which is published alongside the Arabic—or, given the physical layout of the page, before it. The French translation has its own meter and is presented on a page before the Arabic, broken into stanzas, but without regard for the Arabic meter. At the poem's conclusion, Marcel includes a set of annotations to gloss the conventions of Arabic poetry, including reflections on the hemistich and the ending words of the last verses.

Published as the poem is in a journal, it follows an article reporting on a session at the Institut d'Égypte. The sequencing appears almost random, except that each entry follows from another framed within the broad literary-scientific scope that the journal proclaims in its open pages. It is perhaps unsurprising, then, that a mere number of pages later, Marcel's literary skills are turned to a text of another sort: the Qur'an. In an essay on the translation of the Qur'an into verse, "Essai de traduction en vers d'un fragment du Koran," Marcel combines reflections on the status of the Qur'an as a document with his own rendering of Sūrat al-Fātiḥah (The Opening). Similar to the discussion of poetry before his translation of the ode, here, in this entry, Marcel frames the Qur'an for the reader. He does so by situating the Qur'an as the supreme form of eloquence for the Muslim community on behalf of which he claims to speak:

(126)

TRADUCTION.

Au nom de l'Etre unique en pouvoir, en essence ;
Au nom du Dieu clement, du Dieu de bienfaisance,
Dont sur nous chaque jour s'épanchent les présens,
Vers qui nous élevons nos vœux et notre encens.....

Louange au Dieu du ciel, de la terre et des ondes......
Pere de l'univers ! dominateur des mondes !
Arbitre des destins au jour du jugement !
Vengeur de l'opprimé ! soutien de l'innocent !
C'est vers toi que nos cœurs élancent leur priere,
C'est toi que nous osons implorer comme un pere....
Exauce tes enfans ! que toujours l'équité,
Affermissant leurs pas, soit leur guide assuré !
Qu'ils fuient les sentiers de l'erreur mensongère !
Que nul crime sur eux n'appelle ta colère !
Que dirigeant vers toi leurs esprits et leurs cœurs,
Ils se montrent toujours tes vrais adorateurs !

(127)

TEXTE

بسم الله
الرحمن الرحيم

الحمد لله ربّ العالمين
الرحمن الرحيم مالك يوم الدين
اياك نعبد واياك نستعين
اهدنا الصراط المستقيم
صراط الذين انعمت عليهم
غير المغضوب عليهم ولا الضالين

FIGURE 3. Marcel's verse translation of Sūrat al-Fātiḥah from the Qur'an as published in the first volume of *La Décade Égyptienne*.
Source: La Décade Égyptienne, vol. 1 (Cairo, 1798–1799), 126–27.

> Le Koran, ou *le livre par excellence*, est regardé par les Musulmans comme un chef-d'oeuvre d'éloquence: les Arabes pretendent même qu'il n'éxiste point dans leur langue d'oeuvrage mieux écrit. . . .[18]
>
> The Qur'an is regarded by Muslims as a masterpiece of eloquence: the Arabs claim that no work exists in their language better written. . . .

And inasmuch as he offers this framework to the reader, so too does he engage in a comparative analysis of the Qur'an, likening it as a "work" unto other works. In a sort of gesture of comparative religions, he refers to it as though any other work of scripture: "comme la Bible, l'Évangile et les Vedams" (the Bible, the Gospel and the Vedas). He alludes to the prophetic language, its role between a pure morality (*morale pure*) mixed with fiction, philosophy, truth, and dreams, and he continues to highlight the sublime elements of its text in the paragraphs that follow.[19] He notes its richness of images, the abundance of metaphors, its noble manner, and its ultimate sublimity.

His remarks end with a sort of apology in which he confesses not having been able to achieve the beauty of the original, and he warns of the interdiction surrounding the translation of the Qur'an in general, which he nonetheless makes available in writing. Tucked onto the pages of this first issue of *La Décade Égyptienne*, the Qur'an becomes an artifact, a text, a cultural curiosity to be read and admired on account of its literary properties. Like the poem pages before, the Qur'an is transformed into yet another corner of this literary empire, one that textualizes artifacts to attest to the richness of cultures in the provincial domain of scholarly readers.

My point here is not simply to state that the translation of the Qur'an is equivalent to the translation of the Rosetta Stone, but to focus instead on the fact that translation, bringing these texts into French, actually does much more than transpose linguistically. Trained as we are as literary scholars to believe in the materiality of language, we often treat languages as languages without attention to the phenomenological character of the languages themselves: from where and to whom they speak, how they differ in modes of address, and the status of speech they entail. On some level, we see in the translation of the Qur'an a gesture that makes of scripture literature—by which I mean the leveling of registers and qualities of language between the theological and the literary, between the divine and the political. There are some fairly vast implications for this sort of hermeneutic enterprise, which sees texts as windows onto a nascent cultural world but levels the distinctions between languages in doing so.

It is by no means out of place to comment on the Qur'an with literary terms. In fact, for years many key literary theorists have anchored their own reflections on eloquence with a careful consideration of Qur'anic language. Here, for example, we might think of Sayyid Qutb's (Sayyid Quṭb) remarkable *al-Taṣwīr al-fannī fī al-qur'ān*.[20] But Marcel's framework is quite different. It engages the Qur'an as a sort of cultural object whose significance can be mined through the literary analysis of its properties. The end of his study is a more robust understanding of a worldly situation, but such an understanding is gleaned by foreclosing the phenomenological properties through which the text comes to mean differently. In Marcel's entry, we encounter both a translation of Sūrat al-Fātiḥah, and Sūrat al-Fātiḥah framed as a textual artifact, something to be decoded and translated as a matter of language—something, we might say, akin to the Rosetta Stone.

THE CONTOURS OF A LITERARY EMPIRE

In this interchangeable system of objects within the framework of the literary sciences, we thus arrive at what I have been suggesting here is the basis of world literature. If I invite this pairing of the poem, the Qur'an, and the Rosetta Stone, it is because of the ways in which they are each reborn textually and made available to a particular mode of reading. Just as telling as the objects themselves is the phenomenon by which they are each embedded in a descriptive preface. And it is in these descriptive prefaces that the objects are contextualized, and it is precisely how they are contextualized that bespeaks the sort of phenomenological leveling integral to their incarnation as textual artifacts. What is born with the discovery of the Rosetta Stone is this hermeneutic endeavor to make the world intelligible through words.

I have argued in the first section of the chapter that the Rosetta Stone bespeaks an understanding of language that reads equivalence across the various languages printed on the surface. Just as the distinctions between hieroglyphics as the language of the gods and Greek as the language of politics subside in a generalized theory of language as code, so too does the assimilation of textual forms into the Napoleonic journal purport a generalized theory of literature. But to what extent can the Rosetta Stone be understood as a scene of reading at all? Does the text matter in the same way as a poem? Is it not the very unreadability of the Rosetta Stone that makes it a puzzle? My claim here is not to push for *or* against an understanding of the Rosetta Stone as a work of literature. It is rather to point to the community that celebrates it as a site for understanding literary networks. What is asserted at this moment historically is the birth of a particular modality of reading that understands the equivalence between languages as the key to unlocking an ancient world.

When it comes to world literature, then, the Rosetta Stone serves as the affirmation of radical comparison for the audience that comes to value it as a discovery. The slab of stone provides not only a puzzle, but a philosophy of language and the possibilities of translation across place and time. We might consider the implications of this gesture by noting the relationship of particular literary and linguistic traditions within the scope of world literature. Thinking about the place of Arabic literature in world literature, for example, returns us less to the specificity of Arabic than to the ways that the term "literature" is made to accommodate the particularities of varying textual traditions. The quest, then, is not for some native invention of an untranslated Arabic literature, but rather an investigation into how and what literature comes to mean. There are important questions to be asked, but one is to imagine a world outside the literary textualism invited by the Rosetta Stone and Marcel's translation of Arabic texts into the French literary frame.

Part of why I have dealt so extensively here with entextualization is to consider the limits of world literature. For scholars of world literature, there tends to be a shared assumption about the value of literary texts. By foreclosing the classic question of what literature is, in favor of the question of where it takes place, world literature tends to provincialize the frames within which we read. What are the limits to textual understanding, and how else might we delimit the boundaries of world literature? What do we do, for example, when the world in which we situate a text is not the world within which the text is understood (and here we might think of Marcel's excerpt from the Qur'an)? Answering these sorts of questions, reflecting on the scholarly, literary, or philological frame of reading, sheds light on the problem of an object-oriented literary analysis. In the end, it allows us insight into the world within which an object such as the Rosetta Stone comes to matter.

The point, then, on which I would like to conclude is the following: rather than take as a given the stability of the terms within which texts are worldly, we as scholars ought to think across the interpretative worlds the texts make available. My interest in linking together the Rosetta Stone with the translations of poetry and the Qur'an has been to model a means of thinking more robustly about mediation across interpretative worlds. As scholars dealing with texts from a number of traditions, we must ultimately come to terms not only with places depicted but, more crucially still, with the acute ways in which interpretative traditions impact our sensibilities as readers. It is this analytic field that serves as the invitation and the challenge of literary geography and the perennial question of what literature is. What comes to matter, then, has less to do with the status of the object under analysis than the literary culture that determines how and in what ways it ought to be assessed and discussed. Telling this story means shifting from an emphasis on the literary object to an emphasis on the emergent literary sensibility cultivated through the disciplining of how to read. World literature transforms in this process from a collection of objects to a cultivation of readers.

As we move on to the following chapter, we will transition from a discussion of the textual object to consider the disciplines through which reading comes to occur. The emergence of a philosophy of language collapsing the distinction between the political and theological attributes of signification has implications beyond the world of the French savants. As educational policies took shape in colonial Egypt, there was a simultaneous push for literary instruction, on the one hand, and an avoidance of it, on the other. For supporters, literary instruction was seen as integral to the cultivation of a moral, reflective, and democratic polity, and for its critics, an emphasis on literary reading produced an overeducated workforce not necessarily equipped to deal with the technical demands of the Egyptian economy. Within this framework, our discussion considers further the disciplines, practices, and virtues that come to inhere in modern education. The place of literature emerges less from the literary objects gathered than from debates over literary education, the modern state, and the recognition of critical reflection in a colonial setting.

3

EDUCATION

The Moral Imperative of Modernization

> What Europeans mean when they talk of Egyptian self-government is that the Egyptians, far from being allowed to follow the bent of their own unreformed propensities, should only be permitted to govern themselves after the fashion in which Europeans think they ought to be governed.
>
> —LORD CROMER, *MODERN EGYPT*

The common fairy tale of literary modernity in colonial Egypt casts the rise of literacy and new literary forms alongside the development of the modern state, the emergence of modern schools, and the translation, adaptation, and eventual transformation of Western cultural models.[1] Beginning with the scholarly missions established under Muhammad ʻAli and the eventual education of renowned intellectual figures like Rifaʻa al-Tahtawi (Rifāʻah Rāfiʻ al-Ṭahṭāwī) and later Taha Hussein, the modernization narrative reads as an account of cultural enlightenment.[2] Egypt supposedly awakens at the moment it opens up to developments in modern politics, empirical science, as well as arts and literature. And within this account, the failure of the British occupation to bolster national education is seen as a mere stalled moment in a story that eventually culminates with the liberation of the Egyptian state from colonial rule. A myriad of often-conflicting explanations have been offered to account for the limited role of education under the autocratic consul general, Sir Evelyn Baring (Lord Cromer), who oversaw the governance of Egypt from 1883 to 1907; and yet, nearly across the board, the importance of education as an intrinsically modernizing force on the path to self-government goes unquestioned.[3] For the apologists of the British occupation and for the Egyptian nationalists, education's fundamental role was taken as given. If the two sides differed, it was largely over when, in the developmental logic of the modern state, education was to become a priority.

It is perhaps unsurprising, then, that when Alfred Milner published his widely popular *England in Egypt* in 1892, he was defensive about the scant attention paid to education during the British occupation; and that years later, in 1908, when Lord Cromer published his two-volume *Modern Egypt*, he too alluded defensively to education and suggested that other reforms had a more direct impact on the daily life of modern Egyptians. Among many issues that these two imperial accounts held in common, they both shared an underlying assumption that a sound economy was the most crucial step toward the eventual emergence of a self-governing modern Egypt. And even if the deferred goal of Egyptian self-government remained a seemingly distant vision for both, it was nonetheless integral to the overall rhetoric of the British occupation—which saw flawed finances as "international fetters upon Egyptian freedom."[4] Milner was careful to note that the economic priorities were not to be misunderstood: "the interest of the bond holders," he writes, "has never been the inspiring motive of our [British] policy, least of all of our policy during recent years."[5] He continued by proclaiming the humanitarian benefits of the occupation: "The inspiring, the predominant motive of that [British economic] policy, is the welfare of the Egyptian people."[6] Humanitarianism here pertains to a series of governmental and economic policies meant to ensure a particular type of freedom for Egypt—that is, an escape from a seemingly interminable accumulation of debt.

Although education was not an explicit policy in the pursuit of this welfare, it ends up being inseparable from the British occupation. What it means for Egypt to be free is for Egypt to be financially self-determined, and this path to financial self-determination was a lesson overseen by the British administration. When Cromer writes, for example, that Egyptians "should only be permitted to govern themselves after the fashion in which Europeans think they ought to be governed," he gestures to this implicit circularity. Even if he did not pursue educational reform as a direct policy of his administration, he, like Milner, returns time and again to the pedagogical imperatives implicit in how the Egyptians "ought to be governed." What is at stake is the fact that the British occupation implied education by other means—not so much the systematic education of a population in schools, but the transformation of the world within which the colonized population lived and the determination of the freedom toward which the Egyptian people should strive. Moral education was immanent to this process of modernization—and ultimately to the goal of self-government.

Where the chapters thus far have traced the contours of a literary world, this chapter engages most explicitly its limit—that is, it questions how an emergent literacy imagines its other. I draw here from a wealth of scholarship dealing with British imperialism in Egypt—Timothy Mitchell, Mohammad Salama, and Shaden Tageldin, to name a few—but I extend these discussions to consider the role of education within the imagined future of a self-governing state, on the one hand, and the colonial obsession with those seen to be uneducated, hidebound, and fanatical, on the other.[7] Drawing critically from colonial sources, I focus primarily on the arguments for reformed educational policy, often anchored in fears of fanaticism as a counterpart to the moral force of modernization. The question, ultimately, is not why the British underemphasized education in Egypt, for there was always a pedagogic mission to the colonial occupation, but how education comes to be understood (or even transformed) in proclamations of its implicit failure.

Part of explaining the convergence of literary modernity and the rhetoric of educational failure is fairly straightforward: For both defenders of the British administration and its critics, education was seen less in terms of instruction (*taʻlīm*), which implied a set corpus of material to be transmitted to the student, than in terms of cultivation (*tarbiyah*), which implied the students' moral development through learning. As these distinctions play out, both Milner and Cromer understand Qur'anic schools as the domain of instruction, overly concerned with rote memorization at the expense of critical literacy. What emerges is not a developmental historical narrative, where modern schools simply replace Qur'anic schools, but an account that both produces and transforms the terms within which the past comes to be understood, often embodied in a figure deemed ignorant, or in a more extreme variant, fanatical. It is this figure that becomes the unthinkable impediment to the modernizing story and provides the limit to the transformational mission of modern education.

The story of Egypt's path to modernization is thus the story not only of those supposedly redeemed and transformed through modern pedagogy, but also of those outside of its domain. Cromer proclaims some measure of success when he writes, "The Egyptians have, in fact, made one great step forward in the race for a national existence. They have learnt that they are ignorant. They wish to be taught."[8] At play in these brashly paternalistic remarks is a population's self-recognition as "ignorant," but what remains unthinkable is the position from which *not* to wish to be taught. There is a moral force to modernization, and the civilizing mission distinguishes the good from the bad, the future from the past, and the modern from the traditional. The rhetoric of modern self-government entails the shaping of moral dispositions integral to the imagined future it holds in store, and for those who fall outside the parameters of this civilizational transformation, modernization provides other policing forces. In a colonial situation increasingly divided between the educated elite and the uneducated, we are a far cry from a distinction between national populations—we are instead in the moral universe of sensibilities deemed educated, civilized, and modern, and those deemed traditional, fanatic, and uneducated.

In invoking this list of binarisms, I do not want to suggest that there is, in fact, a modern world and a traditional world existing in some unbridgeable divide. I borrow here from an analytical distinction that Talal Asad provides in his effort to link together modernity and secularism. Engaging a number of scholars who rightly note that modernity is not a verifiable object, Asad reframes the issue: "The important question, therefore, is not to determine why the idea of 'modernity' (or 'the West') is a misdescription, but why it has become hegemonic *as a political goal*, what practical consequences follow from that hegemony, and what social conditions maintain it."[9] He emphasizes how modernity entails projects that "account for distinctive sensibilities, aesthetics, moralities," and he notes that "[m]odernity is not primarily a matter of cognizing the real but of living-in-the-world."[10] I draw from Asad's argument in considering what happens to the modernizing story when we refuse the binarism of the modern and traditional, much of which is based on the understanding of modernity as the waning of religion and the rise of the modern state. The modernization narrative produces its counterpart of religious traditionalism, but in doing so, it forecloses a number of critical questions. In what follows, I consider the hegemonic goal of modernization largely from the unintelligibility of the figure of the uneducated. With moral education immanent to the processes of self-government, there is no position from which to counter the seemingly inevitable march toward modernity without being deemed ignorant or fanatical in the process.

FAILURE'S SUCCESS: SECURING THE IMAGINED FUTURE

In 1892, when the British undersecretary of finance, Alfred Milner, published *England in Egypt*, he included a chapter for miscellaneous concerns, titled "Odds and Ends of Reform." In contrast to the historical orientation of preceding chapters, this chapter clusters together various topics for improved rule over Egypt and focuses in large part on the role of education. The inclusion of education in a chapter for miscellaneous concerns underscores a certain hierarchy of priorities within both Milner's reflections and the British governance of Egypt more broadly.[11] During this late Victorian moment of indirect rule, Milner followed his supervisor, Sir Evelyn Baring (later Lord Cromer), who privileged economic self-sufficiency as the factor most essential to an eventual transition to a self-governing state. From 1882 through 1922, Egypt remained under British rule in an explicit manner, and it was not until 1952 that the yoke of the British occupation was formally shed. For Milner and the administration that his writings defended, education was to serve as a mere step toward this ever-deferred goal of Egyptian self-government, but it was by no means primary as an end in itself. There were, Milner famously wrote, other concerns: "People must live before they can be taught. Famine is worse than ignorance."[12]

Milner's remarks embed the staggering Egyptian educational system within a larger historical, and ultimately developmental, narrative. Education was seen as essential for imparting the values, principles, and disciplines of the modern state, but when it came to Egypt, Milner pointed to different, seemingly dire circumstances: "What the Egyptian Government had to fight for, six or seven years ago," he writes, "was the very existence of the people."[13] Seeing the destiny of Egypt in these rather harrowing terms, Milner noted the urgency of public works: "Essential as education is, the provision of education is not such a primary duty of Government as the defence of person and property, the maintenance of justice, or, in a country like Egypt, where human life depends upon Public works, the careful preservation of those works upon which life depends."[14] In Milner's account, education was, by matter of necessity, subordinate to other more basic concerns of government. And perhaps unsurprisingly, years later, the Sub-Committee on Education of the 1920 Milner Commission declared the educational system an outright failure—under the British, barely one percent of the annual Egyptian budget was ever allocated to education, and at the turn of the century, 95 percent of the population was illiterate.[15]

As the story has been inherited, education in Egypt is almost universally understood as a failure.[16] The nationalist movement, casting itself against educational policies of British rule, made education a cornerstone in the struggle to free Egypt for the Egyptians.[17] And even Milner excused the bleak conditions of education as an unfortunate outcome of more pressing priorities—his comments read more as an apology than any proclamation of success. It is worth noting a contrast to the British policies earlier pursued in colonial India. There, literary education (and in particular, the institutionalization of English literature) was seen as integral to effective colonial rule and especially well suited to the cultivation of the moral and ethical sensibilities of the colonized population. Gauri Viswanathan maps "the relationship between the institutionalization of English in India and the exercise of colonial power," and offers a meticulously researched history of how India came to serve as a laboratory for literary pedagogy eventually employed in England.[18] The situation she describes pertains to a historical moment prior to the occupation of Egypt, and by the latter part of the nineteenth century, the methods of literary education in India were increasingly challenged. By many accounts, it was the system of educating colonized Indians that made possible, on some level, the Indian Rebellion of 1857. The failed policies of education in Egypt often explicitly built upon the perceived failure of the model of literary education implemented in colonial India.

One such critic of the educational system in India was Lord Cromer, who served as a finance minister to the Indian viceroy Lord Ripon before becoming a notoriously paternalistic autocrat as consul general of Egypt. It was his contention that training in literature either produces a disgruntled group of overeducated workers or, not entirely unrelated, promotes anticolonial sentiments.[19] He bemoaned the fact that Indian education was "too literary;

insufficient attention [was] paid to professional, technical, and industrial education." In yet another instance, Cromer wrote in a letter to Strachey, "Notably in matters concerned with education, India furnishes rather an object lesson in what should be avoided."[20] And thus, in Cromer's estimation, any program of mass education in Egypt was to consist of "the three R's in the vernacular language; nothing more."[21] By the time the British took over in Egypt, this pragmatism altered the terms in which education was related to the colonial endeavor. No longer a matter of educating the population at large through the institutionalization of literature, the British government in Egypt had other priorities: namely to transform directly the material conditions in which populations lived and operated to enhance the economic self-sufficiency of the state. Gone were aspirations of crafting each individual through literary education, and instead political education became immanent to matters of colonial government.

By the turn of the nineteenth century, even the journalist, writer, and imperialist Valentine Chirol echoed a predominant line of thinking with regard to the British occupation of Egypt. For all of the efforts to stabilize Egypt economically and for all of the paternalism that predominated as a result, the British Empire had, in the domain of education, utterly failed the Egyptians: "By whatever standard we judge the educational system devised for the youth of Egypt under British control," he writes, "it has tended not at all to the salvation of the State. It is unquestionably the worst of our failures."[22] He continued by reprimanding the mere "lip-worship" offered: "If we have made such a poor job of Egyptian education, the great underlying cause is only too clear. There have been very few Englishmen in responsible positions in Egypt who have ever paid more than lip-worship to the importance of education."[23] Chirol was by no means alone in this sentiment—figures ranging from adamant defenders of the British administration to Egyptian nationalists all admit some level at which British educational policy had supposedly failed. For the defenders, failure was an unfortunate outcome of overall financial hardship; and for the administration's critics, failure was the result of a systematic underfinancing of schools. In both cases, the obviousness of failure was not in question.

What exactly was this failure? Was it the failure to achieve goals set by the colonial administration? Was it the failure of the administration to provide for education toward an imagined future of self-government? What would it mean *not* to have failed? What would have constituted success? Focusing on the vision of success over the rhetoric of failure, we arrive at a fairly different situation. Discussions of failure tend to presume what it would mean *not* to fail—and here, embedded in the moral argument of failure, we find a seemingly shared vision of an imagined future. National education reform had been a preoccupation of the emergent state, and the commissioned reports of figures from Edouard Dor, Yacoub Artin, 'Ali Mubarak ('Alī Mubārak Bāshā), Douglas Dunlop, and eventually Sa'ad Zaghlul (Saʿd Zaghlūl) all testify to this quest for a consolidated national education program. Initially, this program focused on the development of specialized schools for an educated elite and then later, particularly under Sa'ad Zaghlul, through the mass reformation of Qur'anic schools at the primary level. In nearly all of these accounts, the desirability of modern education is taken as given, and critics and proponents alike both unite in cementing this rather novel redefinition of what it means to be educated. Curiously, what is at stake in pointing out failure, then, is a moral argument that entails the nonrealization of a specific imagined future. What failed, in other words, was not only the struggling education system under the British, but the step toward the imagined future of a self-governing state.

As the story is told, though, we encounter a split between the British and the nationalists, both of whom recognize failure in somewhat similar terms and both of whom value, at least in principle, the role of education in an imagined future of a self-governing state. In what ways does literature accrue value within this imagined future? The story I tell here and in the previous chapters is meant to draw our attention to literature in a different light—less as a discrete textual object than as a cultivated sensibility integral to recognition as an educated subject. In this understanding, literature is not the domain of a national canon, a particular author, or a specific language, but instead delimits a sensibility closely aligned with presumptions about what it means to be modern, educated, and critical. And in turn, the cultural categories so long the domain of literary study (seen in terms of nations, languages, and peoples) give way to the moral differentiation between the cosmopolitan and the provincial, the liberal and the fanatic, the open-minded and the intolerant. In the terms offered by modern education, learning to recite the Qur'an ceases to be understood as a capacity to read, and instead, reading is closely aligned with the capacity to react and respond to written material in a particular way. The challenge here is asking how and through which practices the literary world secures these distinctions—most often against lifeworlds it deems fanatical, or more recently, fundamentalist. This, it seems to me, is not simply a matter of pointing to stereotypes, caricatures, and misrepresentation in colonial writing, but of analyzing and possibly unsettling the moral presumptions that inhere in the civilizational rhetoric of modernization. This chapter is an effort in these directions.

FROM PREJUDICE TO OPINION

The story of failure and success is merely one aspect of this argument, and it is telling that both Milner and later Cromer frame their remarks with attention to modernization and the specter of the unmodern, delimiting both who is and who is not capable of critique. Milner's account deals, on the one hand, with an emergent class of Egyptians educated in foreign schools and trained for civil service and, on the other, those he describes as "primitive peasantry."[24] While those educated in the modern schools are eventually to constitute the core of Egyptian government, the remainder of the population, "the primitive peasantry," poses Milner challenges of a different sort. In lines brimming with an imperial paternalism, Milner notes, "To govern such a race [the peasantry] is, under ordinary circumstances, a simple task,"[25] but he goes on to explain, "there is always some danger of people being carried away by a spasm of excitement—especially religious excitement."[26] Milner explains this tendency away, claiming, "The Egyptian, if easily governed, is also easily led. He is not by nature in the least fanatical. But he has been brought up in fanatical traditions, and he is greatly under the influence of religious teachers, who are fanatics by profession."[27] This subject of Milner's book, the Egyptian supposedly outside the disciplines of the modern state and easily swayed by religious teaching, actually comes to play a rather crucial role in what follows. The education at stake in government is learning bent on the apparent liberation of the subject from fanaticism. For this population, learning to appreciate the British role is to master appreciating the sensibilities that British governance makes immanent to the procedures of political rule.

At an especially striking moment, Milner considers quite explicitly the emergent distinction between opinion and prejudice. He raises the question of why the Egyptian people were mostly against the British occupation: "I have often been asked," he writes, "whether British influence is popular with the mass of the Egyptian people. It would be absurd to reply to that question in the affirmative."[28] As he continues, he offers the caveat, "But to answer it in the negative would be no less misleading." Having obfuscated the possible lines of response, he goes on to explain, "There is unquestionably a certain prejudice against Englishmen, as there is against all Christians, though that prejudice is easily overcome in individual cases where the people have learned to recognize the stranger as a benefactor."[29] By invoking prejudice, Milner would seem to invite a position critical of "Englishmen," but his remarks do not grant prejudice, in this instance, the weight of an opinion. In fact, as though speaking from utter disbelief at the situation, Milner notes, "prejudice is easily overcome in individual cases." Curiously enough, these individual cases seem to provide one glimpse into the pedagogical imperative at stake in Milner's account: education is implicit both in "*learning* to recognize the stranger as a benefactor" and in "having an opinion" regarding the "broad political issue" of the British involvement in Egypt. In neither case are we dealing with an explicit program by which to educate a population, but instead the implicit assumption that the supposed improvement of material conditions will necessarily lead to overcoming prejudice. In a word, transforming minds by transforming worlds.

As we trace Milner's puzzlement at the impossible response to the question of why the mass of the Egyptian population is dissatisfied, we are led from those with opinions to those with mere prejudice. The movement between these two positions actually underscores a central distinction between those recognizably educated subjects, capable of holding opinions, and those deemed uneducated and disposed toward prejudice. In a most explicit sense, we are dealing here with the social constraints necessary to be *heard* as a modern political subject. For Milner, to be heard as a political subject entails being educated in a particular way: that is, capable of being in "a position to reason about the causes for change" and of having an opinion. The uneducated peasant is not so much voiceless or underrepresented, but fundamentally outside the parameters through which opinion is intelligible within a system of modern governance. Thus, although it might appear that Milner skirts the issue of education, what it means for Egypt to be self-governing ultimately hinges upon this curious pedagogical bind—as regards both the priorities of the Egyptian state and the production of Egyptian subjects. By casting disdain for the British occupation as prejudice, Milner seemingly expels critique from the realm of possibility. Deaf to the world itself, he reserves opinion for those with recognizably sound judgment based on education, and he frames prejudice as a product of fanaticism.

GOVERNING HERMENEUTICS, PRODUCING SUBJECTS

In 1894, a mere two years after the first edition of the book, Milner included a new preface to his reflections on governance in Egypt. "Educational progress," he writes, "has no doubt been retarded by the revival of fanatical prejudice consequent upon the recent political troubles."[30] Fanaticism, previously presented as a parenthetical issue, comes to the fore in the new preface as both a hindrance to educational progress and an occasion to reflect more generally on educational policies. Here the specter of the fanatic is not merely a matter of determining who has the capacity to hold opinions. There is neither any particular subject claiming recognition as a fanatic nor any group claiming exclusion from the parameters of recognition offered by the modern state. Instead, Milner addresses fanaticism as a symptom of circumstances and a threat to the eventual promise of self-government. Without necessarily looking to uproot religious traditions in Egypt, Milner considers how modern government might curtail practices that are seen to lead to the production of the fanatic. If it earlier appears that the British avoided policies of education, then the concern with fanaticism ushers in an occasion for broader reflections on how education might better inculcate a set of disciplines and sensibilities seen as essential to the modern state. In fact, we could say that it is through the specter of the fanatic that the supposedly virtuous, educated, and modern subject comes to be understood.

Even though Milner sees educational reform as an antidote, he places greater weight in his book on descriptions of what he sees to be an utterly outdated education system—often drawing, in the process, from a rather crude characterization of what goes on in Qur'anic instruction. In his discussion,

Milner highlights what he takes to be the three main shortcomings: the first fault, he remarks, is "the practice of cramming the memory instead of developing the powers of thought"; the second, "multiplying the number of subjects taught, and in sacrificing quality to quantity"; and the third, "the want of attention to discipline, to deportment, and to physique."[31] The commentary he dedicates to schooling switches between discussions of al-Azhar and the *kuttāb* system, and in each instance, he focuses in nearly obsessive detail on the apparent shortcomings of this system for the mass of Egyptians. He speaks, though, from a nearly impossible position, for not only did his administration limit funding for education, but as the work of the historians ʿAbd al-Karim and Heyworth-Dunne testifies, the actual number of students enrolled in modern schools fell quite systematically during the period of the British occupation.[32]

The point in dwelling on Milner's remarks is neither to assess their descriptive accuracy nor to relate them to other studies of education, but to consider what the description of the "old system" makes possible as a moral argument. On the one hand, the descriptions enable him to delineate what he sees as "the object of true education": "If the object of true education be intellectual gymnastic, if it be to exercise and render supple the joints of the mind, then this system is its very opposite, for it tends to stiffen them. It is not calculated to enlighten, but to obfuscate,"[33] and quite predictably, to characterize Qur'anic schooling as "an anti-educational process." On the other hand, though, the descriptions redefine education for the purposes of a particular future, securing in its wake the goals and objectives deemed necessary. His descriptions at once misrecognize the *kuttāb* system as a rudimentary educational institution and then, setting up a false equivalence, diagnose their implicit failure to provide skills essential for modern governance. In this curious manner, Milner writes on the cusp of a conquered past, which he himself produces rhetorically, and a promised liberation from it, deferred in the future promise of self-government.

In defining "the object of true education" against Qur'anic instruction, Milner assumes that Qur'anic instruction might possibly share the same goals as the reformed educational system—that is, he assumes that there is enough of an equivalence to recognize Qur'anic instruction as a type of schooling. And in this account, he is hardly alone. As the story is most often told, before the British occupation of Egypt, educational reform had already been enacted under Muhammad ʿAli and promoted again under Khedive Ismaʿil. The educational system, overseen by the Ministry of Public Instruction (*dīwān al-madāris*), entailed two fairly distinct tracks: on the one hand, there was the *kuttāb* system of Qur'anic instruction, which sent successful pupils through to al-Azhar, described in the memoirs of figures like Taha Hussein and Ahmad Amin (Aḥmad Amīn); and on the other hand, there were foreign schools and government schools, which trained an elite group of students to work within the ranks of the civil administration.[34] When Egypt finally gained its independence in 1922, the *kuttāb* system was made free for all students, and education became a main platform for reforms, largely due to the influence of Saʿad Zaghlul, who previously served as education minister under Cromer. In this conventional story, the *kuttāb* system of Qur'anic instruction is seen as the basis of the educational system in Egypt.

There is, however, a certain anachronism to this account. The modernization of the education system transformed the *kuttāb* system, largely by incorporating it within the structures of the emergent Egyptian state.[35] In doing so, it came to be seen as a form of education, when, in principle, the goals of Qur'anic instruction were not necessarily geared to facilitate this specific imagined future. The system of instruction could be recognized as failing only when measured against presumptions of what education should do—in Milner's case, when evaluated against the "object of true education." But if we consider what is meant by "true education," we are drawn to consider not only shifting practices by which to govern the state, but shifting connotations in the sort of character that education was to facilitate. Noting this distinction is not a matter of making relativistic claims, but of clarifying how the Egyptian state came to recognize the *kuttāb* system as a site through which to cultivate the character seen as essential to modern self-government.

Timothy Mitchell's *Colonising Egypt* provides some important insight into the conundrum of recognizing in Qur'anic instruction a flawed mode of schooling. Mitchell focuses on an emergent connotation in nineteenth-century pedagogy for the word *tarbiyah* and describes a fundamental shift in the following terms: "Until perhaps the last third of the nineteenth century *tarbiya* had meant simply 'to breed' or 'to cultivate,' referring as in English, to anything that should be helped to grow—the cotton crop, cattle or the morals of children. It came to mean 'education,' the new field of practices that developed in the last third of the century."[36] The insight Mitchell offers is one that has rich implications for commentary on education, which, in the case of Milner, turns heavily upon a distinction between instruction (*taʿlīm*) and education (*tarbiyah*). But it also has implications for how the story is told. It was not uncommon for colonial writings on education to focus on the figure of the *fiqī*, who is understood as a teacher and who is often depicted as autocratic and abusive.[37] Mitchell notes that the very role of the *fiqī* was *not* that of the teacher. For Mitchell, it is mistaken to make any simple comparison of equivalents:

> To explain the *fiqi* as a school teacher is clearly inappropriate, and leads inevitably once again to observations of the sort that the curriculum of the "school" was restricted to the memorizing of a single text, the Qur'an. Schooling did not exist before the last third of the nineteenth century, and it was not the purpose of any distinct individual

> or institution to give organized instruction. The *fiqi*'s role was formed within an idiom of the power of words and the problems of vulnerability and powerlessness.[38]

By flagging the distinctions between conceptual categories integral to education, Mitchell helps to locate the challenges intrinsic to discussions of nineteenth-century history. The recognition of the *kuttāb* system within the categories of modern education leads time and again to accounts that see it, ultimately, as flawed and in need of a more rigorous delineation of the disciplines.

But because the arguments for education reform are based largely on the specter of fanatical prejudice, they do more than merely collapse contemporary categories for an analysis of the past. Milner's account is less concerned with outlining a program of education than constructing the terms of the past and future, of religious and modern education. Concerned as Milner is with governance, he focuses a lot less on fanatical character than on supposedly antiquated methods of education (such as memorization) that lead to fanatical behavior. And as such, he offers us an account based less on characteristics intrinsic to a subject than on the immanence of procedures productive of moral character. Within these terms, fanaticism is seen to stem from the failure to comply with the methods and demands of a modernizing world—and is not inherent in the subject. Modern education and the rise of the pedagogical sciences make possible not only a shift in what is taught, but the methods that dictate how it is taught.[39]

What is ultimately at stake in Milner's work is not any explicit moral comparison of ends—not, in other words, the modern being compared to the traditional—but instead the presumed superiority of modern means as against the outdatedness of the traditional. Being educated here is *not* a freedom to express opinions, but the discipline of learning *how* to speak in order to be heard as making an educated claim. Milner's remarks on education engage the cultivation of interpretative processes as integral to the uprooting of prejudice and ultimately fanaticism. In a curious twist, both critics and proponents of the British occupation ultimately concede these terms in the rise of the modern state, setting the stage for pedagogical reforms within a transformed understanding of education, its past and its future. Because fanaticism is taken as a symptom of backward processes, it leaves no subject to stand in its place except the specter of the uneducated, the indoctrinated, or the hidebound.

THE COLONIAL CULTIVATION OF CHARACTER

In 1908, years following Alfred Milner's publication, Lord Cromer published his two-volume *Modern Egypt* as an account of his colonial administration. Over the course of more than a thousand pages, Cromer aimed to "record an accurate narrative of some of the principal events which have occurred in Egypt and in the Soudan since the year 1876" and "to explain the results which have accrued to Egypt from the British occupation of the country in 1882."[40] And like Milner, Cromer was suspect of "the true state of native opinion": "I have lived too long in the East," Cromer writes in the opening pages, "not to be aware that it is difficult for any European to arrive at a true estimate of Oriental wishes, aspirations and opinions." And in lines by paradigmatic of an imperial binarism between East and West, Cromer goes on to characterize "the illogical and picturesque East and the logical West" and suggest that "the European and the Oriental, reasoning from the same premises, will often arrive at diametrically opposite conclusions."[41] In a single gesture, Cromer discounts the capacity to hear any possible criticism of British policies as opinion, explaining differences as a matter of differing mind-sets—and so begins his book.

Of the quantity of material included in the two volumes, the issue of education factors in a shorter chapter toward the end of the second volume. And here, as was the case in Milner's account, Cromer is defensive on the topic: "The first and principal obstacle [in the way of rapid progress in education] had been the want of money" and "[t]he idiosyncrasies of the Pashadom constituted the second."[42] His argument outlines some of the efforts for educational reforms, and it also focuses on the role of Qur'anic instruction, of which Cromer writes, "It would be an exaggeration to say that these Mosque schools are absolutely useless."[43] Not only does he explain how the British reformed the curriculum within the *kuttāb* system "based on the teaching of the three R's," but he glosses what he understands to be the improvement and streamlining of the government schools with the "direct personal influence of the new European teachers."[44] In the end, Cromer concedes that there were challenges to the implementation of an education system, but he celebrates those few steps toward reform that occurred under his administration. His remarks on education, though seemingly subordinate to other more pressing matters, engage the system of schooling as a necessary dimension of governance, but as Milner wrote years before, not a pressing priority.

What is remarkable is that Cromer's discussion of education revolves much less around policy concerns than around diagnosing a delicate balance between character and moral development. Prior to the chapter on education, Cromer is careful to distinguish between French and British models of learning. He writes, "[I]f we are to regard education in its true sense, that is to say not merely as a means for imparting certain quantities of information, but as a means for framing the character and for developing the physical qualities of the body and the moral qualities of the mind, the superiority of the English over the French system, when applied to Orientals, is very marked."[45] In this instance, education is understood as it pertains to *tarbiyah*: "a means for framing the character and for developing the physical qualities of the body and the moral qualities of the mind." And in the analysis Cromer offers, the Englishman "instinctively rejects *apriori* reasoning" and "will laboriously collect a number of facts before arriving at any conclusion, and, when he has collected his facts, he will limit his conclusions to the precise point which is proved."[46] Cromer compares this frame of mind to that of "the quick-witted Frenchman, who, on the most slender basis of fact, will advance some sweeping generalisation with an assurance untempered by any shadow of a doubt as to its correctness." He highlights the contrast metaphorically to demonstrate why "the half-educated Egyptian naturally prefers the Frenchman's system." "On the one side," he writes, "is a damsel possessing attractive albeit somewhat artificial charms; on the other side, is a sober, elderly matron of perhaps greater moral worth, but of less pleasing outward appearance."[47]

His remarks continue by pointing to the regretful situation of those Egyptians most taken by the promises of French education. "What the Egyptian most of all requires," Cromer writes, "is, not so much that the mind be trained, as that his character should be formed."[48] The relationship between character and education is further underscored when he writes, "It can scarcely be doubted that, from this point of view, French training has done little to rectify the defects of the Egyptian national character" and then later, "Such, therefore, is the Europeanised Egyptian. His intellectual qualities have, of late years, certainly been developed. His moral attributes have generally been little, if at all, improved by contact with Europe."[49] What Cromer constructs for the reader in this chapter is a division between "intellectual qualities" and "moral attributes," and his discussion of education ultimately turns on a consideration of moral attributes.

When Cromer does address education, he bemoans how long it takes to prepare a population for self-government. "To suppose that the characters and intellects of Egyptians can in a few years be trained to such an extent as to admit of their undertaking the sole direction of one of the most complicated political and administrative machines which the world has ever known . . . is a sheer absurdity."[50] But Cromer does not despair entirely in his imperial endeavors, for there were successes to be claimed. Countering the widespread accusations of the failing educational system, Cromer arrives upon a key question:

> From the political point of view, the most important education question is this: Do the educated Egyptians, whose number is now rapidly increasing, possess the qualities and characteristics of potentially self-governing Egyptians? To put the same question in another way, if we speak of education in the broadest sense of the term—that is to say, if we include the formation, not only of the intellect, but also of the character—if, in a word, we comprise all those manifold mental and moral influences which tend towards preparing a boy or girl for a career of usefulness in after life, has any substantial progress been made?[51]

His questions stack the response in his favor. On the one hand, Cromer emphasizes education as "the formation, not only of the intellect, but also of the character," and on the other, he presupposes the ends of the practice in "preparing a boy or girl for a career of usefulness in after life." He begins by suggesting that the British policies have been far from failing, and he bases his assessment on what he sees as all that has been "done towards forming and elevating the characters of the Egyptians." He initially proposes that language acquisition among the elevated classes is testament enough to developments: "The mere acquisition of the linguistic knowledge, which has enabled a certain number of young Egyptians to study the literature and sciences of Europe, must surely have tended in some degree to engender that accurate habit of thought which is the main characteristic of the Western as opposed to the Eastern mind." But as he continues, he describes specific practices and outcomes that stem from "a partial assimilation of the best European code of morals":

> . . . the abolition of barbarous punishments, the suppression of forced labour and of torture, the introduction of new ideas that the rights of property are sacred and all men are equal in the eyes of the law, the practical abolition of slavery, the discouragement of nepotism, the stigma attached to the worst kinds of vice, and, generally, the fact that the Egyptian social and political atmosphere has for some years been heavily charged with ideas which should act as antidotes against moral degradation.[52]

The move from the first response, which points to the refinement of educated Egyptians, to the second, which describes specific practices that have been undertaken, underscores the practical dimensions of the moral education at stake. Success, for Cromer, is marked not solely in the minds of an elite class of citizen, but in the capacity for governmental policy to abolish what Cromer regards as abhorrent practices. He shifts, as though seamlessly, between discussions of education in terms of intellect and those of education in terms of character, and doing so focuses less on schooling than on the supposed beneficence of colonial rule, the abolition of practices deemed backward, and "antidotes against moral degradation."

Cromer emphasizes the critical importance of sustaining structures of governance both by training the governing class and by modeling virtuous behavior on the part of the occupation. In contrast to the tempered notion of success with which his response to the question of Egyptian education begins, he goes on to caution against the possibility of "a relapse": "Whilst, however, it may reasonably be held that something has been done in the direction of imparting rectitude, virility, and moral equipoise to the Egyptian character, it must be admitted that there is still abundant room for improvement in all these directions. If the moral influences to which the Egyptians are now exposed were withdrawn, or even weakened, a relapse would inevitably ensue."[53] The fascination with national character, on the one hand, and with improvements brought about by instruction leads to a curious confluence. In charting the role and success of education, Cromer draws from examples meant to highlight some of the morally reprehensible dimensions of the uneducated: from corvée labor to corporeal punishment. These practices are distinct from national character in his account, and at the same time, the rise of education is what is attributed to their waning. Through education, it is argued, the natives improve their disposition, learning in the process to respect the sanctity of certain forms of life. Necessary questions arise: Is moral education an adulteration of national character? On what grounds is the moral argument asserted?

In the passages he offers, Cromer shuttles between discussions of education in terms of schooling and sensibilities only to resort to discussions of education in terms of the abolition of immoral practices. Where we might look at the stereotypical nature of these discussions and refute by countering Cromer's claims empirically, it is worth emphasizing that the discussion of character is the starting point for a different descriptive project. The challenge is to identify not only what character is, but how this character came into being; and it is ultimately the obsession with the very techniques by which character is made that underscores most of this writing. There is a moral imperative in the description itself, not only one that depicts character in a certain manner, but one concerned with the techniques by which character emerges. We are no longer in the realm of the timeless and mystical lands of the East, but in the descriptive labor of moral transformation implicit in this story of modernization.

IMMANENTLY MODERN AND UNCRITICALLY CIVILIZED

It would seem that literature and questions of literary education were entirely parenthetical to the British occupation of Egypt. But the fact that both Milner and Cromer are quite defensive on the topic indicates that education, if not enacted as policy, certainly warranted explanation. And for all of the attention given to supposedly pragmatic concerns, Milner's remarks, like those of Lord Cromer, deal extensively with articulating the attributes of character, moral dispositions and sensibilities essential to self-government. Even if their accounts appear to bracket education, there is ultimately a strong pedagogical imperative at play in the rhetoric of self-government. Under the conditions of British occupation, the Egyptian state would be deemed capable of self-government at the moment that it mirrored a set of recognizable goals and principles delineated by the British and deemed crucial to economic self-sufficiency. The pragmatism implicit in this position is not so much an argument against education, but an enactment of education by other means. It was not a matter of training dispositions and sensibilities through literature and schooling, but through the transformation of the social conditions within which the population lived.

When Milner and Cromer defensively allude to the failure of education under the British, they turn to what they see to be the success of a nascent transformation. As though anticipating Cromer's remarks from years later, Milner, for example, unabashedly professed the merits of the English project. He countered critics of the British occupation by suggesting that the terms of neutralization, by which Egypt would be shared among all of Europe, would have neglected the Egyptian people. He suggests, "neutralization misses, in the case of Egypt, the whole point of the difficulty which it is intended to meet."[54] Milner not only emphasized the importance of taking responsibility for the affairs of governance in Egypt, but he went on to ask, as though rebutting his own critics, about what might have happened if nonintervention had been pursued as a policy:

> It is worthwhile to consider how Egypt would look to-day, if this fine-sounding principle had been adopted some years ago. Would neutralization have suppressed the kurbash, or reduced the Corvée? Would it have repaired the Barrage? Would it have created an Egyptian army, or improved the native administration of justice? And would it, if introduced now, afford the slightest guarantee that all the ground gained might not again be lost? It is difficult to believe that Europe would adopt so impotent a policy. For it simply means this—that from unwillingness to allow any one of their number to do the work in which all are interested, the Powers should determine that that work must be left undone.[55]

Much like Cromer, who commends the colonial project on the grounds of the reformation of Egypt, Milner here draws an implicit connection between the occupation and the "suppression" of the kurbash and the "reduction" of the corvée. The apology for the failure in education here derives from the incremental changes that have been made, which are, in this instance, understood as part of a British initiative against the "impotent" policy of neutralization.

So too was the case with Valentine Chirol—he also drew an implicit relation between educational failure and the successes in the reformation of Egypt. For him, even recognizing certain failures, the "material benefits" of British control were "beyond dispute":

> If we have stumbled in our endeavors to promote the intellectual, or moral, or political education of the Egyptian people, the material benefits which he [*sic*] has derived from British control during the last three decades are beyond dispute. They jump to the eye. Long since gone

> is the spectacle I witnessed in the days of Ismail, of whole gangs of wretched peasants being dragged away in chains from their own fields to cultivate the vast estates which the Khedive and his favoured Pashas had systematically filched from the people. Gone is the old system of *corvée*, under which the well-nigh annual task of averting the alternate menace of a dangerously high or dangerously low Nile was carried out by forced labour cruelly recruited and still more cruelly handled. Gone is the *kurbash*, that used to blister the soles of the *fellaheen's* feet until they had disgorged their last piece of hidden silver or wearied the tax-gatherer's arm.[56]

Not only do Chirol's remarks appeal to those incidents that "jump to the eye," but they place the "material benefits" of these transformations "beyond dispute." Again, we see attention drawn to an "old system," aligned with corvée labor and the use of the kurbash, but by placing the abolition of these practices "beyond dispute," he forecloses any possible consideration of the imagined future in store. It is not a matter of being able to question the terms with which modern and civilized are defined—these are instead immanent to the benefits of the modernizing project.

What is curious in all of these remarks is that the presumed good derives from the alteration of set practices, and yet, in all of these accounts, how these practices are upended is not framed as a matter of moral education. The moral, in other words, is carefully deployed both as a criticism of an older system and as a defense of British transformation. When it comes to discussing an educational system, Cromer is inclined to discuss the importance of incremental change from an old system, but when it comes to practices deemed uncivilized and immoral, such as corvée labor or the kurbash, an immediate overhaul is imperative. Both the rhetoric of success and failure come to recognize the intrinsic universality of a supposedly humanitarian sensibility, one whose terms became increasingly instrumental for the governance and production of civilizational difference. By emphasizing a pragmatism of upending practices, the British occupation stymies any position by which to critique the inevitable march toward modernization.

For all of the emphasis that modernization places on the liberation of the subject, it is ultimately quite revealing that the position from which one might argue against education is ultimately unthinkable. We are not in a situation where being civilized entails the possibility of critique; instead, modernization secures a moral world in which critique is foreclosed. There is an inherent political education in learning to recognize the supposed material benefits of the occupation. The transformation of practices deemed immoral becomes, under the imperialist rhetoric, a matter of humanitarian good as opposed to a policy question. And the universality of presumptions about what constitutes modernization makes for a critical limit to the discussion:

there is, in the end, no position from which to think outside the moral universe of modernization. To be perceived as tied to an "old system" is to be positioned outside the terms of being recognizably educated—and ultimately outside the terms of being recognizably critical. Here, then, we spiral back upon the distinction between prejudice and opinion and the imperatives at play in a discussion of national character divorced from the practices and techniques that craft its recognition. To be educated, in this moral universe, is ultimately to be immanently modern and uncritically civilized.

In the next chapter, we shift from debates over education to the question of literariness. If what it means to be self-governing turns on the circularity of being recognizably educated, then what it means for a text to be properly literary turns on a recognition of what literature is. Looking at the emergence of literary institutions and modern literary disciplines, the following chapter pairs together formalist debates over literariness and Orientalist debates over *adab*. Both literature (in the formalist sense) and *adab* (as it comes to be understood) turn on an assertion of how to read properly. What literature means, in this formation, can thus not be abstracted from the practices and institutions through which it comes to be read. The libraries, printing presses, and disciplines integral to producing and promoting a certain model of reader become inseparable from the consolidation of a literary field, one that places Arabic literature squarely within the international commerce of world literature.

4

LITERATURE

How Adab *Became Literary*

In his 1959 essay "The Crisis of Comparative Literature," the Czech-American critic René Wellek takes aim at those who approach literature historically. His remarks explicitly target the work of prominent French comparatists renowned for the social and cultural analysis of literature—figures such as Fernand Baldensperger, Paul Van Tieghem, Jean-Marie Carré, and Marius-François Guyard. Never one to shy away from confrontation, Wellek accuses these French scholars of having "saddled comparative literature with an obsolete methodology and hav[ing] laid on it the dead hand of nineteenth-century factualism, scientism, and historical relativism."[1] He notes that comparative literature "has clung to 'factual relations,' sources and influences, intermediaries and reputations as its only topics," and laments that "the concept of literary study is broadened . . . so radically that it becomes identical with the whole history of humanity."[2] Against these tendencies, Wellek urges that literary scholarship instead "study literature as a subject distinct from other activities and products of man" with attention less to historical situations than to aesthetic form. In a seemingly purifying gesture, he implores the literary scholar to focus on what is fundamentally literary: "we must face the problem of 'literariness,' the central issue of aesthetics, the nature of art and literature."

What precisely is this "literariness" that Wellek invokes? On the one hand, as might be expected, Wellek's emphasis on literariness leads him to understand the work of art formally, as "a stratified structure of signs and meanings which is totally distinct from the mental processes of the author at the time of composition and hence of the influences which may have formed his mind."[3] And yet, on the other hand, fearing a reductive formalism that "confines" literature "to the study of sound, verse, and compositional devices," he makes recourse to a world—one quite distinct from the social context invoked by the French scholars referenced in his essay. He notes that from the analysis of linguistic elements "emerges a 'world' of situations, characters, and events which cannot be identified with any single linguistic element or, least of all, with any element of external ornamental form."[4] Placed as it is in quotes, Wellek's "world" is made thinkable through the literary text ("situations, characters, and events")—and is seemingly distant from the worldly texts that Edward Said celebrates in his remarks on secular criticism. Where for Said texts are "part of the social world, human life, and of course the historical moments in which they are located and interpreted," Wellek's "world" derives from all that the text itself allows the reader to imagine.[5] His "world," in other words, does not make recourse to social or cultural influences, but places the category of literature—and the attributes of literariness—beyond place and time, embedded in the aesthetic encounter with a text.

In recent years, Said's understanding of worldliness has inspired a whole range of scholarship concerned with globalization, postcolonialism, and cultural studies.[6] The explicit impact of Wellek's formalism, however, has remained more muted, even with its widespread translation across numerous languages.[7] What might world literature look like if framed less in terms of Said's worldly texts than in terms of Wellek's literary "world"? What is world literature without the logic of cultural or national particularity? With attention to not only the question of what literature is but also how it ought to be read, Wellek extends the problem of world literature beyond the consideration of when and where a text was written. He considers not so much which texts to include or exclude from a global canon, but how and in what ways to engage with literary texts pedagogically. In an intriguing twist, Wellek's emphasis on literariness (as a quality intrinsic to textual form) calls upon those readers capable of recognizing and valuing literary traits. His formalism presumes a disciplined understanding of what to do with a text deemed literary—that is, how to read, analyze, and ultimately value literature. Taking Wellek's formalism seriously, we could say, ultimately means thinking of world literature in terms of the disciplines and reading practices it comes to imply.

How, we might still wonder, does the concept of literariness level with the variety of traditions in world literature? To what extent does Wellek's formalism (stemming as it does from Latin, French, English, German, and Russian traditions) translate across national borders? These questions might seem to gesture to the potential limits of formal literariness, especially when considered alongside traditions deemed outside the civilizational paradigm of the classical humanities and therefore external to the aesthetic history integral to the analysis of textual form. And yet, as I suggest in what follows, an engagement with differing conceptions of the literary invites a challenge to the conventional understanding of world literature as an accumulation of texts from across the world. It leads us, as Wellek's philological detour will demonstrate, to understand literature in terms of the practices integral to the formation of modern literary study at institutions across the world. An engagement with how literature comes to matter, in other words, helps point us in the direction of seeing literature not merely as a definitional category applied to a set of texts, but as an emergent discipline inflecting how texts come to be read. The notion of literariness, then, becomes both a pedagogical and a theoretical exercise embedded in the emergent discipline of literary study.

Against the backdrop of Wellek's formalism, Orientalist debates on the meaning of *adab* appear to provide a stark counterpoint to the principle of literariness. On one level, Orientalism's commitment to historical, cultural, and linguistic explanation seems to contrast sharply with the techniques of close reading Wellek advocates. And on another level, the Arabic term *adab* appears to introduce a complication to the apparent timelessness of the category of the literary by gesturing to an apparent alternate tradition. In what ways does *adab* challenge the apparent universality of Wellek's literariness?

As a rich range of scholarship notes, *adab* has a semantic register that exceeds and possibly exhausts the contemporary connotations of the word "literature."[8] Texts ranging from Ibn al-Muqaffa''s *Kalīlah wa-Dimnah* to al-Jahiz's *Kitāb al-ḥayawān*, and from al-Hamdani's *Maqāmat* to Ibn Qutaybah and al-Mas'udi's discussions, all attest to a rich discussion of the term during the premodern period. Its significance seems to have stronger echoes of the Greek notion of *pædeia* in that it encompasses manners, education, customs, and behaviors.[9] All of these characteristics seem, at first glance, to atrophy with the more conventional translation of *adab* as literature—and its institutionalization as a modern discipline at places like Dār al-'Ulūm (1871) and, later, the Egyptian University (1908). With the founding of modern departments of literature, curricula emerge around a body of written work spanning poetry, novels, and theater, giving literature its more contemporary application to a category of texts.

And yet, far from erasing previous connotations, discussions of *adab* emerge as a prominent topic from within these institutions of literary instruction, often integral to the shape of the disciplines that result. In the work of Husayn al-Marsafi, who lectured on the topic at Dār al-'Ulūm (Teachers College), or Carlo Alfonso Nallino, based at the Egyptian University (now known as Cairo University), scholarship attuned to the linguistic, social, and cultural context of literary production allows insights into the various registers of *adab*.[10] What emerges is a circularity by which understanding what *adab* means is inseparable from debates on how best to read, understand, and analyze texts. Far from locating debates about *adab* as external to the problem of modern literature, these discussions transpire within the modern institutions supporting this type of inquiry. In a manner not entirely distinct from the pedagogical implications of Wellek's literariness, reflections on *adab* tend also to return to instantiations of how to read. Implicit in the definitional quest to understand the purified category of literature or of *adab*, in other words, is a close link to the disciplines and institutions that structure the training of literary readers.

It is here, caught in the bind between literature understood as a body of texts and as a disciplined manner of reading, that this chapter both departs and returns. Simply to frame *adab* as a matter of translation of the term "literature" is to overlook the transformations in print culture, libraries, schools, discourses on literacy, and the emergence of a literary public, all of which have implications for how texts come to be read and by whom. We could say that by tracing the disciplinary and institutional practices that make literature—and, in turn, literariness—meaningful, we arrive at an understanding of literature that is less an attribute of a text than the archaeology of a discipline (reinforced through institutions, practices, and publics). At a time when scholars move away from models of cultural analysis anchored in contextualization, Wellek's formalism and debates around *adab* allow us to consider alternate trajectories for literary study—focused not on *what* but *how* texts are read. We thus shift away from mimesis as the foundational category of literary theory to consider the disciplines and practices that inscribe how literature comes to matter.

In what follows, my goal is not necessarily to offer an empirical response to how *adab* became literary, nor necessarily to gloss the extensive debates on the historical registers of *adab*. Instead, I note the fold within which defining what literature or *adab* is implies a command about how to read, and I do so to trace the philological, pedagogical, and institutional implications of defining what literature is. This chapter thus considers literary history, on the one hand, as it intersects with literary theory, on the other, to focus on finite moments in the work of Jurji Zaydan, H.A.R. Gibb, and Edward Said. In doing so, I aim less for a comprehensive answer to the question posed in the title than for detailed inquiry into its implications for world literature. How do discussions of world literature relate to the field known as Arabic literature? Is there a concept of literature separate or distinct from formalist conceptions of the literary? We could say that asking about how *adab* becomes literary is to ask about the limits of a purified literariness across space and time. In the end, it is a refusal of the binarism of literary theory and world literature: a gesture toward the worldly existence of the term *adab*, embedded in the question of what literature is, and the imbrication of philology and pedagogy it implies.

A WORLD IN WORDS: PHILOLOGY AS PEDAGOGY

In 1968, just a few years following "The Crisis of Comparative Literature," Wellek published an essay titled "The Name and Nature of Comparative Literature." In a shift from a formalist to a more philological line of argument,

Wellek describes his essay as an exercise in lexicography—or, as he qualifies it, historical semantics.[11] The essay claims to address comparative literature, and the opening section asks about the belated arrival of the term "comparative" in the English language—as compared to French and German, where references to comparative literature occur much earlier. And although he begins by considering the word "comparative," he eventually makes a crucial detour through the mutability of the term "literature." To do so, he tells a story aimed critically at another literary scholar. He points out that Lane Cooper, a professor at Cornell University, insisted on calling the department he chaired the "Comparative Study of Literature"—as opposed to the Department of Comparative Literature. Much like Harry Levin, who would also ask about what one compares in comparative literature, Cooper famously remarked, "You might as well permit yourself to say comparative potatoes or comparative husks."[12] His skepticism of the name attributed to this field of study was not entirely out of place. After all, what could be comparative about literature?

Wellek, of course, has a response to the question and to Cooper's comments in particular. With characteristic barb, Wellek chides Cooper for failing to recognize the basic etymology of the term. The problem with Cooper's remarks, Wellek informs us, is that "in earlier English usage . . . [literature] means 'learning' or 'literary culture,' particularly a knowledge of Latin."[13] He points out that "the meaning of 'literature' as 'literary production' or 'a body of writings' revived a usage of late antiquity."[14] And he notes that the Latin *literatura* was taken as the translation for the Greek *grammatike* and that Tertullian later differentiated the secular and the sacred with a distinction between *literatura* and *scriptura.* The issue, then, is not so much with the term "comparative" as with the increasingly restricted understanding of literature—one that in essence subordinates the disciplinary, ethical, and pedagogical dimensions of the term in favor of its connotation as literary production or a body of writings. In quite a remarkable manner, Wellek turns back upon the problem of what the term might mean—and he does so by noting the historical valence implicit in the term itself. In the end, he appears to bracket his formalism to excavate a pedagogical resonance in the historical meaning of the term "literature."

For a scholar so concerned with literary form, Wellek here broadens his style of argument, turning to philology to note the limits of Cooper's literary world. While his exercise in historical semantics localizes the term "literature" within a French, English, Italian, and German paradigm, it does so, quite intriguingly, to imply the word's dual resonance as learning, knowledge, and study, on the one hand, and literary production or a corpus of texts, on the other. What emerges, in other words, is the distillation of literature as a discipline by which to approach the analysis of texts and literature as a body of works to be compared. He thus seems to insist upon the historical contingency of literature, but does so as a means of defending the intrinsic literariness of the discipline. In the end, then, his vision of comparative literature turns back upon an almost purified presumption of what the literary is—as an aesthetic problem. In anchoring the terms of comparative literature less in the particularities of national traditions than in the generalized framework of literariness, he invites a manner of literary inquiry that draws from philology toward generalizations of a different sort.

Returning to the detail at the heart of Wellek's criticism of Cooper, we might note that there is not simply a translation of the term "literature" (or even of *litteratura* or *adab*). Instead, Wellek's observation hints at the transformations of practices and institutions that help to make this term intelligible in particular ways—in this case, the naming of a department at Cornell University. If Wellek chides Cooper for overlooking that literature means learning, then on some level he chides him for overlooking the pedagogical dimensions implicit in the term. Literature is at once descriptive of education in the fullest sense, which includes pedagogy, learning, and command of language, and of the corpus of texts that it comes to presume. In this exercise, Wellek returns historically to the semantic resonance of the term as an instantiation of a certain type of learning. His essay, with its detour through historical semantics, provides a crucial lesson that destabilizes the apparent obviousness of what literature is. The essay itself becomes a pedagogical performance aimed at the substance of a name for an academic department.

When we shift to consider *adab* with these observations in mind, we arrive at some potentially transformative implications. An invocation of the historical meaning of literature, in the context either of *litteratura* or of *adab*, uncovers the resonance of the term prior to the formation of the modern literary disciplines. And even though literature eventually comes to be understood more as a corpus of texts, it is well worth noting that this corpus of texts impinges upon what is meant by literary education. The return to the historical meaning of literature as learning allows us to consider that world literature (as much as Wellek's understanding here of comparative literature) presumes the framework in which to approach texts. For the literary theorist as for the literary historian, this pedagogical instantiation is implicit in the recognition of an object as literature.

In the models of world literature available, whether David Damrosch's attention to texts across traditions or Pascale Casanova's concern for the dynamics of power in a literary world, Wellek's earlier exercise in historical semantics gestures toward a discipline-based study, reflexive as much about the practices of reading as it is about the literary text.[15] In important ways, Wellek's formalism returns to considerations of what literature is and the question of how it comes to be read. And in this process, we uncover something important for a more formalist conception of world literature. Although it might seem that *adab*'s initial register of etiquette, ethics, and behavior gets muted in discussions of world literature, it is well worth noting that world literature presumes the institutions that define and professionalize reading. It is not simply a discourse that neutralizes registers of textuality or flattens all literary traditions into a common conception of the literary; but it comes to define literature, reading, and the terms of being educated.

LITERARY INSTITUTIONS AND THE INSTANTIATION OF WORLD LITERATURE

In *La Renaissance orientale*, a work of intellectual history seemingly at odds with Wellek's formalism, Raymond Schwab details the explosion of a "new humanism" in the 1870s that undergirds the link between comparative grammar, philology, and the rise of literary studies. Schwab meticulously notes the publication of Theodor Benfy's *Geschichte der Sprachwissenschaften Orientalischen Philogie in Deutschland* in Munich in 1869, the inclusion of the volume "Bibliothèque Orientale" in the series "Chefs-d'oeuvre de l'Espirit Humaine" in Paris in 1870, and the appearance of Max Müller's edited series "Sacred Books of the East" in England in 1875, as just a few examples of the increasingly international scope of literary study—an emergent world literature.[16] He marks the legacy of Silvestre de Sacy, who not only compiled an edition of Arabic grammar and assisted with the decoding of the Rosetta Stone, but also trained a generation of Orientalists and comparative grammarians. And Schwab's account also encompasses the labors of figures ranging from William Jones to Jean-François Champollion, and the study of languages ranging from Sanskrit and Arabic to Aramaic and Hebrew.

When weighed against a concern for literariness—and Wellek's argument against contextual explanation—Schwab's book provides a curious case. Like more recent inquiries into the historical conditions of philology in the scholarship of Tomoko Masuzawa or Maurice Olender, Schawb's pioneering study provides insight into the colonial subtext of many of the key principles undergirding technical reflections on literature.[17] His book, like those of other intellectual historians, does not necessarily engage the particularities of a single literary text, but focuses instead on understanding the rise of a discipline. In this way, though seemingly at odds with formalism, we see in these studies a return to many formal principles, especially as pertains to tracing how it is that literature comes to matter. Much like Wellek's philological exercise in excavating the meaning of literature as learning, Schwab's historical study provides insight into a discipline not solely anchored in the writings of European scholars, but articulated in an emergent institutional framework.

Across the Mediterranean, the scope of Schwab's "new humanism" expanded well beyond the reflections of European scholars to the fashioning of literary cultures. In Cairo, the 1870s was a decade that witnessed the emergence of two formidable literary institutions: on the one hand, the national library, Dār al-Kutub, which was inaugurated in 1870, and on the other hand, Dār al-ʻUlūm (Teachers College), which offered a modernized curriculum for literary studies in 1871. The links between the literary culture of comparative grammar and these literary institutions in Egypt are quite explicit. Khedive Ismail in collaboration with ʻAli Mubarak (ʻAlī Mubārak Bāshā) founded Dār al-Kutub, and two of its first directors were the well-known German Orientalists Karl Vollers and Bernhardt Moritz. Dār al-ʻUlūm was also linked to the visions of ʻAli Mubarak, who helped generate a literary curriculum geared differently than the scholastic traditions taught at the Islamic University, al-Azhar. Here, drawing from the work of comparative studies of Swiss, French, and German education, Dār al-ʻUlūm was set to modernize the literary disciplines for a transformed Egyptian educational program. It helped to spawn the journal *Rawḍat al-mudarris*, and served as a basis from which much of the Arabic literary pedagogy of the twentieth century—and eventually at the Egyptian University—would stem.

Weaving together Schwab's "new humanism," the National Library, and Dār al-ʻUlūm helps us locate sites in the rise of the discipline of modern literature. The ensuing literary institutions bespeak not only a relationship to texts, but the creation of conditions whereby literature (and *adab*) comes to imply a literary world of a particular sort: the training of readers in a canon of texts and modes of textual analysis, the nationalization of libraries and teachers colleges, and the growth of a reading public. And from Cairo to Delhi, literature becomes thinkable as a modern discipline, a corpus of new genres and modes of literary history, as much dependent upon reforms in schooling, the spread of publishing houses, and the circulation of letters as upon the discourse of world literature. In the 1870s as in the years that follow, we find the world of literature both in the accumulation of texts (and series of books dealing with distinct literary traditions), but also in the instantiation of world literary culture (through institutions such as schools and libraries). The relation of these two aspects is what I refer to as world literature—that is, both the institutions and the disciplines that result.

It is worth noting that the emergence of modern literary study in Egypt is not simply a colonial project, but one bound up inseparably with the labor of many Arabic-language scholars. Credit is normally attributed to Husayn al-Marsafi (Ḥusayn al-Marṣafī) as one of the first modern literary critics in Arabic, and his lectures at Dār al-ʻUlūm in the 1870s and 1880s helped to frame a field of study and the modernization of the discipline.[18] Similarly, Muhammad Diyab (Muḥammad Diyāb) is known to have undertaken his own book with the title *Tārīkh ādāb al-lughah al-ʻArabīyah* between the years 1899 and 1901, reflecting on the status of literature in a broad historical frame. In 1911, Mustafa Sadiq al-Rafiʻi (Muṣṭafa Ṣādiq al-Rafīʻī) published *Tārīkh ādāb al-ʻArab*, a study that addressed the meaning of *adab* in its opening pages.[19] Debates about *adab* were famously framed in the lectures of the

Italian Orientalist Carlo Alfonso Nallino, but also in the work of key Egyptian intellectual figures integral to the foundations of modern literary culture, from Dār al-ʿUlūm to the Egyptian University.[20] And as the field of modern Arabic literary scholarship developed on the other side of the Mediterranean, there is a fairly well known course of publications: notably, Carl Brockelmann's *Geschichte der arabischen Litteratur* published in installments at the end of the nineteenth century, Reynold Nicholson's *A Literary History of the Arabs* (1907), and H.A.R. Gibb's *Arabic Literature: An Introduction* (1926).[21]

What is remarkable in these undertakings, reflecting on literature through an analysis of its history, is that they not only help to define what literature is, but also are instrumental in imagining the shape of the discipline. With this in mind, the distinction between theory and pedagogy, between literary history and the question of what is literature, gets entirely blurred. A number of prominent scholars, often working in teams, became directly involved in crafting literary curricula to be taught to a generation of students in a modernized educational system. In 1910, for example, Ahmad Zayyat (Aḥmad Ḥasan Zayyāt) published a treatise on Arabic literary history destined explicitly for use in secondary schools.[22] Then, in 1929, Taha Hussein, Ahmad al-Iskandari, Ahmad Amin, ʿAbd al-ʿAziz al-Bishri, ʿAli al-Jarim, and Ahmad Dayf, collectively published *al-Mujmal fi tārīkh al-adab al-ʿArabī* also for use in schools.[23] How students came to be trained would be inseparable from a literary theory anchored in the particularities of Arabic literary history. In quite an explicit sense, then, the rise of the modern discipline of literary study was closely linked with both defining a corpus of texts, but also the terms within which they would come to be read and understood by generations of literary readers.

This extensive and by no means comprehensive gesture to debates on *adab* was anchored historically, reflexive about issues of canonicity, and ultimately concerned with framing Arabic literature as a scholarly field. And this conversation has continued richly in recent years with scholarship considering the role of Arabic within discourses of comparative literature and world literature. I allude here to the contributions of Ferial Ghazoul and Nadia al-Bagdadi,[24] and even more recently, to a special issue of *Comparative Literature Studies* dedicated to the place of Arabic literature in the context of comparative literary study.[25] We might also think of scholarship dealing explicitly with the classroom, such as Linda Herrera's edited collection of ethnographic studies of Egyptian education.[26] Each of these studies offers a turn in which literature becomes thinkable as a problem—when, in other words, a disciplinary field becomes self-conscious of its endeavors. Institutional history becomes inseparable from what would classically have been understood as literary theory.

And far from being a distinctively Arabic phenomenon, similar transformations have been traced in the context of South Asian studies. Gauri

Viswanathan's *Masks of Conquest* provides a model to think differently about the formation of English as a colonial project by tracing the pedagogical experiments in South Asia eventually applied in England.[27] Aamir Mufti's recent article, "Orientalism and the Institution of World Literatures," and in a different way, Sheldon Pollock's remarkable *Language of the Gods in the World of Men*, both help enrich and ultimately broaden the terms through which world literature comes to be understood.[28] These authors deal with formations of literary culture as generative of the category of literature and help to suggest the philological and governmental dimensions to the production of knowledge, canons, and traditions on and about language and literature. These studies all map different ways in which the convergence of institutional disciplinary questions directly impinge upon the response to the question of what literature is—and ultimately how readers come to make sense of texts.

Rich as the situated studies of literary scholarship are, we might still wonder how they relate to the sorts of questions raised in Wellek's formalism. Is the quest to locate literary study in place and time, historically and culturally, merely a regress to a model of contextualization that jettisons a focus on the literary as an aesthetic experience? What are the implications of institutional histories for the reading of texts? While there may appear to be a fundamental opposition between institutional histories and the analysis of textual form, most of these texts, as written, inscribe precisely the sort of circularity linking what literature is to how one ought to read. Turning now to a formal reading of a moment in the history of Arabic literature, I draw our attention to a text that would seem to delimit how *adab* became literature, which is to say, how *adab* became subject to the protocols of modern literary study.

FOOTNOTING LITERATURE, OR THE LITERARY FOOTNOTE

Between 1894 and 1895, the Lebanese intellectual Jurji Zaydan (Jurjī Zaydān) published *Tārīkh ādāb al-lughah al-ʿArabīyah* as a series of articles in the literary-scientific journal *al-Hilāl*.[29] Taken together, his various articles constitute a monumental literary history, renowned both for its expansive scope and its systematic periodization of Arabic literature. At a time when literary study was being institutionalized at universities across the world, Zaydan helped to situate Arabic literature within and among a number of national traditions. He addressed topics ranging from pre-Islamic poetry to philosophy and linguistics, and he did so within a historical framework attuned to the conventions of political and aesthetic periodization. Just prior to his death in 1914, his accumulated articles were republished in four separate volumes, including an introduction and general index, and collectively provide a sort of textbook for Arabic literary history in the Arabic language.[30] To this day, Zaydan's historical understanding of Arabic literature remains a central influence on the formation of the discipline—as much for the methods he undertakes as for the meticulous cataloguing of sources his work provides.

Situated in dialogue with global scholarship on literary study, *Tārīkh ādāb al-lughah al-ʿArabīyah* furnished a framework for plotting literary history, and ultimately for imagining an Arab literary past in the context of world literature and as part of the global spread of the modern literary disciplines. In this endeavor, "literature" emerges not only as a category, but as a category that demands a certain historicization within a national linguistic tradition. And in Zaydan's case, this history spans centuries of poetry, history, politics, and sciences in the Arab world—from the pre-Islamic period through the Umayyad and Abbasid Caliphates to the end of the nineteenth century. As a testament to the intrinsically comparative thought that inflects this sort of undertaking, Zaydan acknowledges his indebtedness to other literary historians and scholars. He explicitly positions his study alongside a table of influential figures—among them scholars of Greece, India, England, Italy, Spain, and France.[31] For Arabic language resources, Zaydan cites studies ranging from *al-Fihrist* by Ibn al-Nadim (Ibn al-Nadīm) to *al-Muqaddimah* by Ibn Khaldun (Ibn Khaldūn),[32] and he also gestures to the scholarship of Joseph von Hammer-Purgstall, Clément Huart, Carl Brockelmann, and R. A. Nicholson in the context of Arabic literature.[33] But his work is not limited to an Arabic context, and he alludes to prominent French comparatists like Frédéric Loliée and Ferdinand Brunetière, both of whom were incredibly influential in the foundations of comparative literary study in France—and the target of Wellek's criticisms.

In a very concrete manner, Zaydan furnishes a discourse about the study of literature (*ʿilm al-adab*) embedded in the reading practices and disciplines the term itself comes to imply.[34] His work emerges alongside the establishment of modern literary study at universities across the world, about the same time as the founding of a national Egyptian university.[35] But his work also provides insight into the challenges of what it might mean to approach institutional histories with formalism in mind. Even though Zaydan's study might appear to provide the sort of generalized gloss of texts so criticized by Wellek, it also provides an archaeology of the discipline in the various additions to the editions reprinted. Of all of the potential ways of reading or relating to the book, then, I want here to focus on a detail and turn from formalist reading practices to institutional histories. This endeavor, enfolding literary history and literary theory, allows insight into the pedagogical performance at play in reading.

In the 1957 edition of Zaydan's book, reprinted just a few years prior to René Wellek's essay, a crucial footnote appears annotating a key sentence of the introduction. As part of a framework for the volume, the opening section deals explicitly with the definitional problem of what is meant by literature, and is titled, quite simply, "What Is the Meaning of the Language Arts?" (*mā huwa al-murād bi-ādāb al-lughah?*). In this section, Zaydan asks about the status of the language arts generally, and he ponders the distinction between literature as a science and literature as a history of texts: "sciences of the literary arts . . . and the history of the literary arts (*tārīkh ādāb al-lughah*)."[36] At play in both clauses is the use of *adab* in its plural form *ādāb*—the same form invoked in the title of Zaydan's book, and similarly capacious as the term is in Carl Brockelmann's study, which addresses anything written in Arabic. That said, the distinction between the plural and the singular highlights a contrast between what I translate here as "the language arts" (*ādāb*), on the one hand, and "literature" (*adab*), on the other. While the book is careful to note this distinction, it also dwells importantly on the convergence of the plural and the singular, and subsequent citations of the book in French gloss the plural *ādāb* simply as *littérature*.[37] For all of the generative questions the title poses, the introduction is crucial for securing the definition of the term *adab* around which the book itself is structured.

As Zaydan continues, he further amplifies a distinction between the history of the sciences (*tārīkh al-'ulūm*) and the history of "the fruits of the minds of its children (*thimār 'ūqul abnā'ihā*).[38] Analytically, then, this line parses what it is that might be studied in the four volumes, torn between textual objects (a canon of key poems, stories, and manuscripts), and texts as products of the mind. That is to say, already in the opening lines, Zaydan raises a distinction between literature understood as a corpus of knowledge and literature understood as a pedagogical process. For Zaydan, what literature is has everything to do with the sort of knowledge acquired in the minds of readers through the disciplined engagement with texts, history, and language. He returns, in this sense, to the meaning of *adab* in the sense of being educated, and he does not merely subsume the term within the discourse of a canon of texts to be accumulated. In the end, his remarkable opening drives toward a nearly poetic proclamation: that the history of the language arts is "the history of the nation from the literary and scientific point of view" (*fa huwa tārīkh al-ummah min al-wujhah al-adabīyah al-'ulūmiyyah*).

But in the 1957 edition of the book, this opening proclamation is interrupted en route to its destination by a most curious footnote. It is interrupted, in other words, by a form of text set to adapt and qualify the scope and capaciousness of the category of the language arts. Shawqi Dayf assembled and republished the materials for this edition of Zaydan's book and in the process provided annotations to Zaydan's writing. His footnote, marked not numerically but with an asterisk, notably amends and comments upon the term *ādāb*, as though readily acknowledging some of the challenges of presuming its simple translation from the 1911 to the 1957 edition. And in doing so, it appears to clarify the intentions of the writer: "The author uses the term 'history of the language arts' in its widest known meaning as intended by Westerners [*bi-ma'anīhā al-wāsi'ah al-ma'rūfah 'ind al-gharbiyyīn*]."[39] The footnote then goes on to distinguish between the multiple valences of the term "literary," noting its inclusion in science, history, poetry, and all of the modalities of thought in writing.

With the annotation, we are thus welcomed back into a reflection on literature and the language arts, but what is bracketed in the process is the force of Zaydan's performance. On some level, it is possible to say that Zaydan's prose exemplifies the status of *adab* with its elevated language, a celebration of learning and a holistic understanding of the relationship between education and the modern nation. The erudition of the references, the refined manner in which the piece is written, and the overall framework of the study bespeak the meaning of the term *adab* formally as much as thematically. The footnote, however, ushers in an added dimension to this opening paragraph by shifting from an elevated set of questions about the language arts to a sort of historical clarification of what the term *adab* means.

We might say, then, that in the schism between the 1911 and 1957 editions, a footnote glosses, translates, and bespeaks the transformation of the term *ādāb*, returned to its connotation for a readership constrained by the modern disciplines of literature. Here, in other words, in the schism between editions, a footnote points to a moment of reading literature otherwise—when ethics and aesthetics, pedagogy and art, were joined together differently in this term. As Anthony Grafton's work testifies, the footnote offers a clarifying empirical command scribbled at the base of the page, but it is a command entwined with the institutions that come to produce and define what literature is.[40] These same institutions render the residual meaning of the term nearly unintelligible. And so, as though echoing the complex history of the term *adab*, in the footnote of the 1957 edition of Zaydan's *Tārīkh ādāb al-lughah al-'Arabīyah* we find a gesture of returning literature to a moment and context when literature meant differently. Perhaps most importantly, the footnote annotates what is stylistically performed in Zaydan's writing with a style of prose that anchors the claim about *adab* historically and culturally.

This attention to a single footnote might seem an exercise in pure formalist reading, precisely the sort of obsessive detail that needlessly extrapolates significance from something the author had himself never even composed. At the time of the footnote's addition, the book was not in the hands of the author, and the afterlife of the text had been subsumed within a publishing industry dedicated to including the text as part of a larger compendium on the history of literature. It takes this footnoted annotation to amplify what is supposedly Zaydan's intended meaning, but curiously, the footnote offers a mode of historical contextualization, interrupting in the process Zaydan's rhetorical performance of the literary. In this way, we can see the footnote not only as a formal intervention, but also as a confusion of registers: a guide for the reader amid an anachronistic invocation of a literary definition by then out of date.

Easy as it is to point to this detail, I do so not necessarily to make a literary claim, but to point to a genealogy of a different sort—and to point to an implicit circularity invited by this new edition. What is at stake here is both an amplification of intention and a collision between literary writing and demonstrative annotation. The same circularity faced in the schism between the 1911 and 1957 editions is itself a circularity we face as literary scholars writing from a specific formation of discourse on literary study. This is not an exercise in pointing out that literature ought to be rendered more elastic to accommodate the diversity of world literatures, but an exercise in ascertaining the normative force of literature as a category that comes to matter in certain ways pedagogically, ethically, and aesthetically. It is an exercise that helps us understand this footnote in Zaydan's book and the conditions by which a detour through the emergent institutionalization of literary study ends up redefining the meaning of a word.

ORIENTALISM, OR LITERATURE FOR ITS OWN SAKE

In 1931, between the editions of Zaydan's treatise, the Harvard Orientalist H.A.R. Gibb published an essay titled, "Literature," in the volume *The Legacy of Islam.*[41] A key figure in the training of generations of scholars in Arabic literature, Gibb has come to be understood as almost exemplary of Orientalist scholars, committed to the study, engagement, and enriched understanding of Arabic language and culture. It would appear that Orientalism, committed as it is to the historical and cultural understanding of aesthetic phenomena, would sit uncomfortably with the sort of formalism implicit in Wellek's remarks. In fact, Orientalism would furnish the logic in which the universalizing notion of literariness necessarily encountered its civilizational other in a discourse of *adab*. Inadvertently or not, Gibb's scholarship actually offers us something quite different, returning us in ways not entirely dissimilar to Wellek to particular connotations of the word "literature."

The opening line of his essay appears initially to affirm the civilizational binarism classically associated with Orientalism: "The literature of the Muslim Orient," he writes, "seems so remote from us that probably not one reader in a thousand has ever connected it in his mind with our own." And yet, mystifying as this opening line is, Gibb follows it with another—a sort of counterpoint he underscores with the statement "on the other hand." He distinguishes in this second line the "us" of his first sentence to focus on "the student of literary history," adding, "The student of literary history, on the other hand, who knows how much in European literature has at different times been claimed, and how little has ever been proved to be of oriental origin, may well be inclined to regard the whole subject with tolerant skepticism."[42]

In the pages that follow, Gibb traces Arabic influences in literary form, noting both the prominence of *Kitāb alf laylah wa-laylah* and Omar Khayyam (ʿUmar Khayyām), but also highlighting relationships between the *zajal* of Ibn Quzman (Ibn Quzmān) and the Provençal poetry of William of Poitiers as well as the influence of the *maqāmāt* on the Spanish picaresque.[43] Through this exercise, entwining Arabic literature into the foundations of Western literary history, Gibb gradually turns his generalized reader of the opening line (who "has never connected [the literature of the Muslim Orient] in his mind with [his] own") into the student of the second (who approaches such a claim with "tolerant skepticism"). On this level, his essay can be read as a sort of pedagogical instantiation that revises literary history in favor of a more robust understanding of the deeply entwined literary traditions he addresses.

But there is a cost to this generalization. In the last lines of the essay, having traced through generations of Arabic influences on European literature, Gibb pronounces a broadly humanist declaration: "Oriental literature has begun to be studied again *for its own sake*, and a new understanding of the East is being gained." And with an apparent optimism for what may occur, Gibb continues, "As this knowledge spreads and the East recovers its rightful place in the life of humanity, oriental literature may once again perform its historic function, and *assist us to liberate ourselves* from the narrow and oppressive conceptions which would limit all that is significant in literature, thought, and history, to our own small segment of the globe."[44] Couched in what could be seen as the binarism between East and West, Gibb finds a rallying cry for deprovincializing literary study—and it is a rallying cry that appears to transform "the students of literary history" into the generalized "us" to be liberated at the essay's conclusion. Curiously, his Orientalist proclamation is itself a pedagogical instantiation, both modeling what this literary education might do and spreading "knowledge of the East" as a means of recovering "its rightful place in the life of humanity." But ultimately it is a gesture to a sort of liberated self-understanding of the Western scholar as part of a broader humanist realization.

I dwell on Gibb's lines to highlight a curious problem entwining geography and cultural difference within a presumed category for the literary. It is telling that a figure like Gibb would recognize through the study of literature the provincialism of his "small segment of the globe." But it is also telling that, for all of his emphasis on civilizational discourse, his humanist proclamation presumes the stability of the category literature, which can be "studied again for its own sake." It is literature, in other words, that takes on a seemingly secure meaning beneath the shroud of civilization difference. What is performed is a sort of literary phenomenology that secures the place of literature in this "life of humanity." In the end, Gibb's humanism turns as much on the stabilization of the question of what literature is as on any assertion of civilization difference—in the commonality of literature, after all, the opposition between East and West gives way to Gibb's more deeply entrenched humanism.

Years later, Edward Said addresses Gibb's humanist proclamation in *Orientalism.* In the third section, "Orientalism Now," Said suggests that Gibb's call "for humanistic interanimation between East and West reflects the changed political and cultural realities of the postwar era."[45] Said focuses initially on a contrast between Gibb (whom he reads as representative of the interwar period) and Snouck Hurgronje (whom he takes to be characteristic of the prewar period). In doing so, he aligns Gibb with the philological undertakings of scholars such as Louis Massignon—and even Erich Auerbach and Ernst Curtius. But, Said notes, "if the synthesizing ambition in philology (as conceived by Auerbach or Curtius) was to lead to an enlargement of the scholar's awareness, of his sense of the brotherhood of man, of the universality of certain principles of human behavior, in Islamic Orientalism synthesis led to a sharpened sense of difference between Orient and Occident as reflected in Islam."[46] For Said, in other words, Gibb's proclamation only further highlights the role of civilizational binarisms in the self-discovery of the Western scholar through the East.

For all of the recognizable richness of Said's reading of Gibb, it is curious how Said analyzes Gibb's closing lines. Where Gibb writes, "*Oriental literature* has begun to be studied again *for its own sake*," Said glosses it as follows: "Gibb's phrase 'for its own sake' is in diametrical opposition to the string of reasons subordinated to Hurgronje's declaration about European suzerainty over the East. What remains, nevertheless, is that seemingly inviolable over-all identity of something called 'the East' and something else called 'the West.'"[47] Intriguingly, Said's effort to trace a discourse of what he refers to as "the essential Orientality of the Orient" draws him to focus on Gibb's phrase, "for its own sake," and later, the expression, "the Oriental, *en soi*," as key attributes of this Islamic Orientalism.[48] Said helps to highlight the civilizational dimensions of Gibb's writing and the quest for an essential Orient. What gets dropped out in Said's reading, however, is the second term of Gibb's formulation: not just "the Orient" but "Oriental literature." Gibb, after all, writes, "Oriental *literature* has begun to be studied again for its own sake." Easy as it is to characterize Gibb in this manner for the purposes of a sort of civilizational essentialism, it is intriguing that there is an essentialism of a more robust—and perhaps even more insidious—form as pertains to the category of literature. How might we understand Said's apparent oversight of the literary in Gibb's Orientalism?

It is certainly possible to read in Gibb the emergence of a discourse of Oriental literature anchored in the study of the Orient "for its own sake," but it is striking that this same period gives rise to a discourse of the literary: literature "for its own sake." The very figures whom Said cites as exemplars of liberatory philology, Erich Auerbach and Ernst Curtius, find refuge in a particularly provincial conception of the literary—one which is as restrictive philologically (focusing on the literariness of literature) as Orientalism is as a discourse on the Orientality of the Orient.[49]

To take Said's examples: In the preface to his 1948 book *European Literature and the Latin Middle Ages*, Curtius suggests that his book "grew out of a concern for the preservation of Western culture," that "it attempts to illuminate the unity of that tradition," and that all of this is grounded in what he describes as the universal standpoint of Latinity.[50] These civilizational echoes, geared to fix the concept of Western culture as something in need of preservation, also bear closely upon the topic of literature. The civilizational observations lead Curtius to suggest that his book "is not addressed to scholars, but to lovers of literature, that is, to those who are interested in *literature as literature*."[51] A page later, Curtius differentiates his work from that of a comparatist or a literary historian by claiming what he does is "phenomenology of literature."[52] Curiously, then, the very focus of Said's example of a liberatory philologist turns back upon a discourse of literature "for its own sake," precisely the formulation Said himself quotes—but emphasizes quite differently—from Gibb.

The point here is both to note the convergence of a discourse on the literary, but also a certain reification of the term within an emergent field of study. Gibb, Curtius, and Auerbach all work within the modern literary discipline, and each of them commits not only to understanding, but also to producing the object of literary study, training the modality of appreciation. It is here that Gibb's shift from the general audience of the first line to the trained student of the second becomes most meaningful. His essay, employing civilizational distinctions as a manner of self-discovery, produces in the process both an understanding of literature as the common ground and a unique manner of reading, appreciating and valuing texts in the articulation of humanism. This humanism, however, presumes the comparability of texts across place and time, united in the homogenizing discourse of world literature. And it is a humanism that presumes the stability of the category of literature—"for its own sake."

Noting this turn in Gibb's work, and Said's oversight of Gibb's elision of the Orient and literature, both of which come to be understood on their own terms, is meant to highlight a broader problem at play in the convergence of literature and civilizational rhetoric. Where Said helps to highlight and emphasize the dangers of civilizational discourse, noting the manifold problems of entwining literary study with claims of civilizational essence, he does not himself move toward undoing the particularity of the formation "literature" invoked. In the end, Gibb's project does not actually dwell on civilizational distinctions, but has a certain humanistic universalism in mind, one that is not entirely separate of what Said ends up advocating in his own work. And in the quest to secure a humanist discourse beyond the particularity of culture, it is literature, understood as a comparative project, that comes to the fore—for both Said and for Gibb.

I point here to this curious convergence between Gibb and Said because, at base, both actually overlap in their approach to literature. We could say that Gibb's understanding of literature shares in the presumptions of a key trajectory within comparative scholarship. For Gibb, traditions, languages, and territories help to anchor the terms of cultural difference, but the category of literature remains constant, rendering comparisons possible. We can see similar assumptions at play in the works of comparatists, like Ruhi al-Khalidi (Rūḥī al-Khālidī), Qustaki al-Himsi (Qusṭākī al-Ḥimṣī), and Muhammad Ghunaymi Hilal (Muḥammad Ghunaymī Hilāl), each of whom helps think comparatively across regions, languages, and traditions.[53] For someone like Said, who offers us ways of thinking against the civilizational binarism that appears to structure Gibb's thinking, there is still a strong investment in situating the literary text in the world—and even more, a particular investment in the place of literature in cultural analysis.

But Gibb, who uses apparent cultural difference to underscore a common literary heritage, and Said, who reads colonial situations in the subtleties of literary texts, both share an investment in a certain type of contextualization. One could even say that comparison relies on the production of a context in which to make sense of texts. For all of the discussion of universalism and particularism undergirding the cultural analysis of texts, we might wonder whether the stabilization of the category, in this case literature, is implicit in the act of comparing. This investment in the category of literature, whether in the guise of literariness or for its own sake, blurs the apparent opposition not only between Said and Gibb, but also between Orientalism and the sort of formalism undergirding Wellek's project.

DISCIPLINES AND FRAMES OF READING

Considering what literature is means noting the overdetermined ways in which it comes to be understood. Looking at a text, reading a footnote, making sense of the cultures within which we read are not simply matters of pointing to what texts say—or even to how they say it. Instead, they are matters of recognizing the contingency of literary knowledge, the very basis of which was at the heart of the three studies considered here. What is it that we learn when we read? How does literary knowledge differ from historical knowledge? And how does the way in which we read impinge upon what we believe literature to be? Though these questions reach beyond the limits of this chapter, they underscore a broader hope for this sort of inquiry. It is a hope that suspending the answer to the question of what literature is might lead us to contemplate ways that literature might become differently.

We conjoin Wellek with Zaydan and Gibb as examples of a discourse on the literary that is itself literary—in the transformational sense of the term. What is brought together in these three authors is a formulation in which literature is understood less as a canon of texts than as a disciplined manner of reading. And while each of these authors shares in seeing literature as a category through which to understand textual forms, all perform their understanding of the category differently, engaging in the pedagogical act of defining what it is. They all, in turn, offer an understanding of literature that supersedes the logic of cultural particularity. And in doing so, they all help to dissolve the apparent opposition between the abstracted formalist principle of literariness and the historically situated understandings of *adab*. Each of them entangles his questions with the emergent institutions that make literature thinkable as a discipline. And it is as a discipline that *adab*—and literature as such—becomes literary.

And so we might wonder, what is world literature without recourse to the terms of cultural particularity? Given the importance that area studies grants to the social, cultural, and historical analysis of texts, how might Wellek's formalism inflect discussions of literary worlds? Instead of taking world literature to be a mosaic of differing textual traditions, the formalist principle of literariness allows for the consideration of how texts come to be understood as literary—and by extension, incorporated into emergent literary disciplines. At a time when scholars shift from cultural to ethical models of reading, Wellek's formalism ultimately allows for a reorientation away from representation (seen in terms of a relationship between a text and the world) and toward the practices through which a text is understood as literary. Someone like Wellek opens up pathways that far exceed the focus of his early criticism of social and cultural literary analysis. By enfolding literature with questions of reading, Wellek both localizes literature within its disciplines and thereby enables a consideration of its contingencies.

The resulting framework, it strikes me, underscores a critical shift from semiotic analysis (of the sort pursued in the early work of Edward Said and Timothy Mitchell) to a consideration of ethical analysis (in studies such as those of Talal Asad and Saba Mahmood).[54] The issue for the latter group expands the discussions of semiotic ideology to consider the disciplines and practices that make representations intelligible. By way of clarification, we might think of Talal Asad's engagement with Clifford Geertz on the anthropology of religion.[55] Where Geertz, whose body of work informs Stephen Greenblatt's reflections on new historicism, addresses the role of symbols in the context of religion as a cultural system, Asad addresses embodied practices by which symbols become symbolic. He does so by refusing the abstraction of religion and focusing on early Christianity, in particular, to note transformations in the category of religion over time. Asad's influence for literary scholars has implications that shed light on "how social disciplines produce and authorise knowledges," rather than taking the existence of categories as given.[56]

In turn, we could point to Saba Mahmood's article, "Religious Reason and Secular Affect," in which she analyzes the controversial Danish cartoons depicting the prophet Muhammad in terms of both semiotic ideology and positive ethics.[57] The richness of her work, like Asad's, is to provincialize presumptions about the mimetic function of texts and, in doing so, to consider alternate relationships to aesthetic form. Entwining the valences of ethics, embodiment, and discipline, we reinvigorate literary study with those aspects of reading leveled out in discussions of textuality. And as with the discourse around *adab*, defining what literature is becomes inseparable from how it comes to matter. And how it comes to matter turns critically on the institutions that come to frame how we read.

If I began with a confession of my confusion over what literature is, then I end with a confession that I have hopes for thinking about literature differently. I have hopes for what might come of those worlds foreclosed by the disciplines of literary reading. I have tried to highlight not a definition of what literature is, but the conditions of intelligibility at a point in time, and I have suggested that analyzing the term "literature" is not a matter of translation, but an analysis of the literary disciplines into which texts are born. I have done so with hopes that provincializing this literary world might allow for imagining the place of literature otherwise—and the potentials of a discipline to come.

In the next chapter, I explore the relationship of secularism and literature in the context of debates over Charles Darwin in the Arab world. I thus take a step away from the negotiated boundaries of the world republic of letters in order to consider the negotiation between the educated and uneducated within texts deemed literary. The chapter tells the story of a young man trained in the emergent literary disciplines in conversation with his parents who struggle to make sense of his published article. What we encounter in this next chapter is an instance of how literary institutions are embodied, entextualized and enacted in the framework of the modern Arabic novel. It is an effort to demonstrate what sorts of readings are possible when we enfold the problem of words and worlds into the reading of texts, and it is a demonstration of how literature matters not only for those deemed literate but for all of those readers and nonreaders affected by its figuration of the world.

5

CRITIQUE

Debating Darwin

On July 19, 1882, a professor of chemistry and geology, Dr. Edwin Lewis, cited the work of Charles Darwin in a commencement address to the graduating class of medical students at the Syrian Protestant College in Beirut. His reference was part of a talk titled *al-Maʿrifah wa-l-ʿilm wa-l-ḥikmah* (Knowledge, Science, and Wisdom) and centered more broadly on modern science and its relation to knowledge than on any lengthy exploration of Darwin's theories.[1] Nonetheless, in the years to come, this brief allusion ignited an intense series of debates that played out in academic journals, the popular press, and scholarly circles across the Arab world. In most of these discussions what was at stake was not merely Darwin's propositions regarding the origin of man, but key epistemological assumptions about the boundaries of human reason and the explanatory force of empirical science. For Lewis, Darwin's theories were important to an argument for the pursuit of scientific knowledge and, in his estimation, especially well suited to the graduating class. For the director of the college and others in the audience, the speech was heard as wholly inappropriate. The ensuing controversy sparked what would come to be known as the Lewis Affair and threatened to dissolve the Syrian Protestant College entirely.

Darwin's resonance was by no means limited to this college. In 1957, when the Egyptian novelist Naguib Mahfouz published the second volume of his *Cairo Trilogy*, *Qaṣr al-shawq* (Palace of Desire), he devoted a chapter to a discussion of Darwin.[2] The *Trilogy*, overall, becomes the site in which a number of critical philosophical and historical issues are folded into the imagined world of a middle-class Cairene family, whose conflicts, tensions, and triumphs constitute the drama that animates the three volumes of this now canonical piece of modern Arabic prose. Collectively the volumes trace the story of a family patriarch, Sayyid Ahmad ʿAbd al-Jawad, his wife, Amina, his daughters, Khadija and 'A'isha, and his three sons, Yasin, Fahmy, and Kamal.[3] This robust narrative spans the period from 1917 to 1944, gesturing throughout to a number of subplots based roughly around three generations of national history: the first, the Wafdist generation of 1919, the second, a transition between the wars, and the third, marked by tensions between socialism and Muslim activism.[4] In its rather comprehensive span of material, the *Trilogy* serves as a cornerstone of modern Arabic literature: as Hilary Kilpatrick claims, "In its length and the scale of its conception the 'Trilogy' far surpasses any previous Egyptian novel; indeed, in its own genre it has remained unequalled."[5]

Although a seemingly minimal incident in the context of Mahfouz's lengthy novel, the discussion of Darwin not only crystallizes a number of issues in the family—regarding religion, authority, and the role of education—but it also stages a problem of reading at the heart of this realist text. In this particular chapter, the youngest son, Kamal, publishes an article on the work of Darwin and is summoned for a discussion with his parents. For his father, al-Sayyid Ahmad, the matter is one of reprimanding his son and cautioning him against the pursuit of such atheistic thoughts, and for his mother, Amina, the matter is one of asserting the fundamental truth of the Qur'an, a model of scholarship consistent with the grandfather's pursuits. In the contours of the discussion, the reader is offered both an account of what is said between family members and also the terms in which they variously hear and understand one another. As a novel (as against a philosophical argument), the intricacies of the passage frame the issue less as a matter of right and wrong than as the grounds upon which right and wrong are felt. The chapter adeptly animates conflicts at play between one mode of judgment and another, presenting the terms within which various arguments are heard.

With its careful construction of characters and sentiment, Mahfouz's chapter appears to offer us what the historical material on the Lewis Affair does not. Whereas the Lewis Affair serves as a pronounced instance of how strongly certain audiences reacted to Darwin, Mahfouz's novel seems to exceed the dimensions of the historical incident as it is understood through documents, debates, and scholarly articles. In the novel, we are invited to imagine the setting within which Darwin is discussed and to consider the basis from which the controversy stems.[6] Through Mahfouz's lucid prose, we gain an immediate sense of what moves certain characters to respond, and we come to understand how others hear these responses. This Arabic realist novel, it seems, offers us the means through which to understand the complexity of scientific principles as they intersect with competing motivations, sensibilities, and traditions. Woven into the narration of the story, responses to Darwin become not so much true or false as points of view embedded in the attributes of character. This novelistic rendering, we could be led to believe, lends a humanistic texture to scientific debates.

Inasmuch as Mahfouz's novel draws science into the frame of literature, so too does it gesture to the limits of a literary and scientific world.[7] The account of Darwin revolves almost obsessively around the description of readers, few of whom are at all capable of reading in the manner presumed of a modern literary public. On the one hand, there is Kamal, the son who publishes the article, who is both the product of a literary education and an embodiment of its sensibilities. On the other hand, though, are those other readers, al-Sayyid Ahmad, Kamal's father, and Amina, his mother, who are described in their struggles to make sense of their son's article. What is left for us (as readers of Mahfouz's novel) is an article to be known only through the response of others—and notably, others who fall outside or on the margins of novelistic and scientific literacy. Enfolded as we are in the layers of response, reading matters less as an interpretative exercise (engaging with the subtleties of Darwin's argument) than as a sort of narrational limit (gesturing to the horizon of novelistic intelligibility). Here, then, we find ourselves reading a scientific article that passes into the hands of readers who cannot read, but whose responses furnish the basis of the chapter. We encounter not only the limits of the reading public, but also the narrational possibilities of the novel.

As scholars turn increasingly to consider the place of reading in literary history, what might be gained by revisiting the Darwin debates as a historical and literary phenomenon?[8] Both the Lewis Affair and Mahfouz's novel point to a world within which Darwin functions as an index of a particular education—and an education inseparable from the cultivated sensibilities undergirding how this Darwinian world is supposed to matter. What we encounter in these two instances, I argue, is not the perceived schism of the modern, secular intellectual in a struggle against what is deemed traditional and uncompromising. Instead, both accounts offer the passionate terms of a debate that embeds (and subordinates) a world within which Darwinian propositions are cast as out of place. What is at stake is a matter of not simply surface reading or symptomatic reading, but coming to terms with the limits of novelistic knowledge and critical reading. The literary vanishing point of Mahfouz's realist novel and the curious historiography of the Lewis Affair unfurl an additional page in the story of Darwin's resonance. In these two instances, what matters is less a celebration of the literate reader or the supposedly secular intellectual, but the creation of a world within which this schism comes to be imagined in the manner that is does.[9]

There are a number of studies, notably the work of Marwa Elshakry and Shafiq Juha (Shafīq Juḥā), that trace Darwin's reception in the Middle East.[10] What I hope to offer, though, pushes beyond the localization of Darwin in geographical, or even cultural, terms. The schism presented in the Darwin debates is not so much a matter of national, racial, or ethnic identification, but a schism made thinkable primarily through the terms of the scandal itself. In each of the many locations galvanized by Darwin's theories, the conflict is figured as the collision between those deemed literate and those seen as illiterate or uneducated. Pointing to a critical site in the discussion of Darwin, Susan Harding suggests that the famous Scopes Trial was crucial to the emergence of this divide and served as "a moment in which the cultural story of one people was subordinated and reframed by the terms of another."[11] She casts the trial as a "representational event" and offers a careful analysis of this "open-ended cultural process in which participants, including self-appointed observers, created and contested representations of themselves, each other, and the event."[12]

I draw from many of the questions Harding considers, but looking at Mahfouz's novel, I consider representation differently—not simply a matter of representing modernists or traditionalists, but a matter of considering how representation is inseparable from the world certain representational regimes make knowable. The argument I am making is *not* that we have two worlds of readers, culturally distanced one from the other and incapable of coming to any understanding. Instead, I am arguing that the conditions of conversation delimit, on some level, the terms of Darwin's reception. This is not a matter of constructing two worlds so much as a matter of questioning the parameters of a recognizably critical argument or position. The debate over Darwin is as much a contest over the shifting terms of public participation, formulated as persuasive argument, as the actual discussion of the scientist's findings. Enfolding the Lewis Affair and *Qaṣr al-shawq*, then, is an effort to investigate how a literary sensibility delineates what it means to be modern, literate, and knowledgeable, and those sensibilities that remain, in the end, unintelligible to this literate world. In a crucial manner, this story is not entirely literary—it is, rather, a gesture toward literature's limits—what I would call realism from the point of view of its illiterate reader.[13]

SOUNDNESS AND THE POETICS OF THE APPROPRIATE

On the occasion of the commencement in July 1882, the American-born Edwin Lewis spoke in Arabic as he addressed his audience at the Syrian Protestant College. The college had its origins as a missionary institution grounded in American Protestantism—and although it was founded on missionary principles, at the time of the talk it suffered from internal divisions in the faculty based on competing conceptions of what these principles meant.[14] On the one hand, there were professors such as Dr. Cornelius Van Dyke, his son William, who, months before, corresponded with Darwin about a study on Syrian street dogs,[15] and Dr. Edwin Lewis, all of whom tended to espouse liberal conceptions of knowledge; and on the other, there were faculty and administrators, such as Daniel Bliss, who served as the director of the college, David Dodge and George Post, with a different understanding of what constituted "evangelical soundness."[16] The initial conception of the college's mission, professed in a letter to potential donors, emphasized both "the introduction of true science and Christian literature into the language of one tenth of the human race" and the importance of producing "a body of men who will enter into the work of evangelizing and civilizing the millions that speak the Arabic tongue."[17] In the terms of the debate that followed, the college's mission served as the backdrop against which the commencement address would be understood.

In the actual address, Lewis quite explicitly navigated his way through theological debates regarding the proper domain for rational inquiry and the limits of what can be known. He emphasized a distinction between scientific knowledge and faith in the existence of God, noting the difference between science (*al-'ilm*) and wisdom (*al-ḥikmah*). His remarks often turned, almost poetically, to what scientific observation allows us to know and what it does not: "Although through science man may know something of God's existence," Lewis suggested, "it does not permit him to know who or what He is."[18]
فبالعلم يستطيع الإنسان ان يعرف شيئا عن وجود الله . . . ولكنه يقصر عن ادراك من هو الله و ما هو الله.
The address also focused on the impossibility of knowing who or what man is, and bracketed certain aspects of human existence, notably ethics and character, from scientific inquiry. Lewis went on with literary flair to suggest that man is more than science knows of him: "no telescope reveals God, no microscope makes visible the human soul, and chemistry is incapable of explaining the secret of life or of man."[19]
فلا منظر فلكي يرينا الله و لا منظر مكبر يرينا نفس الإنسان ولا كيمياء تكشف لنا سر الحياة ولا سر الإنسان.
Inadvertently or not, Lewis sought a path by which to differentiate various types of knowledge for the graduates, noting what the human mind can learn through science and what is learned through theological reflection. As it played out, only certain aspects of the talk, and notably the rather controversial allusion to Darwin, became subject to rather heated discussion.

Among the members of Lewis's audience was the director of the college, Daniel Bliss, who remained committed to upholding what he understood to be the college's evangelical mission. Shortly following the talk and disgusted by Lewis's oration, Bliss commented in his journal, "Dr. Lewis's address much out of taste: an apology for Bible truth and an acceptance as science unproved theories."[20] The rash nature of these comments evolved into a more polished explanation for his conviction that Lewis's remarks were "at least inappropriate to the occasion."[21] Following the commencement address, Lewis was asked to attend a meeting to discuss his talk with senior administrators. The audacity of the summons led him to announce his resignation from the university, and a wave of professors, students, and lecturers voiced their support of this seasoned professor whom they understood to have been wronged by the administration. In the ensuing controversy, a number of medical students eventually boycotted classes, and two other professors joined Lewis in submitting their resignations. The tumultuous events embroiled students, faculty, and administrators in the Lewis Affair. At the close of the academic year, the Annual Report spoke to the conflict that threatened to pull apart this academic community: "For sixteen years, we have been enabled in presenting the Annual Report, to speak of prosperity, progress and harmony. The year 1882–1883 will long be remembered as one of discord and rebellion."[22]

However much the Lewis Affair animated discussions of Darwin's theory, it also precipitated a certain intellectual genealogy in the Arab world whose effects echoed well into the twentieth century. In the months following the talk, Lewis's comments became a sort of media event with a critical afterlife in the world of Arabic letters. The speech itself was published in the renowned Beirut-based journal *al-Muqtaṭaf*, edited by scholars Faris Nimr (Fāris Nimr) and Yaʿqub Sarruf (Yaʿqub Ṣarrūf), both with strong ties to the academic community of the Syrian Protestant College. In the November issue, Dr. James Dennis, the director of the school of Protestant theology in Beirut, took the speech as an intellectual matter, and published an article countering Lewis on theological grounds, and Lewis participated directly by contributing articles in his own defense.[23] The immediate debate also continued years later, when Jurji Zaydan, a former student at the college, wrote of the affair in his serialized memoirs in *al-Hilāl* in 1924, cementing the story within the annals of late nineteenth-century history.[24] By 1930, Darwin's name was common enough to be the subject of an article by Rashid Rida (Rashīd Riḍā) in the journal *al-Manār*.[25] Darwin's entry into the Arab world became, for many, somewhat inseparable from the discussion of the events of 1882.

At issue in the afterlife of the crisis was not only the educational stakes regarding the proper methods of analysis and observation, but as many of the publications attest, the status of academic freedom in the modern university. The historiography of the incident tends both to cast Lewis as the victim of a traditionalist administration and to celebrate those students he inspired, many of whom, like Ya'qub Sarruf, Faris Namir, and Jurji Zaydan, traveled from Beirut to Cairo to pursue careers as writers and intellectuals. The writings and reflections of these former students help to cement the terms within which the crisis is remembered both in the Middle East and abroad. Glossing the story of Lewis's resignation, one recent scholar draws the following lesson:

> Although this conflict between the students and faculty resulted in a tragic incident as the students attempted to exercise their American-style rights in an Arab country, the spirit those young men generated lived on and was not defeated with the close of the Lewis Affair. The sense of idealism exemplified by their "rebellion" was gained through the broad richness of their secular education at the Syrian Protestant College, and helped them to exert leadership in the great revival of Arab culture, which began to take place in the late nineteenth century.[26]

The allusion to "a tragic incident" and "the spirit those young men generated" underscores the broader implication of Lewis's story within "the great revival of Arab culture."[27] In these sorts of accounts, Lewis's resignation is not only redemptive, but integral to a modernizing narrative in which the defense of scientific inquiry ultimately seems to triumph over the orthodoxy of the missionary college. What emerges is the rhetoric of "American-style rights," the resistance of the subject against the institution and an idealism that inscribes the beneficence of scientific inquiry into the role of modern education.

But for all of the "broad richness" of secular education, it is worth considering how and why Bliss's stance is so impossible within this narrative of cultural revival. The triumphant tone within this "tragic narrative" necessarily subordinates alternate accounts within it, not only by rewriting the terms of the debate, but also by failing to engage the logic of the counterargument. In the narrative accounts of a heroic Lewis, little mention is made of the fact that Lewis was never forcibly removed from his position and that Bliss sought quite diligently to have Lewis continue in his post. Following Lewis's talk, there was an extensive correspondence between Bliss and Dodge, much of which weighed the ethical stakes of the conflict and focused on how to prevent Lewis's resignation.[28] In the triumphant narrative of the Lewis Affair, there is scant attention to the preexisting tensions between various administrators and faculty grounded in matters as much personal as intellectual, especially as pertained to the grievances of medical students about the examination structure.[29] For Bliss and for many on the administration, the matter was never simply understood in terms of rights and freedoms. The problem Lewis's remarks posed revolved primarily around what was appropriate to the occasion of a commencement ceremony. Bliss's response does not make Lewis's talk a matter of academic freedom, but instead seeks to realign Lewis with the mission of college. For Bliss, Lewis had a commitment not only to the virtues of scientific inquiry, but also to the personal responsibility of the intellectual with regard to the audience and occasion of his address.

While the terms of these debates are often understood in the schism between a secular, modern intellectual and a religious, traditional fanatic, Bliss's position reveals more nuance than a simpleminded logic of rights and freedoms allows. For Bliss, what is at stake is less the validity of Darwin's argument and still less the freedom of Lewis to invoke it; instead, the issue is a matter of coming to terms with what it means to be, in Bliss's words, "out of taste." Unlike the debates that played out in the journals, Bliss's personal struggle, gleaned from his rather extensive correspondence, focused on sensibilities and personal judgment. It was widely known that Darwin was controversial, and without engaging the validity of the controversy, Bliss questioned whether Lewis was acting in line with the mission of the university. His concern was not to weigh the subtleties of Darwin's propositions, but to ask whether or not it was appropriate to reference Darwin in the commencement address—and even further, whether or not it was appropriate, in the events that followed, for Lewis to make public a private memo. As the dominant historical narrative developed, the critical actions of Lewis eventually eclipsed these issues of occasion, taste, and responsibility with the logic of rights and freedom. I am not suggesting that Bliss actively rebutted an argument about academic freedom, for he clearly did not. I am suggesting, rather, that we ought to consider different interpretative responses to the talk, not all of which can be understood in the terms the historical narrative offers us.

Approaching the Lewis Affair in this way is less a matter of emphasizing what was said than a matter of understanding the differing ways Lewis's talk was heard. Even though it is quite common to figure Lewis's critics as simpleminded traditionalists opposed to Darwin, we might wonder about what can be gained by hearing the debates differently: What are the arguments that fail to be heard if the matter is only ever understood as the triumph of scientific reason over religious dogma or as the resistance of critically engaged scholars against the intolerant administration? How and in what ways does academic freedom become the hegemonic reading of the Lewis Affair, and what are the limits of an argument based entirely on freedom of speech? How tolerant can the triumphant historical narrative be if it fails to engage descriptively how something is heard before embarking on a prescriptive project of what should be done? These sorts of questions do not necessarily bracket the issue of academic freedom, but they push us to understand with heightened awareness how the dynamics of reception are animated by Lewis's speech.[30]

What is especially telling in the Lewis Affair is that Bliss's response, which weighs responsibility and taste, falls outside of the domain of academic argumentation. Why? For one thing, Bliss's epistolary response does not address an abstracted scholarly public in the same manner as Lewis's argument, which he publishes in journals.[31] Second, Bliss assumes a role that is less critical than it is advisory, reprimanding Lewis on the grounds that he strayed from a common mission.[32] The historiography of the Lewis Affair not only casts the event as the struggle of the modern intellectual against the traditional institution, but also defines the parameters of what modes of response are deemed academic. The terms of this story embed a passionate argument for knowledge of a certain sort and figure other modes of response as traditional, religious, or premodern. In order to understand the historical event of the Lewis Affair and its relation to "cultural revival," we must look at how certain academic, critical positions are inscribed in the telling of this story. In what follows, I consider how, much like these historical accounts, Mahfouz's novel delimits the passionate terms within which this mode of academic understanding comes to be known.

THE FORCE OF THE ILLITERATE READER

Whereas the Lewis Affair frames the struggle over Darwin as an institutional conflict between Bliss and Lewis, Naguib Mahfouz's novel, *Qaṣr al-shawq*, invites us directly into a family's struggle to understand its youngest son's published article.[33] As readers, we are welcomed into the confrontation between an aspiring young intellectual reflecting on Darwin and his parents' concern for his moral well-being—and most of the chapter focuses on the dynamics of reading and responding. In the first few lines of this intricately constructed chapter, al-Sayyid Ahmad summons his son, Kamal, something he only ever does when the matter is of extreme importance. In the lines that follow, we learn that the night before, friends of al-Sayyid Ahmad mentioned his son's article, "The Origin of Man" (*Aṣl al-insān*), published in the scholarly journal *al-Balāgh*.[34] Although none of these men has read the article, they nonetheless praise al-Sayyid Ahmad on the son's publication, drawing reference to other renowned Egyptian writers such as al-Manfaluti, Shawqi, and Hafiz, as though to suggest possible future success for the aspiring young intellectual.[35]

On his way out of the café, al-Sayyid Ahmad places Kamal's article among his belongings, waiting until he is alone to read through it. In these few paragraphs, Mahfouz describes how al-Sayyid Ahmad, following his early morning prayers, reads the article and, a few sentences into it, begins to marvel at the challenge it poses. Mahfouz tells us that al-Sayyid Ahmad is accustomed to reading political articles and understanding without difficulty, but as he reads through this piece, in a loud voice so as to note its style, he grows increasingly agitated by what he understands of its contents: "But this essay made his head turn and agitated his heart." The article describes the findings of Darwin, who, as al-Sayyid Ahmad notes with disgust, claims that man has descended from animals. This proposition alone is sufficient to ground the father's rejection of his son's work, and is, as far as we know, most of what al-Sayyid Ahmad manages to understand of his article. Even though he carefully reads and rereads the "offensive paragraph," he engages with it emotionally and is, in effect, "stunned by the sad reality that his son, his own flesh and blood, was asserting, without objection or discussion, that man was descended from animals." While al-Sayyid Ahmad is initially proud of his son's publication, his attitude transforms in reading it.

This chapter—and especially the description of the father's reading in the ellipsis—offers an intriguing instance when Mahfouz's realism folds upon itself, embedding a reading of a text in a text. While not entirely uncommon—critics including Michael Fried, Nancy Armstrong, and George Levine have focused on a certain self-reflexivity within realism about mediation—this passage does furnish a certain theory of reading, one in which the article's argument, indebted to the discourse of modern science, is weighed within the context of a family discussion.[36] The father's limited understanding of the article places him outside an assumed literacy—he is, as it were, a reader ill equipped to follow the context of the publication. And, all the same, in this richly overdetermined moment in the novel, he is the reader who comes face to face with his son, who is the author of the article. This layered scene in which we read about reading, however, is woven into a narrative style that is itself celebrated as a sort of apex of modern Arabic fiction, one that both incorporates formal attributes of European realism and draws directly upon Arabic sources in doing so. As the novel folds reflexively upon itself, Mahfouz connects an intellectual world known in the history of modern Arab thought together with the responses of those readers written out of this intellectual tradition. We have, in other words, literacy writing its other, delineating the terms through which the otherness of the illiterate is to be understood.

What is crucial to this chapter, though, is not solely the account of reading, but the terms of the response, which present the grounds upon which Darwin is contested within the family. In this particular instance, at the heart of the chapter, animating the discussion as a sort of absent center, is an article that is never cited for the reader and whose contents are only ever obliquely—and arguably improperly—understood. If the staging of the reader in the text casts a certain doubt on the argumentative claims, then there is also an important way in which the chapter performs the terms of response, offering not only reading in the literal sense but also reading in the interpretative sense. In fact, because the article at issue in the discussion is not staged for the reader, it comes to be known through a series of responses: initially, the surprise of al-Sayyid Ahmad's friends, then al-Sayyid Ahmad's frustration, and ultimately Amina's outright disappointment. Mahfouz's novel drops out the content of the text, leaving the terms of response as the grounds from which to imagine the article. What he offers us, then, is both an account of how the article cannot be read, dealing with the father's scene of increasing frustration, and also an account of how the article is discussed, something that transpires among the family members.

Having given the context for the summons in the opening paragraphs, Mahfouz returns us narratologically to the opening line of the chapter when Kamal, the precocious intellectual in the family, is called in to discuss the matter with his father, while his mother listens in. We learn that Kamal had been summoned a few days earlier to be congratulated for his advancement to the third year at the Teachers College and that he did not have "the least idea of what was on his father's mind." As al-Sayyid Ahmad gestures for his son to be seated, Kamal takes a place on the sofa, facing his father, and his mother, over near the wardrobe, "occupies herself folding and mending clothes." Al-Sayyid Ahmad throws down *al-Balāgh* between them and asks, "with feigned composure," about Kamal's article contained in its pages. We move quickly from the prolonged description of the father's reading to the immediacy of his response, which ultimately gives way to a discussion that constitutes the bulk of the chapter.

In the midst of the discussion, Amina, Kamal's mother, chimes in to suggest that Kamal merely correct Darwin by revealing to him the truth that God created Adam from dust and mankind from Adam. She goes on to add that Kamal should be a scholar like his grandfather, who knew the Book of God by heart. After being silenced by al-Sayyid Ahmad, who claims she should not enter discussions she cannot understand, Amina sits quietly, though Kamal and later al-Sayyid Ahmad himself seem to take up the terms of her discussion. She operates outside the parameters of the article being discussed, and yet, the very limits of her literacy make her response to it all the more compelling. At a moment in the novel when Kamal's article meets its unintended public, Amina furnishes a mode of response that is at once part of and foreign to the demands of critical reading.

What is intriguing is how Amina's response shifts the terms of the discussion. Her emphasis is a lot less on the validity of Darwin's argument than on the integrity of Kamal's publication of the article. Unlike al-Sayyid Ahmad, who distances himself from Kamal by appealing to Qur'anic truth, Amina offers advice for how Kamal might have approached the issue differently, echoing a mode of response that Talal Asad characterizes as *naṣīḥah*: "*Naṣīḥah* signifies advice that is given for someone's good, honestly and faithfully . . . since in this context it carries the sense of offering moral advice to an erring fellow Muslim [*manṣūḥ*], it is at once an obligation to be fulfilled and a virtue to be cultivated by all Muslims."[37] Her first suggestion—that Kamal correct Darwin by reminding him of the truth of God—moves from the terrain of critique (*naqd*), which assumes a distance from what is studied, to advice (*naṣīḥah*), which assumes a common ground. If literacy is often understood as the training of critical response, with all of the implications of producing a critical subject, then Amina's response gestures toward the possibility of the uncritical reading, one whose response is a matter of identification with a point of view and advice for how to correct it.[38] Although she is outside the terms of literacy, as someone incapable of both reading and responding as a trained student, she is still affected by her son's published article. If the chapter begins with the limited literacy of the father, then in Amina's illiteracy we approach a limit to the imagined public of the academic article.

Her second suggestion, which advises Kamal to follow the model provided by the grandfather, furnishes yet another instance of advice, negotiating the terms by providing an example of what is a better model of scholarship. Her allusion to the grandfather's memorization of the Qur'an and her suggestion that Kamal might have strayed from the role of a scholar to illuminate God's wisdom in the world point to the incongruity of the intellectual mold to which her son aspires. By correcting him, as though he has deviated from the commonly accepted path, she makes thinkable a mode of response in many ways alien to the properly disciplined mode of reading. In effect, she recognizes her religious duty to correct the wrong—as against the rights of the speaker or intellectual to affirm or deny a set of beliefs. In staging the illiterate reading of Kamal's article, Mahfouz entangles the limits of literature at the heart of realism's epistemological other, the debate over the foundations of science and knowledge itself. The scene is not necessarily an argument for or against Darwin, but is instead an argument for the frame within which knowing occurs, and it is this framing of illiteracy, be it the nonsecular or the traditional, that remains the unspeakable horizon of literature and its presumptions of a supposedly modern literacy.

A PASSION TO BE CULTURED: CONSTRUCTING INTELLECT AND IGNORANCE

Coming to terms with the discussion of Darwin in the novel means not merely understanding the passage as it relates thematically to issues raised in the Lewis Affair, but addressing the relationship between literary knowledge and a certain critical position the passage makes thinkable. Mahfouz's writing offers less an analysis of Darwin than a discussion of how best to understand the tension in the family, and this tension derives, in large part, from the son's ambitions to become a teacher. On one level of analysis, then, we see the acute ways in which Amina's mode of response, rooted in advice and models of virtuous behavior, differs from that of her son. On another level, though, Mahfouz's novel embeds these distinctions in characters whose often-competing motivations are constructed in the omniscient narration of events. Reading is not only something performed in the chapter on Darwin, but it also plays out in the narrative arc of the *Trilogy*, especially as regards Kamal's scholarly ambitions. The omniscient narration comes to embed what it means to be educated in rather particular terms, rooted, as I will argue, in a passionate conviction about the virtue of a certain type of knowledge. Trapped in the circularity of reading about reading, much of the *Trilogy* presents what it means not only to possess literary knowledge, but also to embody literary sensibilities.

Even before publishing the article on Darwin, Kamal's literary engagements are increasingly integral to his interactions with his family, most prominently in his decision to pursue his education at the Teachers College. At the beginning of *Qaṣr al-shawq*, it is his graduation from high school that serves as the occasion for the family to reconvene, making possible a sort of reintroduction of the various components of the narrative after the ellipsis between the first volume and the second. Much of the second volume focuses on Kamal's efforts to decide whether to pursue a practical education in law like his older brother Fahmy, who died during a protest at the end of the first volume, and his friend, Fuad, whom Kamal's father frequently invokes in discussion.[39] Kamal, however, opts to pursue his education at the Teachers College, where he is trained as a scholar of language and literature toward future employment at a state school in Egypt. In the third volume, and in direct contradiction to arguments put forth in the second, Kamal is somewhat jaded with his career and warns his nephews, Ahmad and ʿAbd al-Munʿim, about the challenges of pursuing an intellectual career. The arc of the *Trilogy* appears, at moments, to trace the development of Kamal's education itself.

At an especially tense moment in the fourth chapter of *Qaṣr al-shawq*, Kamal's learning becomes a matter articulated not solely in terms of what is known, but in a professed desire to be cultured. And curiously enough, what it means to be cultured takes on rather particular significance. This chapter, much like the chapter on Darwin, includes references to the names of many prominent intellectuals, the writer al-Manfaluti and poet Ahmad Shawqi being just two, and it lays out the terms in which the pursuit of knowledge is understood as a virtuous end in itself. Much of the chapter focuses on an argument between al-Sayyid Ahmad, who favors law or commerce as a career for his son, and Kamal, who tries to explain his choice to pursue the study of literature. In a certain sense, the focus on Kamal makes the debate a personal matter, and even though he struggles in discussions with his father, he ends up affirmed in his decision, refining his argument by the time he addresses his mother. It is not, then, a matter of depicting an argument to be won or lost, but instead the terms within which Kamal comes to understand his struggle. Similar to the debate over the article on Darwin, this chapter unfolds the dynamics of competing conceptions of knowledge.

Rich in descriptive detail, this chapter not only presents the discussion, but makes possible an understanding of what compels the various interlocutors to speak. Rather unsurprisingly, the debate is the occasion for Kamal to profess what he sees to be the value of his education, and it is through Mahfouz's omniscient narration that much of the texture of Kamal's critical stance comes to be understood. The bulk of the narrative focuses on the construction of Kamal's thinking, and only at the end of lengthy narration does a single line of direct speech emerge:

> كان يؤمن بذلك لا يمكن أن يتزعزع ، كما يؤمن بكفالة الآراء السامية التي يطلع عليها في مؤلفات رجال يحبهم ويعتز بهم ، مثل: المنفلوطي ، والمويلحي وغيرهما. كان يعيش بكل قلبه في عالم "المثال" كما ينعكس على صفحات الكتب ، فلم يتردد فيما بينه وبين نفسه عن تخطئة رأي أبيه رغم جلاله ومكانته من نفسه ، معتذرا عن ذلك بجناية المجتمع المتأخر عليه ، وأثر "الجهلاء" من أصحابه فيه ، وهو ما أسف له كل الأسف ، بيد أنه لم يسعه إلا أن يقول ملتزما غاية ما يستطيع من الأدب والرقة ، و كان في الواقع يردد نصا من مطالعاته:
>
> —العلم فوق الجاه والمال يا بابا. . . .

He was convinced of the inherent merit of the sublime ideas he came across while reading the works of men he loved and respected, such

> as the Egyptian authors al-Manfaluti and al-Muwaylihi. He threw his whole heart into living in the ideal world reflected in the pages of their books. Thus he did not hesitate to reject his father's opinion as mistaken, no matter how much he revered the man. He excused this error by attributing it to their backward society and the influence of his father's ignorant friends. He was sorry but could only repeat, with all the politeness and delicacy he could muster, a phrase he had picked up in his reading: "Learning's superior to prestige and wealth, Papa."[40]

What is remarkable is that the passage draws attention not so much to the position that inheres in Kamal's rejection of his "father's opinion" as to the critical attitude that informs it. To begin with, the invocation of the "backward society" and al-Sayyid Ahmad's "ignorant friends" establishes an identifiable group from which Kamal distances himself. He not only sees himself as distinct from their underlying ignorance and their uninformed opinions, but also is in the position to excuse their error as ultimately mistaken.

In addition to the distance this passage establishes between Kamal and those of whom he is critical, though, it also invokes reading in a curious way. On the one hand, the whole discussion revolves in large part around models provided by authors al-Manfaluti and al-Muwaylihi, who were themselves instrumental in the definition of the literary field in late nineteenth-century Egypt. And on the other hand, the only direct speech is not itself Kamal's—it is, instead, a phrase "picked up in his reading." It is telling that Mahfouz invokes "politeness and delicacy" (*al-adab wa-l-riqqah*) to describe how Kamal recalls this phrase before his father. While the two characteristics are certainly integral to the act of citation that follows, the term for politeness immediately conjures semantic resonance with literature (*al-adab*). Here, at the heart of the realist novel and in a set of reflections on education, what it means to be cultured, polite, and ultimately in good taste is aligned with the sensibilities of the son and his pursuit of a certain type of learning. The one line attributed to him as a speaker in this block of omniscient narration is notably not his own, but "picked up in his reading."

It is worth noting that the English translation glosses the Arabic term *adab* as "politeness," and yet in Arabic the term carries a number of related connotations. On the one hand, the root a-d-b refers to being well bred, well mannered, cultured, urbane, or having refined tastes, and it also entails decorum, decency, social grace, and humanity—in a word, valences of what it means to be polite.[41] On the other hand, though, the word has come to describe literature, drawing in large part from the lineage of a classical understanding of literature. The related term *adabīyāt* refers broadly to the humanities, belles lettres, or literature, and *Adīb* refers to one who has refined tastes, manners, or good breeding, or now an author or a writer. That the term is employed here as Mahfouz describes Kamal's use of the citation draws us, as readers, to the range of associations relating aspirations for an education at the Teachers College with attributes of being well mannered and virtuous in the world of letters. The clustering of literary writers in conjunction with this term allows Mahfouz to fold literature back into its connotation as etiquette, but etiquette here figured in the context of new institutions for higher education.

As the passage continues, al-Manfaluti's name emerges again, and this time al-Sayyid Ahmad pushes his son to explain what specifically makes this writer such an important model. Al-Sayyid Ahmad explains that he has seen al-Manfaluti at al-Husayn mosque on numerous occasions and that the man was trained not at the Teachers College but at al-Azhar, and that he did not work as a teacher, "he was much too distinguished for that."[42] The remarks go on to suggest that what is said of al-Manfaluti is that his education at al-Azhar had nothing to do with him, "he was a gift from God." He then asks, "If you're a gift from God and attain the greatness of al-Manfaluti, why not do so as a prosecutor or a judge?" Kamal's "desperate self-defense" turns upon the distinction between fame and culture: "I don't want to be as famous as al-Manfaluti. I want to be as cultured as he was."[43] Even though, at this point, Kamal seems to falter in his argument, he sustains the impassioned conviction that a life devoted to learning is of supreme importance. He is unable to explain, moments later, what the cultivation of thought means, but his convictions drive the argument—we have here a passion to be cultured and culture itself comes to be understood as a particular type of knowledge.

This discussion provides a crucial backdrop to the emergence of Darwin later in the novel, in large part for how it textures competing conceptions of knowledge aligned with various characters. In a quite explicit sense, Kamal articulates the supposed virtues of a humanities education, including its value as a source of wisdom against the practically-oriented perspective of his father, al-Sayyid Ahmad. There is more, though, than a simple opposition between the humanities and a practically-oriented professionalism, for after all, what drives this debate is again less what is said than the terms within which these arguments come to be felt by the various interlocutors. And it is precisely that Mahfouz's indirect discourse lends the ear, so to speak, to Kamal that the novel's passionate links to the humanist project become pronounced. What emerges over the course of the chapter is the apparent triumph of an individual making a decision, based in large part on the emergence of a particular conception of the subject. The novel, then, at the point of describing decision making, inscribes the conditions not only of how to understand, but the terms through which feeling, sensing, and responding are articulated. The argument for the value of humanist education comes to rest not so much on an analytic defense of it, but on the emergent sensibility that the novel so aptly conveys, animated in large part by its construction of the terms within which speech is felt.

RELATING RELIGION: THE DISCURSIVE LIMITS OF CHARACTER

It is rather unsurprising that many critics have been drawn to Mahfouz's *Trilogy* to consider the relationship between religion and literature. There are not only thematic issues that beg the relation, but throughout the three volumes, there are also formal parallelisms with and invocations of the Qur'an.[44] When asked explicitly, however, Mahfouz himself tended to skirt the question of religion, and his writing stages conflict between characters rather than offering any one specific argument. As we have seen, the Darwin chapter offers one such instance when family members come together with a different understanding of Kamal's publication. In the second example discussed above, Kamal's argument in favor of attending Teachers College demonstrates not only how Kamal understands his own education, but how this education distinguishes him from the rest of the family. He is at once an aspiring intellectual and the youngest son, and because of the nature of his education, he is the character through whom discussions of religion are often staged most explicitly. For those critics concerned with religion in the *Trilogy*, Kamal appears to offer the seemingly perfect case.

In an article exploring Islam and modernity in Mahfouz's work, Rasheed El-Enany quotes an interview in which Mahfouz states, "I will not speak on the thorny question of religion. . . . This is a subject that I prefer to leave open for the investigations of critics." Taking his cue from this line, El-Enany rises to the challenge. His article makes an attempt "at answering this 'thorny question' that the novelist would not be drawn on to comment on explicitly," and he suggests that, in fact, Mahfouz does answer the question "repeatedly, profusely and unequivocally through the one medium that matters: his creative work."[45] El-Enany alludes to historical conditions in Mahfouz's biography, but he focuses most explicitly on various episodes from Mahfouz's extensive corpus of writings in order to explore the position of the author vis-à-vis religion: "To argue that the novelist was merely a neutral recorder, portraying the different socio-political forces at work in Egypt in the thirties and forties is to fail to interpret the first signs of the novelist's social philosophy, which was to be expressed again and again more elaborately and more craftily in later works."[46] The task of isolating the role of religion presumes a direct relationship between the author and the text, one that leads to the rather bold thesis at the end of the discussion: "Let us then establish without further ado that the social creed which the novelist adopts is that of the secularist socialist and the one he discards is that of the revivalist Islamist. The evidence for this conclusion can be found in the terms in which each character is portrayed."[47]

El-Enany's study ultimately opens Mahfouz's work onto the question of religion by addressing "the terms in which each character is portrayed." On the one hand, El-Enany is attentive to Mahfouz's construction of character, but on the other hand, he reads the stance of a character, most often Kamal, as the basis for Mahfouz's views on religion. In El-Enany's analysis, religion is embedded in a point of view, whose terms are related to character as understood through passages and the narration of specific episodes. As El-Enany discusses religion in the *Trilogy,* for example, he draws some rather broad lessons: "In *Qaṣr al-shawq,* the second part of the *Trilogy,* we see religion vanquished by science, while in *al-Sukkarīyah,* the third part, the elements of the picture are completed with socialism seen to join the ranks of science in the fight against the religious outlook on life."[48] The proclamations are possible, on some level, if Kamal is the character through whom these passages are understood, and in large part, as we discussed previously, the narrative voice in the novel often closely aligns with Kamal, lending an ear most explicitly to his view of the various situations. But, as I have been suggesting, there is more to the analysis of the *Trilogy* than we can simply deduce through character analysis.

If we read solely through Kamal's character, we overlook, or at least subordinate, the ways that the various episodes come alive in the *Trilogy*—not only through reflection, but through conflict. Disagreement is the condition of possibility for most of the reflections, and it is also what drives the *Trilogy* forward, pulled as it is between the emotional ups and downs in the family and between various ways of understanding situations. And because the *Trilogy* is a work of realist fiction, it is hard to ascertain a particular argument being made—we have no particular hero, nor any definitive proclamation of right or wrong. With this in mind, the discussion of Darwin in *Qaṣr al-shawq* does not so much offer us, in El-Enany's terms, "religion vanquished by science" as it does acute insight into how positions are recognized by various characters. The very terms of science and religion are only ever introduced in the competing relationships to the article at the empty center of the chapter. Religion, as such, is not something simply embedded in a character, but it constitutes the means through which questions are raised, and in this instance, Darwin is less the focus of discussion than is the fact that, to his parents, Kamal apparently veered from the proper course.

In another article relating the question of religion to Mahfouz's writing, Ronald Judy ends on the same note with which El-Enany begins. He quotes the same lines of Mahfouz's interview and focuses on the *Trilogy* as a site for the negotiation of the "vexed question of religion."[49] Where El-Enany relates structures across novels, linking Mahfouz's earlier writings in *Khān al-Khalīlī* and *al-Qāhirah al-jadīdah* (The New Cairo) to parallelism in *Qaṣr al-shawq* and *al-Sukkarīyah,* Judy focuses on a close and attentive reading of one of Kamal's lengthy soliloquies. Judy provides a careful analysis of an entire intertextual field of references and intimates that the "paramount idea" in the *Trilogy* is: "How can one live a virtuous fulfilling life without faith?"[50] On one level, Judy analyzes references scattered throughout to the Qur'an, al-Ma'arri, and Spinoza, each of which he links to the broader question of Kamal's faith and ultimately his skepticism. And on another level, Judy looks closely at distinctions in Arabic terminology to claim that Kamal offers us a form of "militantly secular" thinking.[51] To make this claim, he suggests that, for Kamal, "*din* designates a profoundly ahistorical way of thinking. In contrast, his [Kamal's] performance of *adab* is a way of thinking that is constitutively critical and immanently historical—in the sense that it questions and explores ceaselessly without venerating its findings as eternally significant."[52] With a close attention to the intricacies of Kamal's soliloquy, Judy ultimately finds in Kamal's character the basis for secular criticism, drawn between emergent distinctions of *dīn*, *adab*, and *thaqāfah*.

Although Judy invokes the "vexed question of religion," then, he focuses more extensively on the secular terms implicit in Kamal's struggle throughout the *Trilogy*. His argument leads him to proclaim that the *Trilogy* is "a literary monument to secular humanism that takes the entirety of human endeavor as its legitimate object of historical criticism."[53] And within this account, Kamal comes to represent "secular skepticism" against the force of his father's "institutional conservatism" and Amina's "popular superstition."[54] Each of the characters comes to be understood in terms that Kamal himself offers in the soliloquy, and Judy helps map out the role of religion accordingly, taking Kamal's struggle against the authority of his family as emblematic of the *Trilogy* as a whole. Even though Judy proposes a method of reading different from El-Enany, he returns us yet again to Kamal as the site from which to consider the *Trilogy*'s seemingly conflicted stance toward religion.

The problem, however, is that Judy's reading deduces this argument from a soliloquy. And as a soliloquy, the passage he examines is structured as a particular point of view and aligned with Kamal. To claim that the novel is secular and to break down the components of the narrative accordingly is, unfortunately, to overlook precisely how the novel constructs religion as a category negotiated between characters. We are dealing not with the triumph of one character over another, but with characters' mutual intelligibility and framework for self-understanding. The very self that comes to be formulated in these passages is crafted through opposition, reaction, and struggle with one mode of perceived authority and subordination to another. Even while Kamal's education incorporates him into the world of letters, it also reformulates his understanding of those around him. The *Trilogy* overall is not Kamal's soliloquy—it offers us instead the various terms through which characters' responses are made intelligible within the narrative logic of the text.

There is, though, an added dimension to the question of how the novel relates to the question of religion. I have highlighted how, in the *Trilogy*, characters emerge relationally in mutually intelligible relationships. In the discussion of Darwin, for example, Mahfouz offers us an account of reading and an extensive focus on response as it plays out within the family. And even Kamal's argument to attend Teachers College is made with the competing audiences in mind—his father's concern, initially, and then his mother's. Kamal does not exist in isolation, but becomes comprehensible as he does by virtue of the dynamic interactions with those who surround him. To suggest that religion is an individuated crisis of faith skirts the role of the novel in offering the terms of the discussion—and in offering the perception of Kamal's distinctiveness from his family. Part of the richness of Mahfouz's account lies in how it frames the terms within which arguments come to be heard by characters and how, in turn, characters become intelligible through their arguments. As with the novel so too with the Lewis Affair, we encounter not only propositions regarding the work of Darwin, but a way of responding that has more to do with advice than it does with assertions of truth or falsity. Where religion rests, then, may have less to do with the beliefs of one character or another than with the ethical practices at play in the respective modes of address and response.

THE BORDERS OF A DARWINIAN WORLD

By enfolding the *Trilogy* and the Lewis Affair into a discussion of address, occasion, and reading, we might begin to consider some of the limits to the public assumed in these accounts of Darwin. Within the context of Victorian studies, a number of scholars have traced Darwin's impact on novelists, noting the close relationship between science, literature, and philosophy during the nineteenth century. The pervasiveness of scientific thought in the Victorian world made it such that whether or not one actually read the scientific theories did not necessarily matter—as Gillian Beer suggests:

> Everyone found themselves living in a Darwinian world in which old assumptions had ceased to *be* assumptions, could be at best beliefs, or myths, or, at worst, detritus of the past. So the question of who read Darwin, or whether a writer had read Darwin, becomes only a fraction of the answer. The related question of whether the reader had read Darwin turns out also to have softer edges than might at first appear. Who had read what does not fix limits. On the face of it, then, a very generous use of evidence would have been possible for this study, which would see it as inevitable that all writers were affected by such theory.[55]

Taken as a point of departure in George Levine's *Darwin and the Novelists*, Beer's argument is quite striking not only for its descriptions of a certain "Darwinian world" but for its insistence on reading.[56] In her discussion, Beer notes the waning of "old assumptions" and the certain inevitability that "all writers were affected by such theory." As her argument develops, she emphasizes the "softer edges" of whether or not the reader had read

Darwin: "One's relationship to ideas depends significantly on whether one has read the works which formulate them. Ideas pass more rapidly into the state of assumptions when they are *unread.* Reading is an essentially question-raising procedure."[57] Here then, at the heart of Beer's discussion of Darwin's importance for nineteenth-century Victorian novels is a Darwinian seed linked to the problem of reading as "an essentially question raising procedure." Her study is as concerned with assumptions, which she situates in the terrain of the "unread," as with Darwin's explicit permeation of the cultural sphere.

Beer's careful articulation of a literary unconscious, rooted in the conditions of a historical reality, allows for her analysis across criticism internal to the novel and criticism of the world from which the novel stems. There is, however, a certain complication to Beer's argument: it presumes a common world in which these manifold experiences of Darwin are lived. Focusing on the Darwin debates, however, reveals a schism between the ways in which competing communities understand this world and their participation in it. The zeitgeist implicit in Beer's Darwinian world, in which "everyone found themselves living," overlooks the fact that, far from unifying the world, reactions to Darwin produce a division within it between those who claim to understand it properly and those who do not, between those deemed modern and literate and those deemed traditional and illiterate. There is also implicit in this schism a shift in interpretative frame that helps to redefine the parameters of reading. Within the terms offered, the illiterate are those who may not have read or have heard of Darwin and those for whom reading is not "a question-raising procedure" with all of its implications of modern critical thought. The very nature of an assumption differs depending upon structures of experiencing the text—even though readers may be geographically and historically in union, it does not necessarily follow that they inhabit the same interpretative world, that is, that they would necessarily pose questions or respond in the same manner.

The literate argument, then, has as much to do with knowing the terms within which to respond to a given work as it does with the actual phenomenological relationship between the reader and the text. If reading is a "question-raising procedure," as Beer suggests, then a literate reading presumes its own critical dimension. It is on this level of analysis that Mahfouz's novel is especially revealing: for, at once, it offers us an instance in which a scientific article is arguably misread on the part of a family, and it furnishes the terms through which to see and understand alternate rubrics of response. Useful and insightful as Beer's work is for drawing together the importance of Darwin's work for nineteenth-century British novelists and the emergence of a specific mode of literary realism, it tends to leave unaddressed the way that Darwin played out for those ultimately unintelligible to the sensibilities of this literate world.

In the two instances highlighted here, the positions of Daniel Bliss and al-Sayyid Ahmad are both cast under the guise of an unenlightened despotism against which the enlightened response must struggle. But more crucially still, the issue for both Daniel Bliss and al-Sayyid Ahmad revolves centrally around the occasion of the claim being made—for Bliss, the integrity of the university, and for al-Sayyid Ahmad, the integrity of the family. The goal is neither to defend nor rebut either argument, but to consider how these characterizations are largely symptomatic of secular criticism. To be critical and reflexive is ultimately to be detached from structures of authority—or to be subject to structures of authority whose antiauthoritarianism is itself entwined with the liberal notion of freedom as social nondetermination. For Edwin Lewis and Kamal, both understood as struggling against the dictates of authority, we get the texture of a more common story, one by now integral to the conventional narrative of modernization.

Looking closely at the response of Daniel Bliss and the reactions in Mahfouz's novel, we encounter modes of response that remain outside what is deemed academic, critical, or modern. What emerges is less a view in favor of or against Darwin than the rise of competing interpretative frames: for those understood to be traditional, Darwin poses a challenge to what it means to be tasteful, appropriate, or responsible as a scholar; and for the modern intellectual, the Darwin debates reveal the argumentative field upon which to refute or accept the propositions in a literate way. We encounter not only the contours of a Darwinian world, but the ever-negotiated terms within which this world is to be perceived, described, and ultimately understood.

In the chapter that follows, we move to a consideration of two writers from across literary traditions and their efforts to engage theological debates in literary form. Looking closely at the epistolary encounter of André Gide and Taha Hussein, we will explore the limits of a literary public in a sense quite different from the Darwin debates.

6

INTELLECTUALS

The Provincialism of a Literary World

We are accustomed to understanding literary cultures as distinctively national phenomena, and literary history tends to recount stories according to the particularities of national traditions. Area studies and comparative literature both emphasize the importance of linguistic, cultural, and historical familiarity, and students of literature are trained to take seriously the particularities of cultural context in the reading of texts. Whether the consideration of canons, influences, and modes of production or the philological and translational activities of close reading, literary study turns in large part on a reverence for communities of readers within national or linguistic frames. The link between the writer and people, literature and society, leads to the sorts of cultural claims that position the relevance of literature at area studies conferences. But what if literature, as a discipline, has more of a unique culture unto itself than its national culture? What if the notion of a writer delimits not so much a distinct spokesperson for a national population, but increasingly a sort of place of intellectual exile? What if, in other words, the supposed cosmopolitanism of the modern writer is itself a form of provincialism?

These questions gesture to a key problem in what has come to be known as world literature. This field, epitomized by ever-proliferating anthologies of geographically-ranging texts, aims to broaden literature beyond the Western civilization paradigm and beyond the conventional constellation of Greek, Latin, French, English, and German. Underlying this supposed global and historical breadth, however, is an assumption that the accumulation of traditions under the rubric of world literature leads to a deprovincialization of literary knowledge. And yet, much as there is an emphasis on broadening the *world* of literature, it is less common to consider what is meant by *literature*—or more specifically, the disciplined manner of reading presumed by this category. Instead, book by book, article by article, empirical studies map, envelop, and adapt traditions into the vocabulary of modern textuality. In the end, there is a fairly provincial literary world that emerges, one that levels out semiotic and phenomenological differences between how texts are lived, embodied, and experienced. All in the name of broadening the world of literature, there emerges an ever more restrictive regard for the literary and the range of texts capable of being marshaled into its domain.

These are some of the questions that have occupied me in the preceding chapters. Whether the analysis of Jean-Joseph Marcel and the Rosetta Stone in chapter 2 or the Darwin debates in Naguib Mahfouz's novel in chapter 5, reading has been understood as a practice that itself has a particular history. In taking reading as the framework for the analysis of world literature, I have wrestled with the relationship between a history of *literature* (as a category with a specific articulation within the modern disciplines, the liberal state, and the secular imagination) and *literary history* (as pertains to the site of nineteenth- and twentieth-century Egypt). Historicizing literature means not simply finding texts deemed literary, but asking about the conditions in which these texts are understood, how they come to matter, and the ends to which they are put.

It is against this theoretical backdrop that I consider here the provincialism of a literary world in early twentieth-century Egypt and France. In doing so, I look closely at two scenes of epistolary exchange: the first, letters exchanged between André Gide and Taha Hussein in 1939, and the second, a series of imagined letters exchanged in the context of Hussein's novella from 1935, titled *Adīb* (A Man of Letters). My claim is that if we consider literature less in terms of cultural systems and meanings (be they national, ethnic, or linguistic) and more in terms of ethical practices of the literate subject, then we arrive at an enriched terrain for the analysis of how literature comes to matter. This terrain may, in the end, have less to do with analyzing categories of textual organization (genre, territory, or national language) than with analyzing normative practices embodied in and crucial for the recognition of the literate subject. In the following stories, I focus on moments of literary interruption—or rather, on how literature both disrupts and enables the dialogical exchange between writers.

THE BONDS OF WORLD LITERATURE

On January 26, 1939, shortly following the death of his wife, the French writer (and later Nobel laureate) André Gide departed from Marseille on a boat destined for Egypt. He arrived in Alexandria four days later and promptly headed to Cairo by car, where he toured a museum and visited a monastery on the outskirts of the city. That same evening he departed on a train for

Luxor to spend two weeks relaxing at the Luxor Hotel and avoiding the activity that surrounded him in France.[1] His two-week escape ended with a brief excursion back up to Alexandria and eventually an Easter visit to Greece, where he met his friend Robert Levesque, a French professor at a college on the island of Spetsai.

At the time of his brief tour of Egypt, Gide's work was already known to Egyptian readers, some of whom were familiar with his books in French and others who knew him through discussions of his work in Arabic—and in particular, the 1936–37 Arabic translation of *La Symphonie pastorale*. As one of the foremost literary figures of his time, he was both a nationally French writer, closely linked to the literary scene in Paris, as well as a world-class author welcomed through translation into modern Arabic literature. Years following his first voyage to Egypt, Gide's *La Porte étroite*, *L'École des femmes*, *Geneviève*, *Robert*, and *Isabelle* would all be available in Arabic translation.[2]

One of Gide's keen Egyptian readers and eventual translators was Taha Hussein, himself an esteemed author, educator, and intellectual.[3] Not only a towering figure in Egyptian cultural life, Hussein had direct ties to France having been partly educated in France and having married a French wife, Suzanne. Hearing of Gide's visit, Hussein had written him a letter, hoping to pass along a copy of his autobiography, *al-Ayyām* (known in French as *Le livre des jours*) and to lure him for a visit in Cairo on his way back to Alexandria.[4]

A short reply written on his last day in Luxor conveyed that Gide was exhausted, and he sent his regrets to Hussein. He did, though, make clear his hopes of returning to Egypt the following autumn, and even more importantly, expressed enthusiasm for Hussein's autobiography, marveling at its composition and subject matter. In the brief note, Gide remarked that he read the book with an intense interest and, turning to a deeply humanistic vocabulary, noted that it breathed a sentiment of humanity that echoed in his heart: "J'ai lu votre beau livre avec une émotion bien vive. Il respire de part en part un sentiment d'humanité, de sympathie profonde—fraternelle, qui trouve aussitôt écho dans mon coeur."[5] His letter ended with a proclamation of his highest regards (*de haute estime*) and friendship for the Egyptian author. And so, on the pages of this preliminary exchange, ultimately the substitution of a book for a personal encounter, a literary friendship was born—and with it a particular bond between institutions of French and Arabic letters.

Even if Gide's 1939 Egyptian voyage did not allow for the direct meeting of these two acclaimed writers, it did lay the groundwork for future correspondence and eventually a series of translations between French and Arabic. More specifically, it is the backstory to Gide's eventual preface to the French publication of Hussein's *al-Ayyām* and Hussein's preface to the Arabic version of Gide's *La porte étroite*.[6] In fact, Gide and Hussein's 1945 letters pertaining to the publication of these two literary texts would themselves constitute the preface to each of the two works. In this sense, the apparently intimate nature of this correspondence, replete with confessions, deep admiration, and friendship, actually functioned to extend the immediacy of one author to another author's reading public. Through Hussein, Gide came to address Arabic readers more broadly, just as Gide facilitated Hussein's address to the French reading public.

The fact that Hussein's son, Claude-Moënis Taha-Hussein, studied in France helped to make possible the delivery of the letters, and Hussein's near yearly visits to Paris kept the bond alive. Thanks to the relationships forged between these two writers, the pages of the intimate correspondence ultimately helped to broaden institutions of publishing, writing, and translating beyond the language and nationality of each writer. The literary friendship seemed to provide an apparent bridge across the particularities of cultures, drawing together two intellectuals united in their common affection and mutual admiration for thinking and writing. These friendships, it would seem, were the sorts of bonds integral to world literature.

Seen in light of recent debates in world literature, the epistolary exchange between Gide and Hussein might appear as a textbook case for transnational dynamics of textual circulation. For one, it seems to exemplify the local dynamics within a world literary system that Pascale Casanova describes, drawing from Braudel, in *The World Republic of Letters.*[7] Alternatively, in the history of modern Egyptian literature, we could see the literary friendship in line with nineteenth-century translation projects, ranging from Rifa'a al-Tahtawi to Muhammad 'Uthman Jalal (Muḥammad 'Uthmān Jalāl) and linking Egypt to a world system of literary circulation.[8] The exchange might even recall Goethe's now-famous remarks on the poetry of Hafiz or the dialogue form for his conversation on world literature with Johann Peter Eckermann.[9] It could be seen to echo the literary friendships between Mohamed Choukri and Paul Bowles described in the work of Brian Edwards.[10] Whichever way we see these letters between Gide and Hussein, they invite us to consider the circulation and dissemination of literary writing—the sorts of transnational exchanges by now integral to discourses of world literature and access to texts across languages and nationalities. In this immediate story, two towering literary figures appear to facilitate the fusion of literary traditions and the expansion of a world republic of letters, drawing Arabic readers into French and French readers into Arabic.

But what precisely is this world into which these readers are welcomed? What does it mean for two writers from different literary traditions to find value in one another? What are the literary attributes valued across differing textual traditions? How might we understand the deep resonance that Hussein's book had for Gide? What follows here focuses on the epistolary exchange between Gide and Hussein in the context of world literature largely to address the place of Arabic literature in a world literary system. What is remarkable about this exchange, I argue, has more to do with the emergence of literature as a common ground for encounter than with the transnational dimension of their address. What is the literature that forms this common ground? What assumptions do both writers share, and how does the internationalization of a literary context redefine the literary field within which they write? This set of questions is meant not to highlight a matter of margin and center, but to ask instead about a constitutive formulation of a field of world literature. What we have in these letters is a site at which world literature asserts its universalizability across the particularities of language and national literary traditions. In the end, it is this literary field that comes to delimit norms for the reading and reception of texts integral to an emergent conception of humanity—and of world literature.

It would be tempting to read the encounter between Gide and Hussein as an encounter between a Western literary modernity and its non-Western component coming together in a common vocabulary of humanity. In Gide, for example, we have the embodiment of a set of principles in the experimentation with the novel as form, and in Hussein, we have continuity with a tradition of autobiography coupled with an interest in narrative and innovations in modern Arabic. When Gide speaks of being touched in his heart or of a text that resonates with broader humanist principles, we might wonder about the forms that ground these assertions—the conditions of being recognizably human—but we might also note some distinctions in the categories of understanding. Rather than insist upon differences between Gide and Hussein, between the unknowability of one to the other, this chapter offers an exploration of some of the unified dynamics of the self-conception of the writer (in this literary world) and its discontinuity with a particular social space.

LITERARY IMAGININGS OF RELIGIOUS DIFFERENCE

Of the many questions addressed in the correspondence between these two towering literary figures, it is striking that much of their discussion focuses a lot less on the categories of national and linguistic difference, so sacred to how comparative literature has come to think of literary systems, than on religion. And insofar as the letters take up the problem of religion, they do so largely to highlight a set of sensibilities, practices, and traditions that possibly limit the reception of the text. Quite explicitly, religion is the occasion through which the writers consider the limits of their address and the terms within which their writing will be received. Much like we witnessed in the debate over the work of Charles Darwin, the letters between Taha Hussein and André Gide refract questions of literacy through broader discussions about sensibilities, readership, and the moral frames through which texts come to be understood.

A few years following their initial correspondence, the two writers exchanged another set of letters. This time Hussein contacts Gide for permission to publish an Arabic translation of his book, *La porte étroite*. Gide seemed to misunderstand that Hussein himself had not translated the text, and much of his letter considers the potential Arabic readers of his novel. In a curious conflation, though, the Arabic language stands in for religion—and far from being concerned with Arabic readers, Gide focuses almost exclusively on religious difference, supposing what his text may have to say to Muslim readers. Recognizing the frequent conflation of Arab and Muslim as categories within Orientalist scholarship of this period, it is striking the extent to which both authors dwell on readership across religious traditions. Translation, figured here as much religiously as linguistically, provides the occasion to consider the limits of audience within the context of world literature.[11]

Gide's letter begins by noting the attraction he has to the Arab world and the wisdom of Islam (*les lumières de l'Islam*).[12] With a dash of Orientalist flourish, he goes on to note that he has spent much time in the company of Arabs and would not have been the same had he "not spent time lounging in the shadows of palms after having tasted to the point of ecstasy the bitter heat of the desert" (*si je ne m'étais jamais attardé sous l'ombre des palmiers après avoir gouté jusqu'à l'extase l'âpre brûlure du désert*).[13] That Gide turns here in the opening lines of the letter to such literary language is telling. Not only is it the basis from which he imagines those readers of his text, but it is also from these opening lines that he frames his reservations about the translation itself.

Gide remarks that he has learned extensively from his contact with the Arab world, and he claims that it is this contact that enabled him to shed "the trappings of our Western culture" (*les revêtements de notre culture occidentale*) in order to find "a lost authentic humanity" (*une authenticité humaine perdue*). But beyond gesturing to a common basis of understanding, Gide reasserts cultural difference by suggesting that although he has learned a great deal from the Arab world, he is not sure that the reciprocal would be possible: "To this day, if I've received a lot, learned a lot from the Arab world, it doesn't seem to me that the reciprocal would be possible." And so, having set up an Orientalist geography in the first clause involving palms and deserts and a Manichean divide between East and West, Gide raises a series of questions about why, of all his works, *La porte étroite* is most strangely suited for translation into Arabic.

For Gide, the question quickly shifts from what he has learned from the Arab world in order to consider who might possibly find any interest in his work. "A translation of my books in your language," he writes, "[t]o which reader might it be addressed? To what curiosity might it respond?"[14] Gide notes, "Of all my books, there would seem to be nothing so strange to your preoccupations as my *Porte étroite*."[15] Gide's remarks, though, are not solely concerned with the readers of his work in Arabic, but they are also instrumental in his own efforts to imagine these readers. He asks, "How could the mystical dissatisfaction described in the book touch souls set in certainty? What resonance could these prayers and these Christian callings find among you?"[16] Gide's reflections turn largely on a supposed opposition between Muslim certainty and questioning Christians. Like a number of French writers of the period, Gide believes that reading the Qur'an leads to an assertion of absolute truth—bracketing an extensive discursive tradition through which debates occur over meaning and relating. Here, then, Gide assumes a particular habit of reading, accompanied by assumptions about readers more generally: "I don't sense much insecurity at all among those trained and educated by the Qur'an. It is a way of thinking that rarely leads to a search, and this is why this training seems quite limited to me."[17]

When it comes to the translation of Gide's own text into Arabic, he again resorts to the language of humanity, pointing to his own limitations and wondering whether or not the particularities of its Christian thematics will be amenable to the Arab reader: "Have I put enough authentic and common humanity, enough love, in my *Porte étroite*, to move those for whom a different training would have sheltered them from such preoccupations."[18] At the moment, then, of considering the intrinsic humanity of texts, he turns to the possible lifeworld of his potential readers as a limit to the message of his work. He thus posits translation less as a matter of language than as a matter of mediating differences across worlds—something that may not be implicit in his work.

The shuttling between allusions to universal humanity, on the one hand, and Muslim difference, on the other, ultimately paves the ground for Hussein's response to Gide's letter. In a rather subtle manner, Hussein concedes the conflation between Arabic and Islam that Gide's letter invites, and then goes on to acknowledge the ignorance of those Gide describes. He gradually casts doubts on those who have been Gide's informants for understanding the Arab world: "The Muslims you have met," Hussein writes, "very simple-minded and very ignorant [*très simples et très ignorants*], couldn't tell you whether the Qur'an proposed responses or raised questions."[19] "As for the Arabists," Hussein continues, "they concern themselves, as they are trained to do, more with the letter than the spirit of texts."[20]

Having thrown into question the status of Gide's informants, Hussein describes Islam differently and ultimately suspends the question of translation until the end of his letter. In his definition, he points to Islamic history, noting the important role of the first five centuries: "far from inviting tranquility, Islam pushes the spirit to the most profound reflection and arouses anguished concerns."[21] He suggests that this anguish, especially apparent in the first two centuries, gives to world literature the most lyrical and the most mystical love poetry (*la plus lyrique et la plus mystique*). Following the move to consider Arabic literature as world literature, situated in the context of Arabic poetry (which had been the subject of one of Hussein's doctoral dissertations), he delineates the interwoven traditions implicit in Arabic. Countering Gide's claim about the nonreciprocity of cultural exchange, Hussein notes that Islam has given much because it has received much (*il a beaucoup donné parce qu'il a beaucoup reçu*) from Judaism and Christianity, and from Hellenic, Persian, and Hindu traditions.[22]

In the closing paragraphs and in light of all that has been said about Islam, Arabic, and literature, Hussein expresses joy to welcome Gide into the Arabic literary tradition "at a moment when two of his works will be made known to the greater Muslim public" (*le grand public musulman*). With Arabic translations of *La Symphonie pastorale* and *L'Ecole des femmes* available and with the publication of *La porte étroite* under way, Hussein concludes the letter by invoking Gide's metaphor of taking and giving, hoping that the Islamic world can receive Gide inasmuch as it has given to him. In the final instance, then, the literary work serves as the bridge between the Arabic language, Muslim readers, and Gide's world-class novel—and his letter, published as the preface, is one step in this direction.

It is telling that neither writer turns to theology to negotiate the terms of the discussion and especially telling that Hussein turns to history in his reply. Gone are the presumptions of negotiating theological questions theologically, and instead, literature here stands in for religious reasoning in a different manner. This is not any simple binarism between East and West, the modern and the traditional, the religious and the secular, but instead a negotiation of the terms through which religious discussion transpires. Hussein's engagement interestingly points to Arabic poetry as part of a retort to Gide's observation of Islam, and both Gide and Hussein find common ground in a shared understanding of literary value across languages—and in this instance, it is poetry that comes to mediate the apparent distinctions between literary publics.

For both Gide and Hussein, the world (whether France or Egypt) is not simply taken as given, but is actively imagined through such literary exchanges—that is to say, literary form, as it comes to be understood, is integral to how the world is figured. These assumptions echo in Pheng Cheah's recent formulation of world literature as a world-making activity that "allows us to imagine the world."[23] Cheah's article focuses on literature's dual function as both figuration and communication: "Literature creates the world and cosmopolitan bonds," he writes, "not only because it enables us to imagine a world through its powers of figuration, but also, more importantly, because it arouses in us pleasure and a desire to share this pleasure through universal communication."[24]

In his argument, weaving together Kant and Goethe, Cheah returns to a curious definitional bind in which assertions of what literature *does* rely on assertions of what literature *is*. When Cheah writes, "Literature enhances our sense of (being a part of) humanity, indeed even brings humanity into being because it leads to sociability," he furnishes a normative definition of the literary in order to secure the world it enables us to imagine.[25] On the one hand, world literature is the occasion to consider the universalization of the literary field across what it perceives as cultural, linguistic, or, in this case, religious differences, but on the other hand, world literature posits a quite restrictive sense of what literature is, predicated here on the legacy of German idealism. That Gide himself would make recourse to humanity and describe his emotional interest in Hussein's book is of little surprise, given how both Gide and Hussein seem to occupy an understanding of literature not entirely distant from the world that Cheah describes.

And yet, it is curious that Cheah makes of literature a matter of imagination precisely when it is the theory of imagination that underwrites the redefinition of the literary in the terms I will be describing—in an epistolary exchange that is as much the grounds for ascertaining religious difference in the secularized discourse of literature as the celebration of literature itself. It is also telling that Cheah's article ends with a curious rendering of *dunyā*, which he glosses as Arabic for world. There is a sort of performative contradiction inasmuch as the translation he offers underscores what he earlier tried to glean from Goethe and Marx. Linguistically speaking, *al-dunyā* invokes worldliness, in contrast to *al-ʻālam*, which has more of a resonance with international and globality. This distinction, it strikes me, is what is at stake in the exchange between Gide and Hussein—an exchange that turns crucially on the establishment of literary grounds from which to imagine religious difference, a subtle shift from the globality of intersecting traditions to the assertion of a quite uniform literary worldliness.

When scholars speak of world literature, they tend to embrace a world literary system organized in social-scientific terms of nations, states, and languages. Not only do Hussein and Gide broach theology through literary history, but they secure a common understanding of what constitutes literature. Literature, then, serves as a curious ground from which they negotiate ways of understanding the specificity of traditions in poetry, language, and the language arts. This is not a simple matter of imagining the world through literature, but of tracing how literature—as a category—dissolves in the translational and transhistorical gaps between writing and reading. What, then, do these letters reveal about the circulation of texts in a supposedly global age? How does this epistolary exchange anticipate the modes of address by now integral to discourses on cultural difference? The letters, it seems to me, are a provocation to consider the limits of a literary world that brackets theology in the service of global literacy—and to consider, in the end, that the world of world literature may be, in effect, a rather small place.

WHISPERS AT THE LIMITS OF LITERARY EXPERIENCE

I turn now to an epistolary exchange of a different sort. In 1935, just a few years prior to the correspondence with Gide, Taha Hussein published another sort of correspondence in the form of a novella. The short piece, titled *Adīb*, recounts the story of a narrator and his friend, both of whom suffer from "an ailment [*'illah*] called literature" and both of whom correspond and converse with an intense intimacy binding them together as intellectuals.[26] Unlike the exchange between Gide and Hussein, the imagined correspondence between Hussein and his friend is written mostly in the form of a first-person narrative and only periodically includes chapters of letters from the imagined friend. Within the narrative arc of the novella, the narrator's friend travels to France, abandoning his wife in the process, and experiences a sort of deep alienation before eventually disappearing. In contrast to the transnational dimension outlined in the letters with Gide, Hussein's imaginary interlocutor is someone from his home village, a sort of long-lost friend, who offers an alienation of a different sort—as much alienated through his status as a writer as through his status as a displaced traveler. If in the friendship with Gide we encounter literary institutions and the spread of a world republic of letters, then in *Adīb* we encounter the limited imaginary of a rather provincializing conception of the modern writer, alienated from his people and destined to a particular form of solitude. In this sense, contextualization in terms of languages and nations seems to fall short of the literary world within which these writers imagine themselves—a world in which the written word, novels and poetry, constitutes a particular mode of address, ethics, and way of experiencing a life.

Part of what renders *Adīb* so fascinating is not so much the nature of the alienation felt in Europe (the source of most critical commentaries on the text), but the nature of the bond between the two friends when in Egypt. It is a sort of imagined exchange of letters that provides a near inverse to Tayeb Salih's (al-Ṭayyib Ṣāliḥ) famous *Mawsim al-hijrah ilā al-shamāl (*Season of Migration to the North*)*. What binds these characters is ultimately their proximity one to the other and the nature of their common interest in learning and then secondarily, their connection to a home place. If Gide and Hussein's letters underscore distinctions between religions, then it is interesting that *Adīb* underscores the imagination of historical and cultural difference within a particular nation, language, and religious tradition. This novella offers us a way of framing not necessarily oppositions between the modern and the traditional, the foreign and the local, the West and the non-West, but transformations within literary culture in Egypt that distinguish a particularly writerly mode of existence—and a set understanding of the role of the intellectual in the face of the national public.[27]

My goal is neither to celebrate the apparently universal reach of world literature, nor to rediscover local literary traditions (with all the nativist implications of such an endeavor). Instead, I hope to consider the limits of literary modernity when seen in terms of character, ethics, and experience, all integral to the ethical formation of the "man of letters" at the heart of Taha Hussein's novella. What semiotic ideology defined relationships to texts prior to the modern moment? Or what social function did literature displace in its emergence? What constitutes literacy in the modern state? Is there a distinction between high literacy and functional literacy—and where does literature factor in this divide? On the other hand, though, we might question what it is that we read for and hope to discover in specific texts. There are distinct ways in which Taha Hussein's *Adīb*, concerned as it is with modernization, constructs a particular world, imagines its reading public, and presents the terms in which reading might transpire.

The opening pages of the novella rather self-reflexively define the prime characteristic of a highly literate man of letters, invoking the social bond linking the writer and the people: "They claim that the most prominent characteristic of a man of letters [*al-adīb*] is his keenness to create a bond between himself and the people [*al-nās*]." As the opening passage continues, the relationship is further intensified: "If he reads a book, goes for a walk, or converses with people, and these actions arouse some impression in his soul, stir some sentiment in his heart, or provoke some thought in his mind, he will find neither peace nor tranquility til he has a recorded this impression, sentiment or thought in a notebook or on a piece of paper." "The reason for this," we are told in the next paragraph, "is that he suffers from an ailment [*'illah*] called literature."[28]

It is especially striking that Taha Hussein's novella invokes literature as an ailment, but does so in order to describe the writer's orientation as its symptom. We immediately shift from the attributes of a literary text to the attributes of one who writes and produces works of literature. We move, in other words, from the world of textual categories to the behavior and dispositions of the modern literate man, the Adīb. Over the course of the twenty-two chapters that follow, the apparent bond between the writer and the people dissolves into an increasingly hermetic dialogue between the writer and his friend—two self-perceived intellectuals. We have an apparent contrast of the writer addressing a world republic of letters in order to address, most intimately, a friend of almost exactly the same background.

A few paragraphs into the novella the seemingly universal characteristics (which are described in terms of an abstracted man of letters) are particularized in the description of the narrator's friend, the Adīb: "If all this is true, then my friend, of whom I wish to speak to you, must be a man of letters. For I know no one among the people I have met and spoken to who was as consumed with this ailment of literature [*'illat al-adab*], whose heart, mind, and soul were as besieged by it as were my friend's."[29] With these opening reflections, we are welcomed to think of literature in terms of the bond it offers between these two characters who self-conceive as educated, modern, and critically inclined in their orientation to the world—and their distance from worlds they deem traditional.

The book overall involves dialogues and letters between the narrator, who lives in Egypt, and his unnamed friend, whom he meets at the university and who eventually travels to France as one of the first Egyptian delegations of students. In its twenty-two chapters, the book shuttles between the urban life of Cairo and a pastoral village in Upper Egypt, the modern Cairene university and the classical education of al-Azhar, as well as the cafes of Egypt and the student quarters in France. On one level, the novella addresses two friends' encounter through education, the sense of alienation they feel from village life, and the challenges and competing ways of coming to terms with modernity; and on another level, the novella deals with the friend's divorce from his village wife Hamida (a precondition of his travels to France), as well as his love interest in a French maid, Fernande, and later Aline, whom he fears conspires against him when Egyptian students are recalled back to Egypt.

In the end, the book might appear to stage a whole set of issues pertaining to the modernization of Egypt in the late nineteenth and early twentieth centuries, at the intersection of the French, British, and Ottoman Empires. One could be tempted to understand the text as a thematic staging of numerous issues pertinent to modernity in both a Western and non-Western context, ranging from education to urbanization in rural and urban Egypt and France at the time of the First World War. An added layer to this thematic understanding of the novella could also point to Taha Hussein's autobiography, eventually published in three volumes as *al-Ayyām*. Like the unnamed friend, Hussein moved to Cairo from a rural village, struggled in his studies to achieve success, and eventually traveled to France.

Seen in these terms, *Adīb* appears to provide an especially rich site through which the autobiographical is apparently fictionalized, projected and transposed into a series of letters that imagine the dialogue between the West and non-West. Here we might think of a range of intertextual echoes: Montesquieu's *Lettres persanes* (Persian Letters), Ahmad Faris Shidyaq's *al-Sāq 'alā al-sāq* (Leg over Leg), Rifa'a al-Tahtawi's *Takhlīṣ al-ibrīz fī talkhīṣ Bārīz aw al-dīwān al-nafīs bi-Īwān Bārīz* (An Imam in Paris), 'Abd al-Rahman al-Jabarti's *'Ajā'ib al-āthār fī al-tarājim wa-al-akhbār*, or more recently Tayeb Salih's *Mawsim al-hijrah ilā al-shamāl* (Season of Migration to the North).[30] Cast against the backdrop of the *nahḍah* or the Renaissance, *Adīb* seems paradigmatic of a set of social and political transformations: the consolidation of the state under Muhammad 'Ali, the delegations of Egyptian students to France, the urbanization of Cairo, the emergence of an effendi class of educated bureaucrats, the rise of the modern disciplines, and the waning of the classical Azharite models of education.

But beyond locating historical resonance in a potentially thematic reading of the text, what is it to turn to a text deemed literary to engage questions about the world of literature? Returning to the opening passage of *Adīb*, I wonder if we might not benefit from a reading less concerned to collapse the various thematic aspects of the story into the dominant historical narrative of literary education than with a consideration for the reimagination of the social function of the literary writer. The novella curiously proceeds not through writing (in the literal sense) at all, but largely through dialogue spoken between the two friends—and it contains moments of whispers, interruptions, disagreement, and laughter, providing a texture to the solitary nature of writing. By the time we reach the ninth chapter, we have the first written letter, sent from the man of letters to the narrator on account of a misunderstanding. The terms of address here are hardly the link between the writer and the people, but rather the intimate terms of personal correspondence uniting two intellectuals. From the abstracted terms of address in the opening lines, the novella contains little discussion of people and consists rather of a series of dialogues and epistolary exchanges between the highly literate narrator (a product of a classical Azharite education who now sits in on classes at the modern university) and his friend (an embodiment of the effendi class of modern intellectual). What ultimately emerges is a sort of manual on the limited social frame of the modern literary life.

A WORLD UNTOUCHED BY LITERATURE

At the outset of the fifth chapter, the narrator and his friend have established that they both come from villages in Upper Egypt, and the intensity of their bond escalates. The chapter itself is uttered "almost in a whisper [*hamsan*], in a voice that bespoke a profoundly affected soul and a heart brimming with love and tenderness."[31] We learn that the narrator is invited into a sort of experiment of imagination, encouraged to flash back to a time when he was young: "Suppose I were now in my village and you were in your city," the friend commands, and then asks, "Where could I meet you?" As the dialogue continues, the friend asks not to have to stand on the ceremony of meeting in a home, he asks the narrator to "throw off his turban" and "return to the gown" he wore before coming to Cairo, and he prompts the narrator to return to a roadside "in front of Sheikh Muhammad Abd al-Wahid's shop on one of those two crates flanking it to the right and left."[32] The man of letters, supposedly a man of the people, here finds his point of return in an interlocutor who shares his background, both in their common village upbringing and in their perceived displacement from it. Their nostalgia is an index of their lost past, but also of their exile in an ever-provincial literary world.

As this remarkable chapter continues, it weaves together a dreamscape of the narrator and his friend constructing the world from which they have fled. They "stop and toy with the hyacinth bean which twines around the *ma'mūr's* gate," they listen to the voices of Aziza and Amina, and they reflect on their pronunciation, seeking a more authentically peasant voice without the twists of the Cairene accents. And as the chapter reaches its conclusion, the friend asks the narrator whether or not he remembers the verse of the fifth-century poet, al-Mutanabbi:

إني من أنصار الحسن الطبيعى الذي لايجتلب، ولا يشترى، وإنما تخلعه الطبيعة وتفضيضه على وجوه النفوس، هذا الحسن الذي تحدث عنه المتنبي. أتذكر بيته؟ إنه مشهور:

حسن الحضارة مجلوب بتطرية   وفي البداوة حسن غير مجلوب

I am a believer in natural beauty, which is neither acquired nor bought, beauty which is provided by nature and lent to souls, this beauty of which al-Mutanabbi spoke. Do you remember his verse? It is famous:

The beauty of urbanity is procured by praise/In the desert, it is beauty unprocured.[33]

With the resounding eloquence of these lines of classical Arabic poetry, the chapter that began with the intimate whisper between two friends ends with the echoes of the distant past—from the memories of rural village to the invocation of the classical poet.

It is the mention of the poet that, in effect, awakens the friend from his soliloquy in the fifth chapter. As the narrator notes,

فما كان لشابين جاهلين من شباب الريف أن يديرا بينهما مثل هذا الحديث أو يذكرا مثل هذا الشعر. وأين حديث الريف الساذج اليسير الذي لافلسفة فيه ولاتعمق من هذا الحديث الطفولي الذي اندفع فيه صاحبى كأنه السيل يرده شيئا، الذي أخذ يتكلف فيه ما تكلف، ويصطنع فيه ما اصطنع على غير شعور من الفلسفة والتعمق والدقة في التفكير والتعبير.

It was not credible for two ignorant village youths to carry on such a conversation or to recite such poetry. For how distant were those naïve, simple conversations of the countryside, devoid of philosophy or profoundness, from this lengthy monologue my friend was pouring forth like an unmanageable torrent, which he inadvertently garnished and embellished with philosophy, profoundness, and precision of thought and expression![34]

At the most eloquent moment in the narration of the provincial past, it is the literary allusion to al-Mutanabbi that shatters the imaginative dream world, the sights, sounds and smells that serve as the apparent antidote to life in the city. As the narrator tells us, "When he [the friend] heard his own voice reciting this verse, he came back to himself, and I came back to myself and to him."[35] فلما سمع صوته ينشد هذا البيت ثاب إلى نفسه، وثبت أنا إلى نفسي وإليه.

What might it mean for literature at this moment to awaken the self unto itself? Is there a nonliterary self in the life of the village? To whom might this experience be communicated? Is there something inherent in modern literary form that bespeaks a particular experience? What experience is no longer thinkable, or left unimaginable, within literary modernity? Just as the dialogue imagining village life is shattered through the invocation of the classical Arabic poet (for "it was not credible for two ignorant village youths to carry on such conversations or to recite such poetry"), so too does the quest for non-Western literary modernity risk such fanciful imaginings of a world untouched by literature (in the sense normalized by an idiom of world literature).

We may be reminded here of the invocation of poetry as it occurs in the conclusion to Hussein's letter to Gide—precisely the point where poetry comes to serve as the bond between these two writers. At a time when comparatists seek to incorporate the world into the purview of the literary (all under the guise of world literature), I wonder what we might gain by considering the particularity of the literate world and the specificity of its categories—and doing so not to assimilate other ways of life into it, but to mark, as does Taha Hussein's *Adīb*, some of the limits to literary imaginings. Only then might the whispers between friends united in common affection for a limited world overcome the pretensions of speaking on behalf of the world or of enfolding all under the assumed liberation of its particular modernist dream.

PROVINCIAL COSMOPOLITANISM

When the French edition of *Adīb* was published in 1960, it was made available thanks to the translation of Hussein's children, including the son who was the conduit of much of the correspondence with Gide. Of the many aspects that might potentially occupy a reader of the two texts side by side, there is one particular detail that seems especially noteworthy in a novella that dwells so extensively on the relationship of the author and his friend. In their adaptation of the Arabic, they provide some key edits, deletions, and transformations, but ultimately translate the people of the Arabic version into the reader of the French: "For the man of letters," they write, translating their father's words in the opening lines, "what is most striking, it is said, is the insistence he places on creating a connection between his reader and himself" (*Chez l'homme des lettres ce qu'il y a de plus frappant, dit-on, c'est l'insistance qu'il met à créer des liens entre son lecteur et lui*).[36] Where the Arabic version places a strong emphasis on the link between the writer and the people (*al-nās*), reserving the possessive only for the relation the author has to himself, here, in the French version, the people are altogether substituted by the figure of the reader (*le lecteur*). And it is not just any reader, it is the writer's reader, *son lecteur*, to whom the writer works to create a particular connection. Here, then, on the pages of this translation of a worldly novella, the people become the reader in the travel from the writer to his children, from one generation to the next, and from Arabic into French.

If this chapter has traced instances of transnational literary exchange alongside the provincial bonds of a writer and his native friend, then in the translation the proclaimed intimacy of this whispered text finds another audience. And it is noteworthy that the translation brings us from the people of the Arabic edition to the reader, in the singular, of the French. Is the notion of the people limited to the scope of a national literary tradition? Can world literature accommodate the people without a sort of anthropological scope? In what ways does the reader here substitute for the people? My goal in pointing out the transformation between the editions is not to insist on the linguistic purity of the original, but instead to inquire differently about what each version engenders by way of thinking through the limits of literary address—made all the more prescient by virtue of what this particular novella broaches on its pages and in its form.[37] Can world literature accommodate a sense of the people? Or is the public of world literature most properly embodied in the reader, replete with presumptions about who or what this reader should be?

In a novella that traces the disappearance of the writer into a state of utter alienation, it is all the more telling that the translation dissolves the category of the people into the individuated reader. The link that emerges, then, is a far cry from the national writer addressing his national community. When Gide writes to Hussein, he does so by invoking his interest in having read his work, and he expresses his concern about not having properly understood the resonance that Hussein's writing might have among his own people. When Hussein replies, he expands his discussion to consider the scope of humanity, but ultimately provincializes what this humanity might mean by bringing literature into the scope of a very particular understanding. This provincial literary domain becomes all the more pronounced in the ailment with which the novella begins, and we arrive here, in the French translation, with the disappearance of the people altogether. The figure of address that initially haunts the nature of the exchange, the contents of the novella, and the role of the writer in general is here eclipsed by that notably global figure of the reader, particularized in the silent practice of staring at a page. Is this, we might wonder, the threshold of world literature?

CONCLUSION

During a workshop at the American University in Beirut, I recall sitting through a talk by a noted Lebanese novelist reflecting on the cultural politics of literature in the Middle East. As he spoke, he bemoaned a literary world in which readership for modern Arabic literature in Arabic seemed to be waning and in which an eagerness for modern Arabic literature in translation was on the rise. The paradoxical situation he presented meant that being translated into French or English was largely a precondition to being read in Arabic by readers of the national public. Being deemed a successful work within a national literary tradition, in other words, demanded being deemed in advance a work of world literature.

The talk, though, did not settle on the commonly discussed problems of translation within a global literary market. Instead, it ultimately went on to address the author's underlying discontentedness with Islamic movements in the region. In a subtle move from literary markets to global politics, he secured a distinction that turned less on the translation between languages than on the distinction between types of readers (or nonreaders) within a given national public. The rise of Islam, he suggested, related quite directly to a declining interest in the modern Arabic novel and to a supposedly disappearing culture of reading in the Middle East more generally. There were few empirical claims to back up his observations, and he dismissed the wealth of reading material available under the auspices of Islam, all of which seemed to elude his definition of what qualified as literature.

While the talk was by no means the impetus for this book, it did force me to reflect on an apparent pattern of thinking. As this novelist had it, not only was religion at odds with literature, but literature itself became the domain through which many global readers (reading Arabic literature in translation) come to understand the situation of religion in the Middle East. For these global readers, the writings of authors ranging from Orhan Pamuk to Azar Nafisi and from Tahar Ben Jelloun to Alaa al-Aswany ('Alā' al-Aswānī) shed light on Islam and its social world.[1] These global authors hold in common access to publishing houses that constitute a sort of world republic of letters, and they also share in being marketed (and called upon) as commentators on the worlds from which they write.[2] As these novels and memoirs are often understood, they offer a legible means through which readers imagine the contours of a social world deemed either radically different or disturbingly familiar. In recent years, these various stories have become a backbone of a world literary canon. It would seem that world literature is to a certain extent revitalized by enveloping these social worlds into its fictional domain, but what are some of the challenges to imagining religion through world literature?

My pause listening to the Lebanese writer stemmed from the claims that were being made on behalf of literature, particularly as it was set in opposition to religion. The modern Arabic novel, in his estimation, wrestles with political problems, engages historical moments, and negotiates the terms of Arab identity. Those familiar with the intertextual dimensions of Arabic literature are deemed learned and educated, and at the same time, those lacking this familiarity are seen as dilettantes, or worse yet, void of any understanding of their own cultural heritage. Although this author expressed his frustrations with the fact that few Arab readers actually turned to modern Arabic literature, he seemed equally unwilling to consider with any degree of sympathy the impact of new media on the reading public. There are broad populations for whom the modern Arabic novel no longer bespeaks national consciousness, but for whom other media impact sensibilities more directly tied to daily practices, be it in the form of cassette sermons, self-help manuals, or serialized television programs. One means of responding to the author's remarks on religion would be to turn to some critical anthropologists, most notably Charles Hirschkind on the circulation of cassette sermons, Lara Deeb and Mona Harb on leisure and Islam, and Lila Abu-Lughod in her exploration of Egyptian serialized melodramas.[3]

My goal, though, has less to do with evaluating the practices of which the novelist was so dismissive than with trying to understand the world from which the novelist spoke—and some of its limitations for thinking about religion. A book such as Azar Nafisi's *Reading Lolita in Tehran* proclaims empathy is a key aspect of learning to read, and at the same time, the memoir offers little if any empathetic reading of counterarguments to the claims the author makes about literature. When it comes to the debate around *The Great Gatsby*, for example, empathy is hardly at play in the depiction of Mr. Nyazi, whom Nafisi presents as a seemingly hidebound zealot. But again, the question at the basis of my work is less to redeem a depiction of Islam in world literature than to question the disciplinary preconditions of world literature and the world it offers. Might it be possible to empathize outside the literary world? What are the conditions for being recognizably human in the world republic of letters—and what is excluded from it? In the end, my response to the Lebanese novelist (and to those writers for whom literature delimits a world at odds with the rise of Islam) was to contemplate the historical specificity of the literary world and the political function the literary text comes to play within it. This set of concerns led me not to a particular canon of novels in search of answers, but to a different analytic terrain engaged with the emergent relationship between secularism, reading, and the rise of modern Arabic literature as a site within world literature.

I have set out in this book to question the relationship between literature and secularism during the reforms of nineteenth- and twentieth-century Egypt. In the various chapters, I have drawn together a range of material to reflect on the transformation of the terms in which literature comes to be understood. The first half of the book analyzed this transformation in terms of the world in which reading occurs: the world republic of letters, the emergence of a literary hermeneutic, and the disciplines of colonial schooling. The second half addressed textual analysis from the standpoint of competing interpretative worlds: in one instance, a discussion of Darwin within the context of a family, and in another, frames for understanding the relationship of literature and religion in the work of Taha Hussein. Each chapter has been an effort to explore textual minutiae as the basis of an interpretative world and to ask about the social conditions of reading against the backdrop of modernizing reforms. At the same time, though, I have avoided the oppositional logic between modernity and its other, largely to highlight the developmental narrative implicit in accounts of world literature and the traditions it gathers in its scope. My goal has been to consider how a certain reading practice sanctions participation in the world republic of letters and comes to delimit both what literature *is* and how it ought to be understood. This is a matter not of celebrating or critiquing an emergent relationship between literature and the modern state, but of asking about how certain distinctions are secured between the literate and the illiterate, the modern and the traditional, and the cosmopolitan and the provincial.

In these concluding remarks, I both draw together some of the underlying arguments at stake across the chapters and consider some of their implications for our work as comparatists. I have been concerned here with the conditions of belonging to the world republic of letters, and in this process, two strategies of representation have been at stake. On the one hand, I have dealt with representation in terms of being recognized within the ambit of the world literature. In doing so, I have focused on what it means to be recognized as a reader, in the case of the protests against Haydar Haydar, and then as a work of literature, in the case of Naguib Mahfouz's Nobel Prize. I have traced a second understanding of representation as a matter of interpretative frames and explored realism in two textual examples: namely, Mahfouz's *Qaṣr al-shawq* and Taha Hussein's novella *Adīb.*

But the book has also pushed differently at these two representational poles largely by taking world literature to be a problem of reading and reception as much as any attribute inherent in the text. I have thus emphasized a mode of analysis that suspends an investment in close reading and investigates instead the world in which the text accrues meaning. Doing so, a crucial thread of this book focused on opinion, critique, and the disciplining procedures of modern literature, which I have taken to be inseparable from literary study, realism, and the consideration of representation as a series of practices. In what follows, I highlight two main trajectories of the project: first, the presumptions of a global public sphere; second, the parameters of critique and opinion in a literary world. I do so not only to summarize some of the claims I have made, but also to pose some questions and challenges regarding the study of literature more generally.

THE DYNAMICS OF A GLOBAL PUBLIC

When listening to the talk in Beirut, I was intrigued by its underlying emphasis on national versus global audiences. The novelist noted that a work being available in English or French had a strong impact on how widely read it was in Arabic, and there was an underlying sense that these circumstances were a given in a global literary market. As comparatists, we often encounter projects that highlight the international dimensions of a given work, be it the reception of the German romantics in France or the influence of Persian poetry on Goethe. The contours of the literary market as underscored by this novelist seemed only to reaffirm the importance of new models for questioning the paradigm of national literature. As we are often told, national literature is not always well suited for addressing the dynamics of readership, publication, and translation in a global framework.

One of the uniting features across the various chapters of this book has been the rather international nature of each of the sites of reading under consideration. The first three chapters, for example, dealt with situations of readership crossing the boundaries from Syria to Egypt and from France, England, and Egypt, respectively. The fifth and sixth chapters dealt with interpretative crises, but did so through a framework linking Beirut to Cairo, on the one hand, and linking France to Egypt, on the other. Bracketing the tendency within world literature to take seriously the site at which a text is written, each of these chapters has drawn attention to an inherent instability situating these texts within a national context. The more I came to terms with the instability of the location of the texts under consideration, the more I was led to rethink the terms of what it means to be situated in general.

Rather than analyze each of these texts in terms of where they were produced, I have been concerned with situating the frameworks through which the texts come to be understood. Is the nation-state the appropriate ground for literary study? How do we account for publics outside the parameters of the nation—or, as in the case highlighted by the Lebanese novelist, for cleavages within a national public? I have analyzed texts in this book by tracing some of the limits of a literary public (with regard to literacy, secularism, and formal characteristics of the genre). I have not been interested in making literature plural (and subsuming an even greater variety of textual traditions within the ambit of literary study), but I have focused on the social negotiation of literature (as it comes to be recognized and valued) through the disciplined practice of reading and the policing function of the public sphere. This framework led me away from presumptions about how literature travels from one location to another and toward the question of how the world republic of letters (and the cosmopolitan public it presumes) transforms textuality and readership. And doing so, I have been concerned with the constitutive exclusions of the literary public and the conditions of belonging to the collectivity it entails.[4]

Over the course of the book, I have thus focused on questions attentive less to the literary object than to the manner in which it comes to be read. And I have taken secularism to be the analytic terrain for my consideration, focusing on emergent fractures within a given national public rather than tensions between national publics. An anchoring point of the argument has been to suggest that whether considering the Rosetta Stone or the Darwin debates, the national context of reception is less meaningful than the axis between the literate and the illiterate, the modern and the traditional, the secular and the religious. In the case of Mahfouz's novel, for example, I explored how realism delimits the terms of the world in which interpretation takes place, and in the case of the novella *Adīb*, I considered ethical formations of the literary writer.

There is across the various chapters an implicit argument regarding our work as comparatists. On the one hand, I have suggested that coming to terms with literature is a matter of grappling with the dynamics of a literary public—bound less to national borders than to the contours and disciplines of the world republic of letters. And on the other hand, I have suggested that the analysis of a global public reframes the question of what literature is. And I have turned in doing so to consider the institutions, practices, and disciplines that structure the ways in which literature accrues meaning. Thinking back to the remarks of the Lebanese novelist, then, we are led to consider both the force of a global literary market and the values he attributes to literary reading.

LITERARY MYOPIA

In addition to highlighting the problem of writing within (and for) a global public, the novelist's talk animated concerns about what it means to participate as a reader in the literary world. As I sat in my chair listening, I was not especially surprised when the rise of Islam became the locus of much frustration for the novelist. In a rather predictable manner, he contrasted the virtues of the literary world to a parallel world of religion. As he lamented the decline of reading, he embraced literature for promoting open-mindedness, critical thinking, and a cosmopolitan outlook on the world. And against these positively inflected attributes, he went on to describe its polar opposite, largely cast under the guise of religion. To read, to be educated and inhabit literary culture, he seemed to suggest, is transformative insofar as it leads to critical thinking and open-mindedness. By implication, not reading means being entrapped within a hidebound worldview, not thinking critically and ultimately being mindlessly subordinate to authority.

This story of the relationship between literature and critical thinking is seemingly intrinsic to the world republic of letters. Simply told, though, the story overlooks the regulatory regimes entailed in learning what it is to become a disciplined reader and what it is to be recognized as such. Chapters 3 and 5, in particular, locate this embedded opposition between the thinking reader and the unthinking nonreader within a history of modern reading practices. And I have suggested that, as comparatists, we ought to reflect on the uncritical basis of much of our scholarship, which often espouses and celebrates a vision of literature to be valued in a particular way. My book overall has tried to chart an alternate literary history attentive to the constraints of the literary world figured largely around conditions of belonging and constitutive exclusions—less literature as the domain of liberation from ignorance than as a set of practices integral to being recognizably educated.

I began the book by considering the protests surrounding the publication of Haydar Haydar's novel—a moment when the literary public appears to fracture between readers of a text engaged with the particularities of the written work, and students protesting on the grounds of accusations of blasphemy. I sought to frame the problem of critique largely around the question of who or what determines the conditions of belonging to the global public of world literature and to consider why religion emerges as a category when speaking of students' uncritical relationship to Haydar Haydar's novel. Said's notion of secular criticism, I argued, is not timeless and universal, but is closely bound to a semiotic ideology that itself begs being situated. The chapters that followed from this introductory frame each sought to analyze critical moments from instances across the colonial past in Egypt in an effort to locate the world within which texts come to be read.

Two chapters, in particular, highlighted problems of being recognizably critical—in one, I addressed the distinctions of the colonial administration between prejudice and opinion, and in another, I considered how debates around Charles Darwin delimit competing conceptions of critical argument. Dealing with prejudice and opinion, I focused on the writings of Alfred Milner, geared largely to defend the British occupation of Egypt to an English-language audience. The framework for discussions of education in Egypt, I argued, largely predetermines the impossibility of dissent—there is no position from which to argue against education without being deemed uneducated and incapable of commentary. I drew from these writings, then, to engage shifting conceptions of education and its relationship to self-government, but also to gesture to the ultimately uncritical dimensions of modernization. Against the presumption that modernization is somehow rationalizing and secular, the chapter considered what the conventional line of argument fails to hear.

Much of the challenge of considering secularism and literature has to do with the close entwinement of the two. When the Lebanese novelist alludes to the supposed challenges facing literature in the Middle East, it is not surprising that he invokes religion as a sort of ominous specter. When Said celebrates situated readings under the rubric of secular criticism, it is perhaps unsurprising that he entitles the apparent opposite of this method religious criticism. My goal has not been to argue for an opposition between religion and secularism, but to consider how secular criticism defines religion as seemingly inimical to critical analysis. I have suggested as comparatists we begin to ask how secularism frames investments in particular definitions of what constitutes literary reading and sanctions ignorance about modes of textuality, dissent, and discussion within traditions deemed religious.

If, as scholars, we remain ultimately wedded to a particular definition of the literary, what are the parameters of exclusion this definition entails? I ask this question not necessarily to call for the assimilation of other textual forms within the fold of world literature, but to consider some of the limits of the literary world and the ways they are secured. Part of what I have tried to ask throughout is to consider the poetics of hearing, listening, and possibly empathizing differently. This is not a matter of generating dialogue, nor a matter of cultural relativism, but an effort to examine the presumptions that govern the production of a supposedly traditional world at the heart of the story of modernization. The intellectual genealogy I have sought here is geared to take Edward Said at his word and consider the worldliness of the reading practices implicit in secular criticism—to situate, in other words, the terms within which the world republic of letters becomes possible.

I would suggest, in a way not to be overtly romanticized, that before we venture to critique, we ought to investigate the grounds from which we know, see, and feel—that is, the very condition of the world itself. It is in this spirit that I aspire for what Talal Asad calls the anthropology of the secular and that I aim for an enriched understanding of the relationship between secularism, reading, and literature.[5] As scholars dealing with texts from a number of traditions, we must ultimately come to terms not only with what these various texts depict, but more crucially still, with the acute ways in which interpretative traditions impact our sensibilities as readers. The conflicted situation of world literature (torn between the dictates of a literary discipline and the traditions it reinvents in its image) is nothing if not a provocation to learn how to read all over again.

HOW TO LOVE THE WORLD PROPERLY

At the conclusion of "Philologie der Weltliteratur," published in 1952, Erich Auerbach reflects explicitly on language and worldliness.[6] His essay was included in a volume honoring Fritz Strich, the author of *Goethe und die Weltliteratur*, and traces the relationship between history, philology, and world literature. And yet, the last few lines move away from general methodical reflections in order to focus on the place of exile. Intriguingly, Auerbach avoids any explicit reference to his time spent at Istanbul State University, when as a Jewish professor he was stripped of his position in Germany in 1935 and followed Leo Spitzer to Turkey.[7] Instead, he turns to a passage from Hugo of St. Victor, whom he cites in untranslated Latin: "The great basis of virtue . . . is for the practiced mind to learn, bit by bit, first to change about in visible and transitory things, so that afterwards it may be able to leave them behind altogether. He who finds homeland sweet is still a tender beginner; he to whom every soil is as his homeland is yet stronger; but he is perfect to whom the entire world is a place of exile."[8] Grasping on the concluding line and addressing "he is perfect to whom the entire world is a place of exile [*perfectus vero cui mundus totus exilium est*]," Auerbach provides his own gloss of the passage, as though clarifying the terms, but actually offering a fairly unique reading. "Hugo intended these lines for one whose aim is to free himself from a love of the world," Auerbach tells us. "But it is a good way also for one who wishes to earn a proper love for the world [*die rechte Liebe zur Welt*]."[9] Almost a direct reversal, then, Auerbach transforms Hugo's abandonment of a love for the world into a dictum about how to love the world properly.

That this exiled scholar himself finds in the Latin citation a universalization and celebration of his own condition is telling. We might note, as well, that he finds the thematization of exile in a medieval text—as against his immediate reality living in Turkey and the United States. Like Ernst Curtius before him, Auerbach finds a pathway for escaping the conditions of his time in the careful reading of medieval texts. He finds in this historical period a manner for complicating the nationalist discourse that so permeated Europe prior to and during the Second World War. What Auerbach's inventive reading offers is a pathway from which to imagine the world differently—a world of exiles. On some level, one could say that Auerbach redeems in this line a sort of critical anthropology geared to estrange the world from itself in order to love it. And he does so not so much by situating Hugo of St. Victor in an imagined past, but by reading him askew, belatedly and against the very world from which he writes. He offers, then, much less a situated reading of the Latin citation than a reading to estrange the world from itself.

In 1969, another young exile, the late Edward Said, published his translation of "Philologie der Weltliteratur" for the *Centennial Review*.[10] In doing so, Said brought Auerbach into a differing context, doing to Auerbach what

Auerbach had done to Hugo of St. Victor years before. Said undertook his translation shortly after arriving at his post at Columbia University, and claims to have drawn inspiration from Auerbach both as the translator of Vico into German and as a proponent of historicist philology. "Historicist philology," Said tells us, "is the discipline of uncovering beneath the surface of words the life of a society embedded there by the great writer's art."[11] It is largely through a reading of figures like Auerbach and Vico that Said elaborates his own concept of worldliness—a principle by which he counters the hermetic relations to textuality espoused by new critics and deconstructionists. For Said, "texts have ways of existing that even in their most rarefied form are always enmeshed in circumstance, time, place, and society—in short, they are in the world, hence worldly."[12] This fidelity to the worldliness of texts is largely what enables Said's readings of literature, colonialism, and politics, but it is also a principle that seems quite curious when read against Auerbach's closing lines.

Remember that when Auerbach cites Hugo of St. Victor, he does not read the passage in context, beyond citing it in Latin. Instead, he borrows the passage and makes it meaningful as a reflection on the importance of exile precisely by bringing it to bear on a contemporary situation and drawing from it a lesson. In fact, there is very little that is philological about this exercise, and it is as though the reflections on exile at the conclusion of Auerbach's essay turn against the proclamation of the essay—with its extensive focus on the relationship among words, history, and meaning. How, then, might we understand that Said's muse for historicist philology so willfully embraces the notion that "he is perfect to whom the entire world is a place of exile"? How, in other words, might we understand that being in the world, for someone like Auerbach, emerges not through reading Hugo of St. Victor in his historical context, but through a transhistorical appropriation of it? How, in the end, might we understand that the world into which we are to be is a world of exile?

I highlight the story of Auerbach's reading of Hugo of St. Victor largely to draw attention to ways that a literary scholar engages tradition against itself and marshals the past in the present. Exile, in this instance, is figured not only as a universal condition of being in the world, but as a particular practice of relating to the text—one in which Hugo of St. Victor is transformed from one "whose aim is to free himself from a love of the world," as Auerbach notes, into "one who wishes to earn a proper love for the world." It strikes me that understanding Auerbach's exilic teetering, between the literal move to Turkey and the figural practice of speaking through Hugo of St. Victor, offers a manner of understanding the world otherwise. If nothing else, the world for which "we earn a proper love" is by no means a world made home. It is instead a place of exile. Note that this is not a claim on behalf of an identity formation either included or excluded, nor the loss of an original identity, but rather a claim to "earn a proper love for the world"—something to be accomplished in the future.

I have drawn attention to Auerbach in order to consider a mode of worldliness not grounded in the discovery of identity, but in an engagement made possible through historicist philology. Auerbach's reading of Hugo of St. Victor elucidates problems of cultural nationalism with the resurrection of a past figure freed from the shackles of context. The interplay of translation, citation, and explication allows for the text to take place, and this taking place is not so much a matter of finding home as one of appreciating the entire world as a place of exile. Coming full circle back to the Lebanese novelist with whom we began, is it the case that world literature itself constitutes a form of exile from national traditions? Does writing a world literary text imply an exile from national culture? For Auerbach, it seems that world literature becomes itself a manner of earning proper love for the world, allowing him to escape his national condition through a longing for a literary internationalism across place and time.

What, though, would it mean to be an exile of world literature? What might the implication be of Auerbach's curious reading? If we take Auerbach's exile seriously, then we might necessarily question the place from which we read, respond, and critique—that is, the values that supposedly inform and inflect a manner of being in the world. As students of languages and literatures, we are not of the periods or texts that we study, nor must we necessarily be at home within them. More than a fight over belonging and unbelonging, consider what it might mean to engage with traditions not to find home, but to appreciate the entire world as a place of exile with "intimacy and distance." Might this be the place from which to question the borders of world literature? In the end, might this be the place not only from which to read, relate, and think differently, but also from which to imagine the world anew?

NOTES

INTRODUCTION

1. First published in serialized form in the periodical *al-Hilāl* between 1925 and 1926, the autobiography would eventually consist of three parts and be published as a single volume known as *al-Ayyām*. My references here are drawn from Ṭāhā Ḥusayn, *al-Ayyām* (Cairo: Dār al-Maʿārif, 1969), 22; and Taha Hussein, *The Days* (Cairo: American University in Cairo Press, 1997), 14. More will be said of this book, its composition, and its reception in chapter 6.
2. The definition of literature is the explicit subject of chapter 4 and is directly linked to the sorts of educational reforms and modern disciplines that will be traced across the various chapters of the book. For reflections on Taha Hussein and loss, see Jeffrey Sacks, *Iterations of Loss: Mutilation and Aesthetic Form, al-Shidyaq to Darwish* (New York: Fordham University Press, 2015).
3. I refer here to Walter Benjamin, "The Storyteller," in *Illuminations*, trans. Harry Zohn (New York: Schocken Books, 1968), 83–110.
4. My use of the term "literary world" draws in part from Eric Hayot, *On Literary Worlds* (Oxford: Oxford University Press, 2013), but also engages quite explicitly the practices, disciplines, and sensibilities that establish literature as a modern discipline with a set of parameters for how to think about literariness and textuality. I benefit from the models of textual analysis performed in Dipesh Chakrabarty, *Provincializing Europe: Postcolonial Thought and Historical Difference* (Princeton: Princeton University Press, 2000) and questions of worldliness raised in pt. 3 of Emily Apter, *Against World Literature* (London: Verso, 2013),
5. What I call literary reading draws from discussions outlined in Michael Warner's essay, "Uncritical Reading," in *Polemic*, ed. Jane Gallop (New York: Routledge, 2004). Critique will play out in differing ways across the various chapters, but key influences for my argument are Talal Asad, "The Limits of Religious Criticism in the Middle East: Notes on Islamic Public Argument" in *Genealogies of Religion: Discipline and Reasons of Power in Christianity and Islam* (Baltimore: Johns Hopkins University Press, 1993); Judith Butler, "What Is Critique? An Essay on Foucault's Virtue," in *The Political: Readings in Continental Philosophy*, ed. David Ingram (London: Basil Blackwell, 2002), 212–26; Michel Foucault, "What Is Critique?," in Ingram, *The Political*, 191–211; Saba Mahmood, *The*

Politics of Piety: The Islamic Revival and the Feminist Subject (Princeton: Princeton University Press, 2005); Edward Said, "Secular Criticism," in *The World, the Text, and the Critic* (Cambridge, Mass.: Harvard University Press, 1983), and "Connecting Empire to Secular Interpretation," in *Culture and Imperialism* (New York: Knopf, 1993).

6. Among a number of titles on schooling in the Middle East, more of which will be the subject of chapter 3, I draw from Ami Ayalon, *Reading Palestine: Printing and Literacy, 1900–1948* (Austin: University of Texas Press, 2004); Benjamin Fortna, *Imperial Classroom: Islam, the State, and Education in the Late Ottoman Empire* (New York: Oxford University Press, 2002); Nelly Hanna, *In Praise of Books: A Cultural History of Cairo's Middle Class, Sixteenth through the Eighteenth Century* (Syracuse, N.Y.: Syracuse University Press, 2003); Linda Herrera and Carlos Alberto Torres, *Cultures of Arab Schooling: Critical Ethnographies from Egypt* (Albany: State University of New York, 2006); and Gregory Starrett, *Putting Islam to Work: Education, Politics, and Religious Transformation in Egypt* (Berkeley: University of California Press, 1998).
7. I draw inspiration in doing so from Natalie Melas, *All the Difference in the World: Postcoloniality and the Ends of Comparison* (Palo Alto: Stanford University Press, 2006). Where Melas weaves together a disciplinary history with literary readings around the question of commensurability, I turn in the chapters that follow to a fundamental question of what literature is and how this definition comes to anchor readings across traditions. I have also benefitted from questions raised in the collection of essays in Rita Felski and Susan Stanford Friedman, eds., *Comparison: Theories, Approaches, Uses* (Baltimore: Johns Hopkins University Press, 2013).
8. I refer here to the title of George Antonius's classic study, *The Arab Awakening: The Story of the Arab National Movement* (London: H. Hamilton, 1938).
9. A standard account is offered in Albert Hourani, *Arabic Thought in the Liberal Age, 1798–1939* (New York: Cambridge University Press, 1983), and a recent inquiry into its significance can be found in Abdulrazzak Patel, *The Arab Nahdah: The Making of the Intellectual and Humanist Movement* (Edinburgh: Edinburgh University Press, 2013). It is well worth noting that this conventional *nahḍah* story is not without its critics, and much critical work in the humanities and social sciences of the past few decades has been importantly undoing this account. The Middle East historian Peter Gran, for example, notes that this *nahḍah* paradigm not only relies on theories of emulation (in which what is modern is necessarily foreign) and on presumptions of Oriental despotism (in which Muhammad ʿAli enacts reform through a consolidated state), but also forecloses the analysis of transformations that were already under way within the Arab world. See Peter Gran, "Rediscovering al-ʿAttar," *Al-Ahram Weekly*, no. 770 (November 24–30, 2005). What follows in chapters 3, 5, and 6, in particular, draws from Gran and a number of other scholars in questioning the predominant force and oversights of the *nahḍah* paradigm.
10. My work benefits from that of the scholars in the social sciences who trace the emergence of disciplines such as psychology, history, and law in Egypt: see Omnia El Shakry, *The Great Social Laboratory: Subjects of Knowledge in Colonial and Postcolonial Egypt* (Palo Alto: Stanford University Press, 2007) and Samera

Esmeir, *Juridical Humanity: A Colonial History* (Palo Alto: Stanford University Press, 2012).

11. See Roger Allen, *An Introduction to Arabic Literature* (New York: Cambridge University Press, 2000); ʻAbd al-Muḥsin Ṭāhā Badr, *Taṭawwur al-riwāyah al-ʿarabīyah al-ḥadīthah fī miṣr* (Cairo: Dār al-Maʻārif, 1963); Sabry Hafez, *The Genesis of Arabic Narrative Discourse: A Study in the Sociology of Modern Arabic Literature* (London: Saqi Books, 1993); André Miquel, *La littérature arabe* (Paris: Presse universitaire de France, 1969) and Matti Moosa, *The Origins of Modern Arabic Fiction* (Boulder, Colo.: Three Continents Press, 1997).
12. Here I draw, in part, from Timothy Mitchell's *Colonising Egypt* (Berkeley: University of California Press, 1991), but also from Webb Keane, "Signs Are Not the Garb of Meaning: On the Social Analysis of Material Things," in *Materiality*, ed. Daniel Miller (Durham, N.C.: Duke University Press, 2005), and *Christian Moderns: Freedom and Fetish in the Mission Encounter* (Berkeley: University of California Press, 2007); as well as Michael Silverstein and Greg Urban, eds., *Natural Histories of Discourse* (Chicago: University of Chicago Press, 1996). I discuss the term further in chapters 1 and 2.
13. *Adab* is the topic of chapter 4, and a more extensive list of sources is available there. For general reference, see the entry for "adab" in the *Encyclopaedia of Islam* as well as the classic works of Gustave von Grunebaum. Additional sources can be found in ʻIzz al-Dīn Ismāʻīl's anthology, *al-Adab wa-funūnuh: Dirāsah wa-naqd* (Cairo: Dār al-fikr al-ʿarabī, 1965); Iman Farag, "Private Lives, Public Affairs: The Uses of *Adab*," in *Muslim Traditions and Modern Techniques of Power*, ed. Armando Salvatore (Münster: Lit Verlag, 2001); Philip Kennedy, *On Fiction and* Adab *in Medieval Arabic Literature* (Wiesbaden: Harrassowitz Verlag, 2005); Ellen McLarney, "The Islamic Public Sphere and the Discipline of *Adab*," *International Journal of Middle East Studies* 43 (2011): 429–49; and Barbara Daly Metcalf, ed., *Moral Conduct and Authority* (Berkeley: University of California Press, 1984).
14. See, for example, Charles Pellat, "Variations sur le thème de l'adab" and "Al-Gahiz: Les Nations civilisées et les croyances religieuses," in *Etudes sur l'histoire socio-culturelle de l'Islam (VIIe–XVe s.)* (1964; repr., London: Variorum Reprints, 1976).
15. I borrow from some of the arguments in Tomoko Masuzawa, *The Invention of World Religions; or, How European Universalism Was Preserved in the Language of Pluralism* (Chicago: University of Chicago Press, 2005).
16. For the variety of ways in which scholars read this material, see Edward Said, *Orientalism* (New York: Vintage, 1978); Emily Haddad, *Orientalist Poetics* (Aldershot: Ashgate, 2002); Shaden Tageldin, *Disarming Words: Empire and the Seductions of Translation in Egypt* (Berkeley: University of California Press, 2011).
17. See, for example, Said, *Culture and Imperialism*; Bill Ashcroft, Gareth Griffiths, and Helen Tiffin, eds., *The Empire Writes Back* (London: Routledge, 1994); Homi Bhabha, *The Location of Culture* (London: Routledge, 1994). And as pertains to Egypt, see Samia Mehrez, *Egyptian Writers between History and Fiction* (Cairo: AUC Press, 2005); Samah Selim, *The Novel and the Rural Imaginary in Egypt, 1880–1985* (London: Routledge, 2004); Muhammad Siddiq, *Arab Culture and the Novel: Genre, Identity and Agency in Egyptian Fiction* (London: Routledge, 2007).

18. Of a number of allusions to this work, see Michael Gasper, "Abdallah al-Nadim, Islamic Reform, and 'Ignorant' Peasants: State-Building in Egypt?," in Salvatore, *Muslim Traditions*; Eve Troutt Powell, *A Different Shade of Colonialism: Egypt, Great Britain, and the Mastery of the Sudan* (Berkeley: University of California Press, 2003).
19. See Chris Baldick, *The Social Mission of English Criticism: 1848–1932* (Oxford: Clarendon, 1983); Benjamin Fortna, "Learning to Read in the Late Ottoman Empire and Early Turkish Republic," *Comparative Studies of South Asia, Africa and the Middle East* 21, nos. 1–2 (2001): 33–41; and Phyllis Stock-Morton, *Moral Education for a Secular Society* (Albany: State University of New York Press, 1988).
20. For an elaboration on some of these questions, see Michael Allan, "Reading Secularism: Religion, Literature, Aesthetics," *Comparative Literature* 65, no. 3 (2013): 257–64.
21. Talal Asad, "Limits of Religious Criticism"; Saba Mahmood, "Secularism, Hermeneutics, Empire: The Politics of Islamic Reformation," *Public Culture* 18, no. 2 (2006): 323–47; David Scott and Charles Hirschkind, eds., *Powers of the Secular Modern: Talal Asad and His Interlocutors* (Stanford: Stanford University Press, 2006); Charles Taylor, "Modes of Secularism," in *Secularism and Its Critics*, ed. Rajeev Bhargava (Delhi: Oxford University Press, 1998); Michael Warner, "Secularism" in *Keywords: A Vocabulary of American Cultural Studies*, ed. Bruce Burgett and Glenn Hendler (New York: New York University Press, 2007).
22. I refer here to a line of argument pursued in Winnifred Fallers Sullivan, *The Impossibility of Religious Freedom* (Princeton: Princeton University Press, 2005).
23. Charles Taylor, *A Secular Age* (Cambridge, Mass.: Harvard University Press, 2007), 26.
24. Talal Asad, *Formations of the Secular: Christianity, Islam, Modernity* (Stanford: Stanford University Press, 2003); "Trying to Understand French Secularism," in *Political Theologies: Public Religions in a Post-secular World*, ed. Hent de Vries and Lawrence Sullivan (New York: Fordham University Press, 2006), 494–526; *On Suicide Bombing* (New York: Columbia University Press, 2007). See also Mayanthi Fernando, *The Republic Unsettled: Muslim French and the Contradictions of Secularism* (Durham, N.C.: Duke University Press, 2014) and Kabir Tambar, *The Reckoning of Pluralism: Political Belonging and the Demands of History in Turkey* (Palo Alto: Stanford University Press, 2014).
25. Said, "Secular Criticism," and "Connecting Empire to Secular Interpretation," in *Culture and Imperialism*.
26. Buṭrus al-Bustānī used the word *'almānīyah* in *Kitāb Quṭr al-Muḥīṭ* (1869; repr., Beirut: Maktabat Lubnān, 1966), and more recently, Fauzi Najjar notes that the Arabic Language Academy in Cairo links the etymology of secularism to *'ālam* (world) and not *'ilm* (science) in "The Debate on Islam and Secularism in Egypt," *Arab Studies Quarterly* 18, no. 2 (1996). Contemporary discussions of the term can be found in 'Azīz al-'Aẓmah, *Al-'Almānīyah fī manẓūr mukhtalif* (Beirut: Markaz Dirāsat al-Waḥdah al-'Arabīyah, 1992); 'Abd al-Wahhāb Muḥammad al-Misīrī and 'Azīz al-'Aẓmah, *al-'Ilmānīyah taḥta al-majhar* (Beirut: Dār al-Fikr al-Mu'āsir, 2000); Andrew Davidson, "Turkey, a 'Secular' State? The Challenge of Description," *South Atlantic Quarterly* 102, nos. 2/3 (2003): 333–50; and Driss Maghraoui, "'Ilmaniyya, Laïcité, Sécularisme/Secularism in Morocco," in *Words*

in Motion: Toward a Global Lexicon, ed. Carol Gluck and Anna Lowenhaupt Tsing (Durham, N.C.: Duke University Press, 2009). More will be said on the etymology of the term in chapter 6.

27. Colin Jager, "After the Secular: The Subject of Romanticism," *Public Culture* 18 (2006): 301–21, and *The Book of God: Secularization and Design in the Romantic Era* (Philadelphia: University of Pennsylvania Press, 2006); Jean-Luc Nancy and Philippe Lacoue-Labarthe, *The Literary Absolute: The Theory of Literature in German Romanticism*, trans. Philip Barnard and Cheryl Lester (Albany: State University of New York Press, 1988).
28. Hans Frei, *The Eclipse of Biblical Narrative: A Study in Eighteenth and Nineteenth Century Hermeneutics* (New Haven: Yale University Press, 1974); Jonathan Sheehan, "Enlightenment, Religion, and the Enigma of Secularization," *American Historical Review* 108 (2003): 1061–80, and *The Enlightenment Bible: Translation, Scholarship, Culture* (Princeton: Princeton University Press, 2005); Deborah Shuger, *The Renaissance Bible: Scholarship, Sacrifice and Subjectivity* (Berkeley: University of California Press, 1994).
29. Marcel Gauchet, *The Disenchantment of the World: A Political History of Religion*, trans. Oscar Burge (Princeton: Princeton University Press, 1997); Claude Lefort, "The Permanence of the Theologico-Political," in de Vries and Sullivan, *Political Theologies*, 148–87.
30. I refer here to Gauchet, *Disenchantment of the World*; Jean-Luc Nancy, "Church, State, Resistance," in de Vries and Sullivan, *Political Theologies*, 102–12; and Taylor, *Secular Age*.
31. See Johann Gottfried Herder, "Results of a Comparison of Different Peoples' Poetry in Ancient and Modern Times," in *The Princeton Sourcebook in Comparative Literature*, ed. David Damrosch, Natalie Melas, and Mbongiseni Buthelezi (Princeton: Princeton University Press, 2009); and Karl Marx and Friedrich Engels, *The Communist Manifesto* (1888; repr., London: Penguin, 2002). For an extended reading of Marx on world literature, see Aijaz Ahmad, "The Communist Manifesto and World Literature," *Social Scientist* 28, nos. 7/8 (2000): 3–30.
32. For reflections on the relationship between Arabic literature and literary theory more generally, see Alexander Key, "Arabic: Acceptance and Anxiety," *ACLA State of the Discipline*, http://stateofthediscipline.acla.org/entry/arabic-acceptance-and-anxiety, accessed June 10, 2015, and Mohammad Salama, "Arabic and the Monopoly of Theory," *ARCADE*, http://arcade.stanford.edu/blogs/arabic-and-monopoly-theory, accessed June 10, 2015. Both of these authors offer important contributions to the place of Arabic literature and make the case for the inclusion of Arabic within general training in comparative literature.

1. WORLD

1. Martin Seymour-Smith, *The New Guide to Modern World Literature* (New York: Peter Bedrick Books, 1985), xii.
2. Among a number of possible titles, I refer here to Sarah Lawall, *The Norton Anthology of World Literature* (New York: Norton, 2001); Franco Moretti, *Atlas of the European Novel, 1800–1900* (New York: Verso, 1999) and "Conjectures on World Literature," *New Left Review* (January/February 2000); Pascale Casanova,

The World Republic of Letters, trans. M. B. DeBovoise (Cambridge, Mass.: Harvard University Press, 2004); and David Damrosch, *What Is World Literature?* (Princeton: Princeton University Press, 2003). See Theo D'haen, David Damrosch, and Djelal Kader, eds., *The Routledge Companion to World Literature* (London: Routledge, 2011) for a rich range of essays devoted to the historical and theoretical dimensions of this field.

3. Sabry Hafez, "The Novel, Politics and Islam," *New Left Review*, September/October 2000.
4. As quoted in ibid., 133.
5. Ibid., 138. Hafez repeats the terms "secular" and "rationalist" at various places in the article, most explicitly in his suggestion that the "affair is now divided into two different fronts: on the one hand, the right of the Islamicists to express their views; on the other, the character of their crusade against secular and rationalist culture."
6. Ibid., 135.
7. Of a number of essays on the topic, my thinking draws heavily from Asad, *Genealogies of Religion*, 239–306, and *Formations of the Secular*, 160–80. It is worth noting that Hafez contrasts Haydar Haydar to Salman Rushdie, and my relating of the two incidents has less to do with the immediate situation of the respective novels than with the response of critics to protests in both cases.
8. In using the term "semiotic ideology," I allude here to the work of the anthropologist Webb Keane. In his article, "Semiotics and the Social Analysis of Material Things," *Language and Communication* 23 (2003), he writes, "By *semiotic ideology*, I mean basic assumptions about what signs are and how they function in the world. It determines, for instance, what people will consider the role that intentions play in signification to be, what possible kinds of agents (humans only? Animals? Spirits?) exist to which acts might be imputed, whether signs are arbitrary or necessarily linked to their objects, and so forth" (419).
9. See Khaled Dawoud, "Banquet Serves Up Indigestion," http://weekly.ahram.org.eg/2000/483/eg13.htm, accessed December 14, 2013.
10. It is worth noting an echo in the work of Tarek El-Ariss, who explores the dynamic relation of scandal and literary publics in the context of contemporary Arabic literature. He provides a model of reading that takes scandal itself as constitutive of relations between authors and readers: see "Fiction of Scandal," *Journal of Arabic Literature* 23 (2012): 510–31. For an especially rich analysis of the social field of twentieth-century literary production in Egypt, see Richard Jacquemond, *Conscience of the Nation: Writers, State and Society in Modern Egypt*, trans. David Tresilian (New York: American University in Cairo Press, 2008). And for analysis of literature and religion in modern Arabic literature, see Muhsin al-Musawi, *Islam on the Street: Religion in Modern Arabic Literature* (Lanham, Md.: Rowman & Littlefield, 2009).
11. For an insightful exploration of moral injury and semiotic ideology, see Saba Mahmood, "Religious Reason and Secular Affect: An Incommensurable Divide?," *Critical Inquiry* 35, no. 4 (2009): 836–62.
12. Hafez, "Novel, Politics and Islam," 119.
13. Ibid., 119.
14. Ibid., 118.
15. Ibid., 135.

16. Ibid., 138.
17. Asad, *Genealogies of Religion*, 283.
18. Ibid., 283.
19. Sture Allén, ed., *Nobel Lectures, Literature 1981–1990* (Singapore: World Scientific, 1993), 118.
20. *Nobel Lectures, Literature*, 122.
21. "Tārīkh Miṣr wa-adabuhā lā yudarrasān ḥattā l-ān fī al-jāmiʿah al-Miṣrīyah," *al-Siyāsah al-usbūʿīyah* 3, no. 146 (December 28, 1928): 5.
22. See, of a number of possible sources, J. Brugman, *An Introduction to the History of Modern Arabic Literature in Egypt*, Studies in Arabic Literature vol. 10 (Leiden: Brill, 1984), 240, 250–51.
23. For a study that addresses Mahfouz's influence by and within Arab culture, see Siddiq, *Arab Culture and the Novel.*
24. *Nobel Lectures, Literature*, 124.
25. Ibid., 122.
26. For an insightful analysis of literary awards, see James English, *The Economy of Prestige: Prizes, Awards, and the Circulation of Cultural Value* (Cambridge, Mass.: Harvard University Press, 2009).
27. Ibid., 118.
28. Casanova, *World Republic of Letters*, 150.
29. See "Presentation Speech by Harald Hjärne, Chairman of the Nobel Committee of the Swedish Academy, on December 10, 1913," http://nobelprize.org/nobel_prizes/literature/laureates/1913/press.html, accessed March 24, 2014. The presentation speech claimed, ". . . after exhaustive and conscientious deliberation, having concluded that these poems of his most nearly approach the prescribed standard. . . ."
30. "Presentation Speech by Harald Hjärne," which states, ". . . the Academy thought that there was no reason to hesitate because the poet's name was still comparatively unknown in Europe, due to the distant location of his home. There was even less reason since the founder of the Prize laid it down in set terms as his 'express wish and desire that, in the awarding of the Prize, no consideration should be paid to the nationality to which any proposed candidate might belong."
31. Casanova, *World Republic of Letters*, 3.
32. Casanova describes *littéralisation* as follows: "For texts that come from literarily disinherited countries, the magical transmutation that consecration brings about amounts to a change in their very nature: a passage from literary inexistence to existence, from invisibility to the condition of literature—a transformation that I have called *littéralisation.*" Ibid., 127.
33. Ibid., 94.
34. *Nobel Lectures, Literature*, 117.
35. Casanova, *World Republic of Letters*, 3.
36. Said, *The World*, 2.
37. Ibid., 2.
38. Ibid., 2.
39. Ibid., 2.
40. Ibid., 5.
41. Ibid., 2.

42. Ibid., 3.
43. Ibid., 3.
44. Ibid., 3.
45. Ibid., 3.
46. Ibid., 3.
47. Ibid., 4.
48. Ibid., 4.
49. Ibid., 4.
50. Ibid., 30; Foucault, "What Is Critique?," 191–211.
51. Said, *The World*, 24.
52. Ibid., 26.
53. Ibid., 29.
54. Ibid., 29.
55. Ibid., 290.
56. Ibid., 290.
57. Ibid., 292.
58. David Damrosch, "Secular Criticism Meets the World," http://weekly.ahram.org.eg/2005/769/bo2.htm, accessed January 14, 2014. See also Gil Anidjar, "Secularism," *Critical Inquiry* 33, no. 1 (2006): 52–77; Talal Asad, "Historical Notes on the Idea of Secular Criticism," http://blogs.ssrc.org/tif/2008/01/25/historical-notes-on-the-idea-of-secular-criticism/, accessed June 14, 2015; W.J.T. Mitchell, "Secular Divination: Edward Said's Humanism," in *Edward Said: Continuing the Conversation*, ed. Homi Bhabha and W.J.T. Mitchell (Chicago: University of Chicago Press, 2005); Aamir Mufti, ed., "Critical Secularism," special issue, *boundary 2* 31, no. 2 (2004).

2. TRANSLATION

1. My use of the term "entextualization" draws from Michael Silverstein—and, with a slight variation, from Michael Warner. See Michael Silverstein, "Contemporary Transformations of Local Linguistic Communities," *Annual Review of Anthropology* 27 (1998): 401–26, and Warner, "Uncritical Reading," 13–38. In his chapter, "Entextualization, Replication, and Power," Greg Urban contrasts entextualization to replication: "If entextualization is understood as the process of rendering a given instance of discourse a text, detachable form its local context, replication is one way, seemingly, of implementing detachment." See chap. 1 of Silverstein and Urban, *Natural Histories of Discourse*, 21.
2. For a sense of the historiography of archaeological debates, see Holger Hoock, "The British State and the Anglo-French Wars over Antiquities, 1798–1858," *Historical Journal* 50, no. 1 (March 2007): 49–72. In addition to the sources cited later in this chapter, general debates around archaeology and colonialism can be found in Lynn Meskell, ed., *Archaeology Under Fire* (London: Routledge, 2002) and Colin Renfrew, *Loot, Legitimacy and Ownership: The Ethical Crisis in Archaeology* (London: Duckworth Press, 2000).
3. Competing accounts exist for the exact date.
4. The recordings of the actual sessions are no longer extant, but notes exist in Jean-Joseph Marcel, *La Décade Égyptienne*, vol. 3 (Cairo, 1798–1800), 292.

5. See *La Description de l'Égypte*, vol. 5, *Antiquités*, nos. 52, 53, and 54, http://descegy.bibalex.org/fr/index1.html, accessed March 24, 2014.
6. R. B. Parkinson, ed., *Cracking Codes: The Rosetta Stone and Decipherment* (Berkeley: University of California Press, 1999), 20.
7. As quoted in Robert Solé and Dominique Valbelle, *The Rosetta Stone: The Story of the Decoding of Hieroglyphics* (New York: Profile Books, 2005), 7.
8. Elliott Colla, *Conflicted Antiquities: Egyptology, Egyptomania, Egyptian Modernity* (Durham, N.C.: Duke University Press, 2008), 90; see also Donald Reid, *Whose Pharaohs? Archaeology, Museums and National Identity from Napoleon to World War I* (Berkeley: University of California Press, 2004).
9. Okasha El Daly, *Egyptology: The Missing Millennium* (London: University College of London Press, 2005).
10. Damrosch, *What Is World Literature?*, Casanova, *World Republic of Letters*, and Moretti, *Atlas of the European Novel.*
11. See Anonymous, "Report of the Arrival of the Rosetta Stone in England," *Gentleman's Magazine*, 1802.
12. Edward Daniel Clarke, *Travels in Various Countries of Asia, Europe and Africa* (London: Cadwell and Davies, 1810–23). See also his letter quoted in Nina Burleigh, *Mirage: Napoleon's Scientists and the Unveiling of Egypt* (New York: HarperCollins, 2007), 212.
13. Marcel, *La Décade Égyptienne*, 3:293.
14. Jean-Joseph Marcel, *Les Fables de Lokman* (Cairo: Éditeurs d'Erpénius et de Golius, 1803).
15. Cheikh El-Mohdy, *Les dix soirées malheureuses, contes d'Abd-Errahman, el-Iskanderany; ou Contes d'un endormeur*, trans. Jean-Joseph Marcel (Paris: Jules Renouard, 1829).
16. Marcel, *La Décade Égyptienne*, vol. 1 (Cairo, 1798–1799), 84–85.
17. Ibid., 85.
18. Ibid., 124.
19. Ibid., 124.
20. Sayyid Quṭb, *al-Taṣwīr al-fannī fī al-qur'ān* (Cairo: Dār al-Ma'ārif, 1945).

3. EDUCATION

1. See Badr, *Taṭawwur al-riwāyah*; Moosa, *Origins of Modern Arabic Fiction*; and Hafez, *Genesis of Arabic Narrative Discourse*. For a constructive overview of new directions in "nahḍah studies," see Stephen Sheehi, "Towards a Critical Theory of the Nahdah: Epistemology, Ideology, Capital," *Journal of Arabic Literature* 43, nos. 2–3 (2012): 269–98.
2. Rifā'ah Rāfi' al-Ṭahṭāwī, *Takhlīṣ al-ibrīz fī talkhīṣ Bārīz aw al-dīwān al-nafīs bi-Īwān Bārīz* (Cairo: al-Hay'ah al-Miṣrīyah al-'Āmmah li-l-Kitāb, 1993); Ḥusayn, *al-Ayyām.*
3. Sir Evelyn Baring was awarded the title Earl of Cromer in 1901. I refer to him as Lord Cromer throughout the chapter for the sake of consistency with his published book, even though I occasionally refer to moments prior to his receiving this title.
4. Alfred Milner, *England in Egypt* (London: Edward Arnold, 1894), 443.

5. Ibid., 444.
6. Ibid., 444.
7. See Mitchell, *Colonising Egypt*, Mohammad Salama, *Islam, Orientalism and Intellectual History: Modernity and the Politics of Exclusion since Ibn Khaldun* (London: I.B. Taurus, 2011), and Tageldin, *Disarming Words*.
8. Evelyn Baring Cromer, *Modern Egypt, II* (New York: Macmillan, 1916), 532.
9. Asad, *Formations of the Secular*, 13.
10. Ibid., 14.
11. P. J. Vatikiotis, *The History of Modern Egypt: From Muhammad Ali to Mubarak* (Baltimore: Johns Hopkins University Press, 1991), 172–73.
12. Milner, *England in Egypt*, 372.
13. Ibid., 372. For accounts of contrasting policies in India and Egypt, see, for example, Robert Tignor, "The 'Indianization' of the Egyptian Administration under British Rule," *American Historical Review* 68, no. 3 (1963): 636–61.
14. Milner, *England in Egypt*, 372.
15. Vatikiotis, *History of Modern Egypt*, 469.
16. A wealth of scholarship exists on this topic, but see, for example, documents compiled in the mid-nineteenth century on the status of education: Yacoub Artin, *L'Instruction Publique en Égypte, Considérations sur l'éducation publique en Égypte* (Paris: Ernest Leroux, 1890); Edouard Dor, *L'Instruction publique en Égypte* (Paris: A. Lacroix, Verboeckhoven et Cie, 1872). I have also drawn here from Aḥmad ʿIzzat ʿabd al-Karīm, *Tārīkh al-taʿlīm fī Miṣr: 1848–1882* (Cairo: Dār al-Maʿārif, 1917); J. Heyworth-Dunne, *An Introduction to the History of Education in Modern Egypt* (London: Luzac, 1939); David C. Kinsey, "Egyptian Education under Cromer: A Study of East-West Encounter in Educational Administration and Policy, 1883–1907" (PhD diss., Harvard University, 1965); Mona Russell, "Competing, Overlapping, and Contradictory Agendas: Egyptian Education under British Occupation, 1882–1922," *Comparative Studies of South Asia, Africa and the Middle East* 21, nos. 1–2 (2001): 50–60; Starrett, *Putting Islam to Work*; Robert L. Tignor, *Modernization and British Colonial Rule in Egypt, 1882–1914* (Princeton: Princeton University Press, 1966).
17. I borrow here from an observation by Mona Russell: "Much of the historiography on Egyptian education pits Egyptian nationalists, who are seeking widespread educational reform, against the British, who are bent on restricting education." And she continues, "Nevertheless, this seeming gap between British and Egyptian nationalist positions is not as large as it appears when we examine the various factions composing the Egyptian nationalist position." Russell makes an important claim that class has much to do with the convergence of the British and Egyptian nationalist positions. See Russell, "Competing, Overlapping, and Contradictory Agendas," 51–52.
18. Gauri Viswanathan, *Masks of Conquest: Literary Study and British Rule in India* (New York: Columbia University Press, 1989), 3. In addition to Viswanathan's rich study, I have also benefitted from Patrick Brantlinger, *Rule of Darkness: British Literature and Imperialism, 1830–1900* (Ithaca, N.Y.: Cornell University Press, 1988) and Priya Joshi, *Another Country: Colonialism, Culture and the English Novel in India* (New York: Columbia University Press, 2002).

19. Tignor is quite explicit: "In their policy of education in Egypt the British attempted to avoid mistakes they felt had been made in India. Indian officials in the 1880's generally believed that Indian education had been too European, literary, and not practical enough, thereby creating a class of intellectuals not trained to perform a definite function in their society, constantly discontented with British rule." Tignor, "'Indianization' of the Egyptian Administration," 657.
20. Cited by Kinsey, "Egyptian Education under Cromer," 195 (letter to Strachey, April 13, 1906, FO633VIII).
21. Tignor, "'Indianization' of the Egyptian Administration," 658.
22. Valentine Chirol, *The Egyptian Problem* (London: Macmillan, 1920), 221.
23. Ibid., 231.
24. Milner, *England in Egypt*, 386. It is worth noting that this distinction is also integral to Cromer's account of the Egyptian population; see Afaf Lutfi al-Sayyid, *Egypt and Cromer: A Study in Anglo-Egyptian Relations* (London: John Murray, 1968), 63. For especially rich accounts of how the category of the peasant plays out in Egyptian politics and literature, see Michael Gasper, *The Power of Representation: Publics, Peasants and Islam in Egypt* (Palo Alto: Stanford University Press, 2009) and Selim, *Novel and the Rural Imaginary.*
25. Milner, *England in Egypt*, 389.
26. Ibid., 390.
27. Ibid., 390.
28. Ibid., 390.
29. Ibid., 390.
30. Ibid., xi.
31. It is well worth noting that Milner's characterizations are in line with common Orientalist conceptions of Qur'anic schooling. For an important study of Arab accounts of Orientalism, see Muḥsin Jāsim al-Mūsawī, *al-Istishrāq fī al-fikr al-'Arabī* (Beirut: al-Mu'assasah al'Arabīyah lil-Dirāsāt wa-al-Nashr, 1993).
32. See al-Karīm, *Tārīkh al-ta'līm fī Miṣr* and Heyworth-Dunne, *Introduction.*
33. Milner, *England in Egypt*, 370.
34. See Aḥmad Amīn, *Ḥayātī* (Cairo: Maktabat al-Adab, 1952), and Ṭāhā Ḥusayn, *al-Ayyām.*
35. Khaled Fahmy, *All the Pasha's Men: Mehmed Ali, His Army and the Making of Modern Egypt* (Cambridge: Cambridge University Press, 1997); Timothy Mitchell, *Colonising Egypt*; Starrett, *Putting Islam to Work.*
36. Mitchell, *Colonising Egypt*, 88.
37. See, for example, Dor, *L'Instruction publique en Égypte*, 83.
38. Mitchell, *Colonising Egypt*, 87.
39. For a remarkable study on the rise of the pedagogical sciences, see Farag, "Private Lives, Public Affairs."
40. Cromer, *Modern Egypt, I*, 1
41. Ibid., 7.
42. Cromer, *Modern Egypt, II*, 527/528.
43. Ibid., 533.
44. Ibid., 535–36.
45. Ibid., 238.

46. Ibid., 237.
47. Ibid., 238. For an extended reading of this passage, see Tageldin, *Disarming Words.*
48. Cromer, *Modern Egypt, II*, 238.
49. Ibid., 238, 242–43.
50. Ibid., 527.
51. Ibid., 537.
52. Ibid., 537.
53. Ibid., 537–38.
54. Milner, *England in Egypt*, 429.
55. Ibid., 430.
56. Chirol, *Egyptian Problem*, 160.

4. LITERATURE

1. René Wellek, "The Crisis of Comparative Literature (1959)," in Damrosch, Melas, and Buthelezi, *Princeton Sourcebook in Comparative Literature*, 162.
2. Ibid., 169.
3. Ibid., 170.
4. Ibid., 170.
5. I allude here to Edward Said's famous reflections in *The World*, 4: "[T]exts are worldly, to some degree they are events, and, even when they appear to deny it, they are nevertheless part of the social world, human life, and of course the historical moments in which they are located and interpreted."
6. Here I think of those who cite Said's influence explicitly and scholars who draw from his methods in the cultural analysis of texts: Aamir Mufti, Paul Bové, Gauri Viswanathan, Donald Pease, Anne McClintock, and Timothy Brennan, to name a mere few. The contrast of Wellek and Said is not meant to suggest an outright opposition in their approaches. Said was by no means unconcerned with formalism, and as I show later in this chapter, the apparent tension he has with it seems to recede, especially when weighed against his understanding of what literature is in works like *Humanism and Democratic Criticism* (New York: Columbia University Press, 2004).
7. Wellek's writings have been extensively translated, and *Theory of Literature*, which he cowrote with his colleague Austin Warren at the University of Iowa, has alone been translated into twenty-two languages. Austin Warren and René Wellek, *Theory of Literature* (Orlando, Fla.: Harcourt Brace, 1949).
8. A systematic overview of the extensive scholarship on *adab* is beyond the scope of this chapter. For readers interested in historical studies, see, for example, Fedwa Malti-Douglas, *Structures of Avarice: The Bukhalā' in Medieval Arabic Literature* (Leiden: Brill, 1985), 7–14; Bo Holmberg, "Adab and Arabic Literature," in *Literary History: Towards a Global Perspective*, ed. Anders Pettersson (Berlin: Walter de Gruyter, 2006), 180–206; and S. A. Bonebakker, "Adab and the Concept of Belles-Lettres," in *'Abbasid Belles-Lettres*, ed. Julia Ashtiany et al. (Cambridge: Cambridge University Press, 1990), 16–30. For references to the influential work of Wolfhart Heinrichs, Charles Pellat, and Gustave von Grunebaum, see Bilal Orfali, "A Sketch Map of Arabic Poetry Anthologies up to the Fall of Baghdad," *Journal of Arabic Literature* 43 (2012): 29–59.

9. See Paul Starkey, *Modern Arabic Literature* (Edinburgh: University of Edinburgh Press, 2006), 8–10; Tarif Khalidi, *Arabic Historical Thought in the Classical Period* (Cambridge: Cambridge University Press, 1994), 83–181; and Georges Makdisi, *The Rise of Humanism in Classical Islam and the Christian West* (Edinburgh: University of Edinburgh Press, 1990), 99–105.
10. See, for example, Ḥusayn al-Marṣafī, *al-Wasīlah al-adabīyah ilā al-ʿulūm al-ʿArabīyah* (Cairo: al-Hayʾah al-Miṣrīyah al-ʿĀmmah li-l-Kitāb, 1981). Carlo Alfonso Nallino's lectures were published initially in Italian in 1948 and then as *La littérature arabe des origins à l'époque de la dynastie umayyide*, trans. Charles Pellat (Paris: Maisonneuve, 1950).
11. René Wellek, "The Name and Nature of Comparative Literature," in *Discriminations* (New Haven: Yale University Press, 1970).
12. See Harry Levin, "Comparing the Literature," in *Grounds for Comparison* (Cambridge, Mass.: Harvard University Press, 1972), and cited in Wellek, "Name and Nature," 4.
13. Wellek, "Name and Nature," 4.
14. Ibid., 4.
15. See Damrosch, *What Is World Literature?*; Casanova, *World Republic of Letters*.
16. Raymond Schwab, *Oriental Renaissance: Europe's Rediscovery of India and the East 1680–1880* (New York: Columbia University Press, 1987), 8.
17. See Masuzawa, *Invention of World Religions*; and Maurice Olender, *The Languages of Paradise* (Cambridge, Mass.: Harvard University Press, 2003).
18. See al-Marṣafī, *al-Wasīlah al-adabīyah*.
19. Muṣṭafa Ṣādiq al-Rafīʿī, *Tārīkh ādāb al-ʿArab* (Cairo, 1911).
20. See, for example, Nallino's lectures. Numerous articles on behalf of the Egyptian University were published in *al-Hilāl* between 1906 and 1914; see, for example, "Al-Madrasah al-kullīyah al-Miṣrīyah," *al-Hilāl* 15, no. 4 (January 1907): 217–24; or "Al-Jāmiʿah al-Miṣriyya wa-l-taʿlīm al-lāzim li-l-bilād," *al-Hilāl* 17, no. 5 (February 1909): 272–79.
21. Carl Brockelmann, *Geschichte der arabischen Litteratur* (Weimar: E. Felber, 1898–1902); Reynold Nicholson, *A Literary History of the Arabs* (London: T.F. Unwin, 1907); and H.A.R. Gibb, *Arabic Literature: An Introduction* (London: Oxford University Press, 1926).
22. Aḥmad Ḥasan Zayyāt, *Tārīkh al-adab al-ʿArabī li-l-madāris al-thānawīyah wa-al-ʿulyā*, 5th ed. (Cairo: Lajnat al-Ta'līf wa-l-Tarjamah wa-l-Nashr, 1930).
23. Ṭāhā Ḥusayn et al., eds., *al-Mujmal fi tārīkh al-adab al-ʿArabī* (Egypt: Maṭbaʿat al-Iʿtimād, 1929).
24. Ferial Ghazoul, "Comparative Literature in the Arab World," *Comparative Critical Studies* 3, nos. 1–2 (June 2006): 113–24; and Nadia al-Bagdadi, "Registers of Arabic Literary History," *New Literary History* 39, no. 3 (Summer 2008): 437–61.
25. See, in particular, Mara Naaman, Muhammad Siddiq, and Shaden Tageldin's articles in *Comparative Literature Studies* 47, no. 4 (2010).
26. See, for example, Herrera and Torres, *Cultures of Arab Schooling*.
27. Viswanathan, *Masks of Conquest*.
28. Aamir Mufti, "Orientalism and the Institution of World Literatures," *Critical Inquiry* 36 (2010): 458–93; and Sheldon Pollock, *Language of the Gods in the World of Men* (Berkeley: University of California Press, 2006).

29. The articles were published serially between the years 1894 and 1895, and were republished again in collected forms in numerous editions. In what follows I draw primarily from the four volumes published from 1911 to 1914 and then republished in 1957. Editions are noted in the notes. For the initial series, see Jurjī Zaydān, "Tārīkh ādāb al-lughah al-ʻArabīyah," in *al-Hilāl* (Cairo, 1894–95).
30. Jurjī Zaydān, *Tārīkh ādāb al-lughah al-ʻArabīyah* (Cairo: Maṭbaʻat al-Hilāl, 1911–14).
31. See ibid., 7–8.
32. As Anne-Laure Dupont's biography of Zaydan notes, much of Zaydan's understanding of *adab* can be traced to his formation at the Syrian Protestant College in Beirut. His arguments for literary education are quite explicit in his statements on behalf of the Egyptian University—and even in the form of education espoused in the opening charter, which privileged literary over scientific foundations for incoming students. See Anne-Laure Dupont, *Gurgi Zaydan: Ecrivain réformiste et témoin de la renaissance Arabe* (Paris: IFPO, 2006).
33. It is unclear whether or not Zaydan would have actually been able to read the German sources he lists in his introduction. That said, there were scholars who accused him of plagiarizing from Brockelmann in the initial reviews of the second volume of his book: see *al-Mashriq* 15, no. 8 (August 1912): 597–610.
34. See chap. 6, sec. 44 of Ibn Khaldūn, *al-Muqaddimah* (1332–1406; repr., Beirut: Dār al-Qalam, 1977).
35. The Egyptian University was founded in 1908, and Zaydan was a key figure in its history. See Donald Reid, *Cairo University and the Making of Modern Egypt* (Cambridge: Cambridge University Press, 1990).
36. Zaydān, *Tārīkh ādāb.*
37. I note here that Anne-Laure Dupont translates the title of Zaydan's work as simply *L'Histoire de la littérature arabe* in her book, *Gurgi Zaydan: Ecrivain réformiste et témoin de la renaissance Arabe.*
38. Zaydān, *Tārīkh ādāb.*
39. Ibid.
40. Anthony Grafton, *The Footnote: A Curious History* (Cambridge, Mass.: Harvard University Press, 1999).
41. H.A.R. Gibb, *The Legacy of Islam* (Oxford: Oxford University Press, 1974), 180.
42. Ibid., 180.
43. Ibid., 189.
44. Ibid., 189.
45. Said, *Orientalism*, 257.
46. Ibid., 265.
47. Ibid., 257, my emphasis.
48. See ibid., 255, 257, 271.
49. For two studies on Auerbach in the context of comparative literature, see Aamir Mufti, "Auerbach in Istanbul: Edward Said, Secular Criticism, and the Question of Minority Culture," *Critical Inquiry* 25 (Autumn 1998): 95–125; and chap. 3 in Emily Apter, *The Translation Zone: New Comparative Literature* (Princeton: Princeton University Press, 2006), 41–64.
50. Ernst Curtius, "Preface to *European Literature and the Latin Middle Ages* (1948)," in Damrosch, Melas, and Buthelezi, *Princeton Sourcebook in Comparative Literature*, 122.

51. Ibid., 122.
52. Ibid., 123
53. See Rūḥī al-Khālidī, "Tārīkh ʻilm al-adab ʻinda-l-frank wa-l-ʻarab wa fiktur hūkū," serialized beginning in *al-Hilāl* 4, no. 11 (November 1902), and then as a book in 1904 under the title *al-Maqdisi*. See also H. al-Khateeb, "Ruhi al-Khalidi: A Pioneer of Comparative Literature in Arabic," *Journal of Arabic Literature* 18 (1987): 81–87; Qusṭākī al-Ḥimṣī, *Manhal al-wurrād fi ʻilm al-intiqād*, vol. 3 (Aleppo: Matbaʻat al-ʻAṣr al-Jadīd, 1935); and Muḥammad Ghunaymī Hilāl, *Al-Adab al-muqāran* (1950; 3rd ed., Cairo: Maktabat al-Anglo al-Misriyya, 1962).
54. See, for example, Said, *Orientalism*, and Mitchell, *Colonising Egypt*. For models of ethical analysis, I refer here to Asad, *Genealogies of Religion* and *Formations of the Secular*, and Mahmood, *Politics of Piety*.
55. Talal Asad, "Anthropological Conceptions of Religion: Reflections on Geertz," *Man*, New Series, 18, no. 2 (June 1983): 237–59.
56. Ibid., 252.
57. Saba Mahmood, "Religious Reason and Secular Affect: An Incommensurable Divide?," *Critical Inquiry* 35, no. 4 (2009): 836–62.

5. CRITIQUE

1. Lewis's speech was reprinted as "al-Maʿrifah wa-l-ʿilm wa-l-ḥikmah," *al-Muqtaṭaf* 7 (1882).
2. Mahfouz was most likely familiar with an extensive line of commentary regarding Darwin in the Arab world. In 1930, when he was still quite young, he published an article wrestling with faith and modern science in Salama Musa's journal, *al-Majallah al-Jadīdah*. See Najīb Maḥfūẓ, "Iḥtiḍār muʿtaqadāt wa-tawallud muʿtaqadāt" [The dying of old beliefs and the birth of new beliefs], *al-Majallah al-Jadīdah* 1, no. 12 (October 1930): 1468–70.
3. Where the first volume is cast against the backdrop of student revolts, the Milner Commission, and Fahmy's tragic death, the second and third volumes chart Kamal's intellectual development from his decision to attend the Teachers College to his negotiated position in an Egyptian intellectual scene, textured by his infatuation with Aida, who both speaks French and eventually moves to France. The third volume is perhaps most pronounced in its exploration of Ahmad and ʻAbd al-Munʻim, the sons of Khadija and Ibrahim, who, in the end, both end up imprisoned on account of their beliefs: the former a communist and the latter a member of the Muslim Brotherhood. In each of the rich dimensions of the three novels, there is a gesture toward an intertextual body of Arabic literature, political events, and historical phenomena, much of which seeps into the family's life in often the most oblique manner.
4. A large number of studies gloss these three generations, noting how Mahfouz skillfully animates many of the conflicting sentiments between them: see, for example, Brugman, *Introduction to the History of Modern Arabic Literature in Egypt*, 301.
5. Hilary Kilpatrick, "The Egyptian Novel from *Zaynab* to 1980," in *Modern Arabic Literature*, ed. M. M. Badawi (Cambridge: Cambridge University Press, 1992), 243. On Mahfouz's significance for modern Arabic letters, see the work

of scholars such as Roger Allen, Gaber Asfour, Sabry Hafez, Matti Moussa, Muhammad Siddiq, and Sasson Somekh.

6. I note here a range of rich scholarship on the complexity of the novel as a literary form. For efforts to think about the novel across the boundaries of specific national traditions, see Nancy Armstrong's special issue, "Theories of the Novel Now," *Novel: A Forum on Fiction* 42, nos. 2–3 and 43, no. 1 (2009–10). In the context of Victorian studies, in particular, see Nicholas Dames's *The Physiology of the Novel* (Oxford: Oxford University Press, 2007).
7. Here I use the terms "scientific" and "literary" somewhat interchangeably on account of the reading public that they imply. In Arabic-language print culture in the late nineteenth and early twentieth centuries, many journals covered scientific and literary issues together. For an insightful analysis of this phenomenon, see Stephen Sheehi, "Arabic Literary-Scientific Journals: Precedence for Globalization and the Creation of Modernity," *Comparative Studies of South Asia, Africa and the Middle East* 25, no. 2 (2005): 118–48.
8. As a testament to the rich range of scholarship on reading, I gesture here to Steven Best and Sharon Marcus's special issue of *Representations* 108, no. 1 (Fall 2009), "The Way We Read Now," as well as Rachel Ablow's anthology, *The Feeling of Reading* (Ann Arbor: University of Michigan Press, 2010).
9. Saba Mahmood's "Religious Reason and Secular Affect" offers an insightful way to read beyond the conventional binarism of religion and secularism. For one, she notes that secularism is the condition through which religion comes to be defined, and second, she traces the implications of secular reading practices in the context of the Danish cartoons. See Mahmood, "Religious Reason and Secular Affect."
10. Marwa Elshakry, *Reading Darwin in Arabic, 1860–1950* (Chicago: University of Chicago Press, 2014); and Shafīq Juḥā, *Dārwin wa-azmat 1882 bi-l-dāʾirah al-ṭibbīyah* (Beirut, 1991).
11. Susan Harding, *The Book of Jerry Falwell* (Princeton: Princeton University Press, 2000), 65.
12. Ibid., 65.
13. As I hope will be clear in what follows, my use of the term "illiterate" refers both to those incapable of reading or writing in the conventional sense, but also to readers outside of the educational conventions of an emergent literary world.
14. Stephen B. L. Penrose, *That They May Have Life: The Story of the American University of Beirut, 1866–1941* (Beirut: American University in Beirut, 1970).
15. In 1882, following months of research, Van Dyck sent Darwin an article summarizing his findings, titled "On the Modification of a Race of Syrian Street Dogs." While initially Van Dyck received a response from one of Darwin's sons, who explained his father was too ill to reply, Darwin himself did eventually reply and informed Van Dyck that he was sending along the article to the London Zoological Society for publication: see William Van Dyck, "On the Modification of a Race of Syrian Street Dogs by Means of Sexual Selection," *Proceedings of the Zoological Society of London* 25 (1882): 367–70, published with a prefatory notice by Charles Darwin. The report of this correspondence between Van Dyck and Darwin was eventually referenced in the Arabic literary journal of Yaʿqub Sarruf and Faris Nimr, *al-Muqtaṭaf*, drawing what could well have been a fairly

obscure interaction into an emergent sphere of intellectual debate: see "Charles Darwin" [in Arabic], *al-Muqtaṭaf* 7, no. 1 (June 1882): 4–5.

16. Nadia Farag, "The Lewis Affair and the Fortunes of al-Muqtataf," *Middle Eastern Studies* 8, no. 1 (1972): 73–83.
17. Letter to potential donors from Daniel Bliss, July 27, 1865, Archives of the American University in Beirut.
18. Lewis, "al-Maʿrifah," 165.
19. Ibid., 165.
20. Quoted in Farag, "Lewis Affair," 78.
21. "A Statement 1883 by the President to the Board of Managers," Archives of the American University in Beirut.
22. "Annual Reports, Board of Managers, Syrian Protestant College," Archives of the American University in Beirut.
23. James Dennis, "Darwinism" [in Arabic], *al-Muqtaṭaf* 7, no. 4 (November 1882): 233.
24. Jurjī Zaydān, "Tadhkirat al-Madrasah," *al-Hilāl* 33 (1924–25).
25. Rashīd Riḍā, "Nazariyat Darwin wa-l-Islām" *al-Manār* 30, no. 8 (March 1930): 593–600.
26. Donald Leavitt, "Darwinism in the Arab World: The Lewis Affair at the Syrian Protestant College," *Muslim World* 71, no. 2 (April 1981): 98.
27. The *nahḍah* tends to be understood as the sweeping reforms of the nineteenth century that lead both to political modernization and to the rise of modern Arabic letters, stemming from the infusion of European literary forms into Arabic as well as reforms in education, unsettling the authority of al-Azhar and making possible the modern universities, be it Dār al-ʿUlūm or eventually, at the beginning of the twentieth century, Egyptian University.
28. The letters written between Daniel Bliss and David Dodge reveal a separate set of concerns. A letter from June 14, 1882, focuses on Lewis's public disclosure of a personal memo from the administration: "If Dr. Lewis had replied quietly and privately to a letter not designed for public use, but written to him as an individual and a friend, and if his reply had been just—what has now received little or nothing would have been said." Letters from June 20, July 14, and even August 1 all focus extensively on Lewis's public circulation of a letter that was "private and personal."
29. A number of issues came to the fore during faculty meetings around the time of the Lewis Affair, and many of them are included in the student letters to Daniel Bliss. "A Statement 1883 by the President to the Board of Managers" summarizes many of the concerns and even quotes a student letter in its entirety. Medical students were intent upon altering the requirement that they travel to Constantinople for the certifying examination.
30. See Charles Hirschkind, "Heresy or Hermeneutics: The Case of Nasr Hamid Abu Zayd," *Stanford Humanities Review* 5, no. 1 (1995).
31. I draw inspiration here from Michael Warner's current work on reading practices, some of which has been presented in lectures on "The Evangelical Public Sphere," presented at the University of Pennsylvania. See also his essay "Uncritical Reading."
32. Talal Asad's observations on distinctions between critique (*naqd*) and advice (*naṣīḥah*) have helped inform my observations—see Asad, *Genealogies of Religion.*

For broader reflections on the place of critique, see his entry, "Historical Notes on the Idea of Secular Criticism," *Immanent Frame*, January 25, 2008, http://blogs.ssrc.org/tif/2008/01/25/historical-notes-on-the-idea-of-secular-criticism/, accessed June 14, 2015.

33. Arabic citations are drawn from Najīb Maḥfūẓ, *Qaṣr al-shawq* (1956–57; repr., Cairo: Dār al-Shurūq, 2006), 428–37. The English translation is largely based on Naguib Mahfouz, *The Cairo Trilogy*, trans. William Hutchins (New York: Knopf, 2001), 888–95.
34. As part of Mahfouz's engagement with modern Arabic letters, he includes the title of a well-known Wafdist publication from the period.
35. These few lines bear a certain richness, not only in their execution, but also in their invocation of specific literary figures who help to delimit the literary field. Al-Manfaluti, whose name is often cited in the *Trilogy*, was both a master essayist and a key figure in the consolidation of modern Arabic letters. Shawqi and Hafiz, renowned for their poetry, also call to mind a certain generation of romantic poets quite integral, by the time the novel is written, to conceptions of Arabic, and specifically Egyptian, literature. Collectively, the writings of these figures constituted a basic corpus of texts regularly incorporated into curricula at the Teachers College, a training college for teachers of Arabic separate from the traditional Islamic university, al-Azhar. Rather intriguingly, the very lines that delineate the terms of belonging and participation in a reading public construct an intertextual field at once familiar to the literate Arabic reader and perhaps foreign to the international reader more familiar with Balzac, Dickens, or Tolstoy than a modern Arabic tradition.
36. I refer here to Michael Fried, *Courbet's Realism* (Chicago: University of Chicago Press, 1992), Nancy Armstrong, *Fiction in the Age of Photography: The Legacy of British Realism* (Cambridge, Mass.: Harvard University Press, 2000), George Lewis Levine, *The Realistic Imagination: English Fiction from Frankenstein to Lady Chatterley* (Chicago: University of Chicago Press, 1981), 18.
37. Asad, "Limits of Religious Criticism," 214.
38. See, for example, Amy Hollywood's "Reading as Self-Annihilation," in Gallop, *Polemic*, 39–63, and Warner's "Uncritical Reading."
39. Both Matti Moosa and Omar Saghi comment on this aspect of the *Trilogy*: see Moosa, *Origins of Modern Arabic Fiction* and Omar Saghi, *Figures De L'engagement: Le Militant Dans La Trilogie De Naguib Mahfouz* (Paris: Harmattan, 2003).
40. Maḥfūẓ, *Qaṣr al-shawq*, 63; Mahfouz, *Cairo Trilogy*, 587.
41. See the entry in J. M. Cowan, ed., *The Hans Wehr Dictionary of Modern Written Arabic* (Ithaca, N.Y.: Spoken Language Services, 1994), 11.
42. Mahfouz, *Cairo Trilogy*/*Qaṣr al-shawq*, 591/68.
43. Ibid., 592/68.
44. I refer here to Siddiq, *Arab Culture and the Novel* and Ronald T. Judy, "Some Thoughts on Naguib Mahfouz in the Spirit of Secular Criticism," *boundary 2* 34, no. 2 (2007): 21–54.
45. Rasheed El-Enany, "The Dichotomy of Islam and Modernity in the Fiction of Naguib Mahfouz," in *The Postcolonial Crescent: Islam's Impact of Contemporary Literature*, ed. John Hawley (New York: Peter Lang, 1998), 71.
46. Ibid., 72.

47. Ibid., 73.
48. Ibid., 74.
49. Judy, "Some Thoughts," 54.
50. Ibid., 25.
51. Ibid., 32.
52. Ibid., 38.
53. Ibid., 53.
54. Ibid., 53.
55. Gillian Beer, *Darwin's Plots: Evolutionary Narrative in Darwin, George Eliot, and Nineteenth-Century Fiction* (London: Routledge & Kegan Paul, 1983), 6.
56. George Lewis Levine, *Darwin and the Novelists: Patterns of Science in Victorian Fiction* (Cambridge, Mass.: Harvard University Press, 1988).
57. Beer, *Darwin's Plots*, 6.

6. INTELLECTUALS

1. Gide's voyages are well documented both in his journals and letters and in studies of his life. Among a range of resources, I have drawn from André Gide, *Souvenirs et voyages*, ed. Pierre Masson (Paris: Gallimard, 2001) and André Gide, *Journal II*, ed. Martine Sagaert (Paris: Gallimard, 1997). I have also benefited from Alan Sheridan's *André Gide: A Life in the Present* (London: Hamish Hamilton, 1998); Gabriel Michaud's *Gide et l'Afrique* (Paris: Editions de Scorpion, 1961); and Michael Lucey's *Gide's Bent: Sexuality, Politics, Writing* (New York: Oxford University Press, 1995).
2. Claude-Moënis Taha-Hussein, ed., "André Gide: Lettres à Taha Hussein et sa famille," *Bulletin des Amis d'André Gide* 25, nos. 114–15 (April–July 1997): 169.
3. Hussein would eventually publish his Arabic translations of Gide's *Thésée* and *Oedipe* in 1947.
4. The first section of his autobiography—dealing with his time at al-Azhar—was initially published in serialized form in *al-Hilāl* between 1926 and 1927. The second part—dealing with his studies in France—was also published serially in 1940, and the last volume emerged in 1967.
5. Taha-Hussein, "André Gide," 169.
6. Taha Hussein, *Le livre des jours*, trans. Jean Lecerf and Gaston Wiet (vol. 2) (Cairo: Dār al-Maʿārif, 1940–43). For a broader discussion of this work in the context of both its Egyptian and French reception, see Luc-Willy Deheuvels, "Tâhâ Hussein et *Le livre des jours*; Démarche autobiographique et structure narrative," *Revue des mondes musulmans et de la Méditerranée*, July 1, 2013, 95–98, http://remmm.revues.org/236.
7. Casanova, *World Republic of Letters*, 115.
8. See, for example, Carol Bardenstein, *Translation and Transformation in Modern Arabic Literature* (Wiesbaden: Otto Harrassowitz Press, 2005); Tageldin, *Disarming Words*; and Tarek El-Ariss, *Trials of Arab Modernity* (New York: Fordham University Press, 2013).
9. J. K. Moorhead, ed., *Conversations of Goethe with Johann Peter Eckermann* (Cambridge: De Capo Press, 1998).
10. Brian Edwards, *Morocco Bound* (Durham, N.C.: Duke University Press, 2005).

11. Ibrahim Ibrahim quotes these letters at the conclusion to a chapter dedicated to Taha Hussein. See Ibrahim I. Ibrahim, "Taha Hussein: The Critical Spirit," in *Problems of the Modern Middle East in Historical Perspective*, ed. John Spagnolo (Reading: Garnet and Ithaca Press, 1996), 118.
12. The citations are drawn here from Gide's letter to Taha-Hussein in Taha-Hussein, "André Gide," 146–47.
13. Gide's letter, ibid., 147.
14. Gide's letter, ibid., 147: "Une traduction de mes livres en votre langue. . . . À quelle lecteur pourra-t-elle s'adresser? À quelle curiosité peut-elle répondre?"
15. Gide's letter, ibid., 147: "Enfin, de tous mes livres, il n'en est point, eussé-je pensé, de plus étranger à vos próccupations que ma *Porte Etroite*."
16. Gide's letter, ibid., 147: "En quoi cet insatisfaction mystique que j'ai peinte ici peut-elle toucher des âmes assises dans la certitude? Quel écho ces prières et ces appels chrétiens pourront-ils trouver parmi vous?"
17. Gide's letter, ibid., 147: "Mais je ne sens point grande inquiétude chez ceux qu'a formés et eduqués le Coran. C'est une école d'assurance qui n'invite guère à la recherche; et c'est même par quoi cet enseignement me semble limité!"
18. Gide's letter, ibid., 147: "Ai-je mis dans ma *Porte Etroite* assez d'humanité authentique et commune, assez d'amour, pour émouvoir ceux qu'une instruction différente aura su maintenir à l'abri de semblables tourments?"
19. Hussein's letter, ibid., 148–49.
20. Hussein's letter, ibid., 148–49.
21. Hussein's letter, ibid., 148–49.
22. Hussein's letter, ibid., 148–49.
23. Pheng Cheah, "What Is a World? On World Literature as a World Making Activity," *Daedalus* 137, no. 3 (2008): 26–38.
24. Ibid., 27.
25. Ibid., 27.
26. See Ṭāhā Ḥusayn, *Adīb* (1935; repr., Cairo: Dār al-Maʿārif, 1961); and for the English translations, I cite Taha Hussein, *A Man of Letters*, trans. Mona El-Zayyat (Cairo: American University in Cairo Press, 1994).
27. For two especially insightful analyses, see Rashīdah Mahrān, *Ṭāhā Ḥusayn bayn al-Sīrah wa-l-Tarjamah al-Dhātīyah* (Alexandria: al-Hayʾah al-Miṣrīyah al-ʿĀmmah li-l-Kitāb, 1979); Pierre Cachia, *Taha Hussein: His Place in the Arab Literary Renaissance* (London: Luzac, 1956).
28. Hussein, *Man of Letters*, 3.
29. Ibid., 4.
30. Montesquieu, *Persian Letters*, trans. C. J. Betts (New York: Penguin, 2004); Aḥmad Fāris al-Shidyāq, *al-Sāq ʿalā al-sāq fī mā huwa al-fāryāq: aw Ayyām wa-shuhūr wa-aʿwām fī ʿajam al-ʿArab wa-al-aʿjām*, ed. N. W. Khāzin (Beirut: Dār Maktabat al-Ḥayāh, 1966); Rifāʿah Rāfʿi al-Ṭahṭāwī, *An Imam in Paris: Account of a Stay in France by an Egyptian Cleric*, trans. Daniel Newman (London: Saqi, 2004); ʿAbd al-Raḥmān al-Jabartī, *ʿAjāʾib al-Athār fī'l-Tarājim wa'l-Akhbār*, trans. Thomas Philip and Moshe Perlman (Stuttgart: Franz Steiner Verlag, 1994); and Tayeb Salih, *Season of Migration to the North*, trans. Denys Johnson-Davies (London: Penguin, 2003).
31. Hussein, *Man of Letters*, 15/23.

32. Ibid., 17.
33. Ibid., 24/35.
34. Ibid., 25/36.
35. Ibid., 25/36.
36. Taha Hussein, *Adīb: ou l'aventure occidentale*, trans. Amina and Moenis Taha-Hussein (Cairo: Dār al-Maʿārif, 1960), 5.
37. For an extended treatment of world literature in the context of literary address, see Michael Allan, "Reading with One Eye, Speaking with One Tongue: On the Problem of Address in World Literature," *Comparative Literature Studies* 44, nos. 1–2 (2007): 1–19; and "You, the Sacrificial Reader: Poetics and Pronouns in Mahmoud Darwish's 'al-Qurban,'" in *Commitment and Beyond*, ed. Friederike Pannewick and Georges Khalil (Berlin: Reichert-Verlag, 2015).

CONCLUSION

1. Orhan Pamuk, *Snow*, trans. Maureen Freekly (New York: Faber and Faber, 2004); Azar Nafisi, *Reading Lolita in Tehran* (New York: Random House, 2003); Tahar Ben Jelloun, *L'Enfant de sable* (Paris: Editions du Seuil, 1985); Alaa al-Aswany, *The Yacoubian Building* (New York: Harper Perennial, 2006). For an example of a study engaging religion in literature, see John Erickson, *Islam and Postcolonial Narrative* (Cambridge: Cambridge University Press, 1998), and Justin Neuman, *Fiction Beyond Secularism* (Evanston, Ill.: Northwestern University Press, 2014).
2. For an insightful account exploring the prevalence of Muslim women's memoirs marketed to American readers, see Saba Mahmood, "Feminism, Democracy, and Empire: Islam and the War on Terror," in *Women's Studies on the Edge*, ed. Joan Scott (Durham, N.C.: Duke University Press, 2008).
3. Charles Hirschkind, *The Ethical Soundscape* (New York: Columbia University Press, 2006); Lara Deeb and Mona Harb, "Sanctioned Pleasures: Youth, Piety, and Leisure in Beirut," *Middle East Report*, Winter 2007; Lila Abu-Lughod, *Dramas of Nationhood: The Politics of Television in Egypt* (Chicago: University of Chicago Press, 2005).
4. For reflections on the dynamics of globalization and publics, see Emily Apter, "On Translation in a Global Market," *Public Culture* 13, no. 1 (2001): 1–12, and Susan Buck-Morss, *Thinking Past Terror: Islamism and Critical Theory on the Left* (New York: Verso, 2006).
5. Asad, *Formations of the Secular*.
6. Published originally in German as Erich Auerbach, "Philologie der Weltliteratur," in *Weltliteratur: Festgabe für Fritz Strich zum 70. Geburtstag*, ed. Walter Muschg and E. Staiger (Bern: Francke, 1952), 39–50. The citations here come from the English translation: "Philology and Weltliteratur," trans. Edward and Marie Said, *Centennial Review* 13, no. 1 (1969): 1–17.
7. For insightful analysis of Auerbach's relation to secularism, see "Auerbach's *Welttheologie*," in Apter, *Against World Literature*.
8. Auerbach, "Philologie der Weltliteratur," 49–50: "ut discat paulatim exercitatus animus visibilia haec et transitoria primum commutare, ut postmodum possit etiam derelinquere. Delicatus ille est adhue cui patria culcis est, fortis autem cui omne solum patria est, perfectus vero cui mundus totus exilium est."

9. Ibid., 50: "Hugo meinte das für den, dessen Ziel Loslösung von der Liebe zur Welt ist. Doch auch für einen, der die rechte Liebe zur Welt gewinnen will, ist es ein guter Weg."
10. Auerbach, "Philology and Weltliteratur."
11. Edward Said, *Reflections on Exiles and Other Essays* (Cambridge, Mass.: Harvard University Press, 2000), 456.
12. Said, *The World*, 35.

BIBLIOGRAPHY

Ablow, Rachel, ed. *The Feeling of Reading*. Ann Arbor: University of Michigan Press, 2010.

Abu-Lughod, Lila. *Dramas of Nationhood: The Politics of Television in Egypt*. Chicago: University of Chicago Press, 2005.

Ahmad, Aijaz. "The Communist Manifesto and World Literature." *Social Scientist* 28, nos. 7/8 (2000): 3–30.

Allan, Michael. "Reading Secularism: Religion, Literature, Aesthetics." *Comparative Literature* 65, no. 3 (2013): 257–64.

——. "Reading with One Eye, Speaking with One Tongue: On the Problem of Address in World Literature." *Comparative Literature Studies* 44, nos. 1–2 (2007): 1–19.

——. "You, the Sacrificial Reader: Poetics and Pronouns in Mahmoud Darwish's 'al-Qurban'." In *Commitment and Beyond*, edited by Friederike Pannewick and Georges Khalil. Berlin: Reichert-Verlag, 2015.

Allen, Roger M. A. *An Introduction to Arabic Literature*. New York: Cambridge University Press, 2000.

Amīn, Aḥmad. *Ḥayātī*. Cairo: Maktabat al-Adab, 1952.

Anidjar, Gil. "Secularism." *Critical Inquiry* 33, no. 1 (2006): 52–77.

Antonius, George. *The Arab Awakening: The Story of the Arab National Movement*. London: H. Hamilton, 1938.

Apter, Emily. *Against World Literature*. London: Verso, 2013.

——. "On Translation in a Global Market." *Public Culture* 13, no. 1 (2001): 1–12.

——. *The Translation Zone: New Comparative Literature*. Princeton: Princeton University Press, 2006.

Armstrong, Nancy. *Fiction in the Age of Photography: The Legacy of British Realism*. Cambridge, Mass.: Harvard University Press, 2000.

——, ed. "Theories of the Novel Now." Special issue, *Novel: A Forum on Fiction* 42, nos. 2–3 and 43, no. 1 (2009–10).

Artin, Yacoub. *L'Instruction Publique en Égypte, Considérations sur l'éducation publique en Égypte*. Paris: Ernest Leroux, 1890.

Asad, Talal. "Anthropological Conceptions of Religion: Reflections on Geertz." *Man*, New Series, 18, no. 2 (June 1983): 237–59.

——. *Formations of the Secular: Christianity, Islam, Modernity*. Stanford: Stanford University Press, 2003.

——. *Genealogies of Religion: Discipline and Reasons of Power in Christianity and Islam*. Baltimore: Johns Hopkins University Press, 1993.

——. "Historical Notes on the Idea of Secular Criticism." *Immanent Frame*, January 25, 2008. http://blogs.ssrc.org/tif/2008/01/25/historical-notes-on-the-idea-of-secular-criticism/. Accessed June 14, 2015.

——. *On Suicide Bombing*. New York: Columbia University Press, 2007.

——. "Trying to Understand French Secularism." In de Vries and Sullivan, *Political Theologies*, 494–526.

Ashcroft, Bill, Gareth Griffiths, and Helen Tiffin, eds. *The Empire Writes Back*. London: Routledge, 1994.

al-Aswany, Alaa. *The Yacoubian Building*. New York: Harper Perennial, 2006.

Auerbach, Erich. "Philologie der Weltliteratur." In *Weltliteratur: Festgabe für Fritz Strich zum 70. Geburtstag*, edited by Walter Muschg and E. Staiger, 39–50. Bern: Francke, 1952.

——. "Philology and Weltliteratur." Translated by Edward and Marie Said. *Centennial Review* 13, no. 1 (1969): 1–17.

Ayalon, Ami. *Reading Palestine: Printing and Literacy, 1900–1948*. Austin: University of Texas Press, 2004.

al-ʻAẓmah, ʻAzīz. *al-ʻAlmāniyyah fī manẓūr mukhtalif*. Beirut: Markaz Dirāsat al-Waḥdah al-ʻArabīyah, 1992.

Badawi, M. M., ed. *Modern Arabic Literature*. Cambridge: Cambridge University Press, 1992.

Badr, ʻAbd al-Muḥsin Ṭāhā. *Taṭawwur al-riwāyah al-ʻarabīyah al-ḥadiīhah fī miṣr, 1870–1938*. Cairo: Dār al-Maʻārif, 1963.

al-Bagdadi, Nadia. "Registers of Arabic Literary History." *New Literary History* 39, no. 3 (Summer 2008): 437–61.

Baldick, Chris. *The Social Mission of English Criticism: 1848–1932*. Oxford: Clarendon, 1983.

Bardenstein, Carol. *Translation and Transformation in Modern Arabic Literature*. Wiesbaden: Otto Harrassowitz Press, 2005.

Beer, Gillian. *Darwin's Plots: Evolutionary Narrative in Darwin, George Eliot, and Nineteenth-Century Fiction*. London: Routledge & Kegan Paul, 1983.

Benjamin, Walter. "The Storyteller." Translated by Harry Zohn. In *Illuminations*, 83–110. New York: Schocken Books, 1968.

Ben Jelloun, Tahar. *L'Enfant de sable*. Paris: Editions du Seuil, 1985.

Best, Steven, and Sharon Marcus, eds. "The Way We Read Now." Special issue, *Representations* 108, no. 1 (Fall 2009).

Bhabha, Homi. *The Location of Culture*. London: Routledge, 1994.

Bhabha, Homi, and W.J.T. Mitchell, eds. *Edward Said: Continuing the Conversation*. Chicago: University of Chicago Press, 2005.

Bhargava, Rajeev, ed. *Secularism and Its Critics*. Delhi: Oxford University Press, 1998.

Blunt, Wilfrid. *My Diaries: Being a Personal Narrative of Events, 1888–1914*. New York: Knopf, 1923.

Bonebakker, S. A. "Adab and the Concept of Belles-Lettres." In *'Abbasid Belles-Lettres*, edited by Julia Ashtiany et al., 16–30. Cambridge: Cambridge University Press, 1990.

Brantlinger, Patrick. *Rule of Darkness: British Literature and Imperialism, 1830–1900*. Ithaca, N.Y.: Cornell University Press, 1988.

Brockelmann, Carl. *Geschichte der arabischen Litteratur*. Weimar: E. Felber, 1898–1902.

Brugman, J. *An Introduction to the History of Modern Arabic Literature in Egypt.* Studies in Arabic Literature vol. 10. Leiden: Brill, 1984.
Buck-Morss, Susan. *Thinking Past Terror: Islamism and Critical Theory on the Left.* New York: Verso, 2006.
Burgett, Bruce, and Glen Hendler, eds. *Keywords: A Vocabulary of American Cultural Studies.* New York: New York University Press, 2007.
Burleigh, Nina. *Mirage: Napoleon's Scientists and the Unveiling of Egypt.* New York: HarperCollins, 2007.
al-Bustānī, Buṭrus. *Kitāb Quṭr al-Muḥīṭ.* 1869. Reprint, Beirut: Maktabat Lubnān, 1966.
Butler, Judith. "What Is Critique? An Essay on Foucault's Virtue." In Ingram, *The Political*, 212–26.
Cachia, Pierre. *Taha Hussein: His Place in the Arab Literary Renaissance.* London: Luzac, 1956.
Casanova, Pascale. *The World Republic of Letters.* Translated by M. B. DeBovoise. Cambridge, Mass.: Harvard University Press, 2004.
Chakrabarty, Dipesh. *Provincializing Europe: Postcolonial Thought and Historical Difference.* Princeton: Princeton University Press, 2000.
Cheah, Pheng. "What Is a World? On World Literature as a World Making Activity." *Daedalus* 137, no. 3 (2008): 26–38.
Chirol, Valentine. *The Egyptian Problem.* London: Macmillan, 1920.
Clarke, Edward Daniel. *Travels in Various Countries of Asia, Europe and Africa.* London: Cadwell and Davies, 1810–23.
Colla, Elliott. *Conflicted Antiquities: Egyptology, Egyptomania, Egyptian Modernity.* Durham, N.C.: Duke University Press, 2008.
Cowan, J. M., ed. *The Hans Wehr Dictionary of Modern Written Arabic.* Ithaca, N.Y.: Spoken Language Services, 1994.
Cromer, Evelyn Baring. *Modern Egypt, I.* New York: Macmillan, 1908.
——. *Modern Egypt, II.* New York: Macmillan, 1916.
Curtius, Ernst. "Preface to *European Literature and the Latin Middle Ages* (1948)." In Damrosch, Melas, and Buthelezi, *Princeton Sourcebook in Comparative Literature*, 120–24.
Dames, Nicholas. *The Physiology of the Novel.* Oxford: Oxford University Press, 2007.
Damrosch, David. "Secular Criticism Meets the World." http://weekly.ahram.org.eg/2005/769/bo2.htm. Accessed February 17, 2008.
——. *What Is World Literature?* Princeton: Princeton University Press, 2003.
Damrosch, David, Natalie Melas, and Mbongiseni Buthelezi, eds. *The Princeton Sourcebook in Comparative Literature.* Princeton: Princeton University Press, 2009.
Davidson, Andrew. "Turkey, a 'Secular' State? The Challenge of Description." *South Atlantic Quarterly* 102, nos. 2/3 (2003): 333–50.
Dawoud, Khaled. "Banquet Serves Up Indigestion." http://weekly.ahram.org.eg/2000/483/eg13.htm. Accessed December 14, 2007.
Deeb, Lara, and Mona Harb. "Sanctioned Pleasures: Youth, Piety, and Leisure in Beirut." *Middle East Report*, Winter 2007.
Deheuvels, Luc-Willy. "Tâhâ Husayn et *Le livre des jours*; Démarche autobiographique et structure narrative." *Revue des mondes musulmans et de la Méditerranée*, July 1, 2013, 95–98. http://remmm.revues.org/236.
Dennis, James. "Darwinism" [in Arabic]. *al-Muqtaṭaf* 7, no. 4 (November 1882): 233.

de Vries, Hent, and Lawrence Sullivan, eds. *Political Theologies: Public Religions in a Post-secular World.* New York: Fordham University Press, 2006.

D'haen, Theo, David Damrosch, and Djelal Kader, eds. *The Routledge Companion to World Literature.* London: Routledge, 2011.

Dor, Edouard. *L'Instruction publique en Égypte.* Paris: A. Lacroix, Verboeckhoven et Cie, 1872.

Dupont, Anne-Laure. *Gurgi Zaydan: Ecrivain réformiste et témoin de la renaissance Arabe.* Paris: IFPO, 2006.

Edwards, Brian. *Morocco Bound.* Durham, N.C.: Duke University Press, 2005.

El-Ariss, Tarek. "Fiction of Scandal." *Journal of Arabic Literature* 23 (2012): 510–31.

——. *Trials of Arab Modernity.* New York: Fordham University Press, 2013.

El Daly, Okasha. *Egyptology: The Missing Millennium.* London: University College of London Press, 2005.

El-Enany, Rasheed. "The Dichotomy of Islam and Modernity in the Fiction of Naguib Mahfouz." In Hawley, *Postcolonial Crescent,* 71–83.

El-Mohdy, Cheikh. *Les dix soirées malheureuses, contes d'Abd-Errahman, el-Iskanderany; ou Contes d'un endormeur.* Translated by Jean-Joseph Marcel. Paris: Jules Renouard, 1829.

Elshakry, Marwa. *Reading Darwin in Arabic, 1860–1950.* Chicago: University of Chicago Press, 2014.

El Shakry, Omnia. *The Great Social Laboratory: Subjects of Knowledge in Colonial and Postcolonial Egypt.* Palo Alto: Stanford University Press, 2007.

English, James. *The Economy of Prestige: Prizes, Awards, and the Circulation of Cultural Value.* Cambridge: Harvard University Press, 2009.

Erickson, John. *Islam and Postcolonial Narrative.* Cambridge: Cambridge University Press, 1998.

Esmeir, Samera. *Juridical Humanity: A Colonial History.* Palo Alto: Stanford University Press, 2012.

Fahmy, Khaled. *All the Pasha's Men: Mehmed Ali, His Army and the Making of Modern Egypt.* Cambridge: Cambridge University Press, 1997.

Farag, Iman. "Private Lives, Public Affairs: The Uses of *Adab.*" In Salvatore, *Muslim Traditions and Modern Techniques of Power,* 93–120.

Farag, Nadia. "The Lewis Affair and the Fortunes of al-Muqtataf." *Middle Eastern Studies* 8, no. 1 (1972): 73–83.

Felski, Rita, and Susan Stanford Friedman, eds. *Comparison: Theories, Approaches, Uses.* Baltimore: Johns Hopkins University Press, 2013.

Fernando, Mayanthi. *The Republic Unsettled: Muslim French and the Contradictions of Secularism.* Durham, N.C.: Duke University Press, 2014.

Fortna, Benjamin C. *Imperial Classroom: Islam, the State, and Education in the Late Ottoman Empire.* New York: Oxford University Press, 2002.

——. "Learning to Read in the Late Ottoman Empire and Early Turkish Republic." *Comparative Studies of South Asia, Africa and the Middle East* 21, nos. 1–2 (2001): 33–41.

Foucault, Michel. "What Is Critique?" In Ingram, *The Political,* 191–211.

Frängsmyr, Tore, and Sture Allén, eds. *Literature, 1981–1990.* Singapore: World Scientific, 1993.

Frei, Hans W. *The Eclipse of Biblical Narrative: A Study in Eighteenth and Nineteenth Century Hermeneutics.* New Haven: Yale University Press, 1974.

Fried, Michael. *Courbet's Realism.* Chicago: University of Chicago Press, 1992.
Gallop, Jane, ed. *Polemic: Critical or Uncritical.* New York: Routledge, 2004.
Gasper, Michael. "Abdallah al-Nadim, Islamic Reform, and 'Ignorant' Peasants: State-Building in Egypt?" In Salvatore, *Muslim Traditions and Modern Techniques of Power,* 75–92.
———. *The Power of Representation: Publics, Peasants and Islam in Egypt.* Palo Alto: Stanford University Press, 2009.
Gauchet, Marcel. *The Disenchantment of the World: A Political History of Religion.* Translated by Oscar Burge. Princeton: Princeton University Press, 1997.
Ghazoul, Ferial. "Comparative Literature in the Arab World." *Comparative Critical Studies* 3, nos. 1–2 (June 2006): 113–24.
Gibb, H.A.R. *Arabic Literature: An Introduction.* London: Oxford University Press, 1926.
———. *The Legacy of Islam.* Oxford: Oxford University Press, 1974.
Gide, André. *Journal II.* Edited by Martine Sagaert. Paris: Gallimard, 1997.
———. *Souvenirs et voyages.* Edited by Pierre Masson. Paris: Gallimard, 2001.
Grafton, Anthony. *The Footnote: A Curious History.* Cambridge, Mass.: Harvard University Press, 1999.
Gran, Peter. "Rediscovering al-'Attar." *Al-Ahram Weekly,* no. 770 (November 24–30, 2005).
Haddad, Emily. *Orientalist Poetics.* Aldershot: Ashgate, 2002.
Hafez, Sabry. *The Genesis of Arabic Narrative Discourse: A Study in the Sociology of Modern Arabic Literature.* London: Saqi Books, 1993.
———. "The Novel, Politics and Islam." *New Left Review,* September/October 2000. http://newleftreview.org/II/5/sabry-hafez-the-novel-politics-and-islam.
Hanna, Nelly. *In Praise of Books: A Cultural History of Cairo's Middle Class, Sixteenth through the Eighteenth Century.* Syracuse, N.Y.: Syracuse University Press, 2003.
Harding, Susan. *The Book of Jerry Falwell.* Princeton: Princeton University Press, 2000.
Hawley, John C., ed. *The Postcolonial Crescent: Islam's Impact on Contemporary Literature.* New York: Peter Lang, 1998.
Haykal, Muḥammad Ḥusayn. "Ta'rikh Misr wa 'adabuha la yudarrasan hatta l-an fi al-jami'a al-misriyya." *Al-Siyasa al-Usbu'iya* 3, no. 146 (December 28, 1928): 5.
Hayot, Eric. *On Literary Worlds.* Oxford: Oxford University Press, 2013.
Herder, Johann Gottfried. "Results of a Comparison of Different Peoples' Poetry in Ancient and Modern Times." In Damrosch, Melas, and Buthelezi, *Princeton Sourcebook in Comparative Literature,* 3–9.
Herrera, Linda, and Carlos Alberto Torres. *Cultures of Arab Schooling: Critical Ethnographies from Egypt.* Albany: State University of New York, 2006.
Heyworth-Dunne, J. *An Introduction to the History of Education in Modern Egypt.* London: Luzac, 1939.
Hilāl, Muḥammad Ghunaymī. *Al-Adab al-muqāran.* 1950. 3rd ed., Cairo: Maktabat al-Anglo al-Misriyya, 1962.
Hirschkind, Charles. *The Ethical Soundscape.* New York: Columbia University Press, 2006.
———. "Heresy or Hermeneutics: The Case of Nasr Hamid Abu Zayd." *Stanford Humanities Review* 5, no. 1 (1995): 464–77.
Hollywood, Amy. "Reading as Self-Annihilation." In Gallop, *Polemic,* 39–63.
Holmberg, Bo. "Adab and Arabic Literature." In *Literary History: Towards a Global Perspective,* edited by Anders Pettersson, 180–205. Berlin: Walter de Gruyter, 2006.

Hoock, Holger. "The British State and the Anglo-French Wars over Antiquities, 1798–1858." *Historical Journal* 50, no. 1 (March 2007): 49–72.

Hourani, Albert Habib. *Arabic Thought in the Liberal Age, 1798–1939.* New York: Cambridge University Press, 1983.

al-Ḥimṣī, Qusṭākī. *Manhal al-wurrād fi 'ilm al-intiqād.* Vol. 3. Aleppo: Matba'at al-'Asr al-Jadīd, 1935.

Ḥusayn, Ṭāhā. *Adīb.* 1935. Reprint, Cairo: Dār al-Ma'ārif, 1961.

——. *al-Ayyām.* Cairo: Dār al-Ma'ārif, 1969.

Ḥusayn, Ṭāhā, et al., eds. *Al-Mujmal fi tārīkh al-adab al-'Arabī.* Egypt: Maṭba'at al-I'timād, 1929.

Hussein, Taha. *Adīb: ou l'aventure occidentale.* Translated by Amina and Moenis Taha-Hussein. Cairo: Dār al-Ma'ārif, 1960.

——. *The Days.* Cairo: American University in Cairo Press, 1997.

——. *Le livre des jours.* Translated by Jean Lecerf and Gaston Wiet (vol. 2). Cairo: Dār al-Ma'ārif, 1940–43.

——. *A Man of Letters.* Translated by Mona El-Zayyat. Cairo: American University in Cairo Press, 1994.

Ibrahim, Ibrahim I. "Taha Hussein: The Critical Spirit." In *Problems of the Modern Middle East in Historical Perspective,* edited by John Spagnolo, 105–18. Reading: Garnet and Ithaca Press, 1996.

Ingram, David, ed. *The Political: Readings in Continental Philosophy.* London: Basil Blackwell, 2002.

Ismā'īl, 'Izz al-Dīn. *Al-Adab wa-funūnuh: Dirāsah wa-naqd.* Cairo: Dār al-fikr al-'arabī, 1965.

al-Jabartī, 'Abd al-Raḥmān. *'Ajā'ib al-Athār fi'l-Tarājim wa'l-Akhbār.* Translated by Thomas Philip and Moshe Perlman. Stuttgart: Franz Steiner Verlag, 1994.

Jager, Colin. "After the Secular: The Subject of Romanticism." *Public Culture* 18 (2006): 301–21.

——. *The Book of God: Secularization and Design in the Romantic Era.* Philadelphia: University of Pennsylvania Press, 2006.

Jacquemond, Richard. *Conscience of the Nation: Writers, State and Society in Modern Egypt.* Translated by David Tresilian. New York: American University in Cairo Press, 2008.

Joshi, Priya. *Another Country: Colonialism, Culture and the English Novel in India.* New York: Columbia University Press, 2002.

Judy, Ronald T. "Some Thoughts on Naguib Mahfouz in the Spirit of Secular Criticism." *boundary 2* 34, no. 2 (2007): 21–54.

Juḥā, Shafīq. *Dārwin wa-azmat 1882 bil-dā'irah al-ṭibbīyah.* Beirut, 1991.

al-Karīm, Aḥmad 'Izzat 'Abd. *Tārīkh al-ta'līm fī Miṣr: 1848–1882.* Cairo: Dār al-Ma'ārif, 1917.

Keane, Webb. *Christian Moderns: Freedom and Fetish in the Mission Encounter.* Berkeley: University of California Press, 2007.

——. "Semiotics and the Social Analysis of Material Things." *Language and Communication* 23 (2003): 409–25.

——. "Signs Are Not the Garb of Meaning: On the Social Analysis of Material Things." In Miller, *Materiality,* 182–205.

Kennedy, Philip. *On Fiction and* Adab *in Medieval Arabic Literature.* Wiesbaden: Harrassowitz Verlag, 2005.

Key, Alexander. "Arabic: Acceptance and Anxiety." *ACLA State of the Discipline*. http://stateofthediscipline.acla.org/entry/arabic-acceptance-and-anxiety. Accessed June 10, 2015.

Khaldūn, Ibn. *al-Muqaddimah*. 1332–1406. Reprint, Beirut: Dār al-Qalam, 1977.

al-Khālidī, Rūḥī. "Tārīkh ʻilm al-adab ʻinda-l-frank wa-l-ʻarab wa fiktur hūkū." *al-Hilāl* 4, no. 11 (November 1902).

Khalidi, Tarif. *Arabic Historical Thought in the Classical Period*. Cambridge: Cambridge University Press, 1994.

al-Khateeb, H. "Ruhi al-Khalidi: A Pioneer of Comparative Literature in Arabic." *Journal of Arabic Literature* 18 (1987): 81–87.

Kilpatrick, Hilary. "The Egyptian Novel from *Zaynab* to 1980." In Badawi, *Modern Arabic Literature*, 223–69.

Kinsey, David C. "Egyptian Education under Cromer: A Study of East-West Encounter in Educational Administration and Policy, 1883–1907." PhD dissertation, Harvard University, 1965.

Lawall, Sarah. *The Norton Anthology of World Literature*. New York: Norton, 2001.

Leavitt, Donald. "Darwinism in the Arab World: The Lewis Affair at the Syrian Protestant College." *Muslim World* 71, no. 2 (April 1981): 98.

Lefort, Claude. "The Permanence of the Theologico-Political." In de Vries and Sullivan, *Political Theologies*, 148–87.

Levin, Harry. "Comparing the Literature." In *Grounds for Comparison*, 74–91. Cambridge, Mass.: Harvard University Press, 1972.

Levine, George Lewis. *Darwin and the Novelists: Patterns of Science in Victorian Fiction*. Cambridge, Mass.: Harvard University Press, 1988.

——. *The Realistic Imagination: English Fiction from Frankenstein to Lady Chatterley*. Chicago: University of Chicago Press, 1981.

Lewis, Edwin. "al-Maʿrifah wa-l-ʿilm wa-l-ḥikmah." *al-Muqtaṭaf* 7 (1882).

Lucey, Michael. *Gide's Bent: Sexuality, Politics, Writing*. New York: Oxford University Press, 1995.

Maghraoui, Driss. "'Ilmaniyya, Laïcité, Sécularisme/Secularism in Morocco." In *Words in Motion: Toward a Global Lexicon*, edited by Carol Gluck and Anna Lowenhaupt Tsing, 109–28. Durham, N.C.: Duke University Press, 2009.

Mahfouz, Naguib. *The Cairo Trilogy*. Translated by William Hutchins. New York: Knopf, 2001.

Maḥfūẓ, Najīb. "Iḥtiḍār muʿtaqadāt wa-tawallud muʿtaqadāt." *al-Majālah al-Jadīdah* 1, no. 12 (October 1930): 1468.

——. *Palace of Desire*. Translated by William Hutchins. New York: Knopf, 2001.

——. *Qaṣr al-shawq*. 1956–57. Reprint, Cairo: Dar al-Shuruq, 2006.

Mahmood, Saba. "Feminism, Democracy, and Empire: Islam and the War on Terror." In *Women's Studies on the Edge*, edited by Joan Scott, 81–114. Durham, N.C.: Duke University Press, 2008.

——. *Politics of Piety: The Islamic Revival and the Feminist Subject*. Princeton: Princeton University Press, 2005.

——. "Religious Reason and Secular Affect: An Incommensurable Divide?" *Critical Inquiry* 35, no. 4 (2009): 836–62.

——. "Secularism, Hermeneutics, Empire: The Politics of Islamic Reformation." *Public Culture* 18, no. 2 (2006): 323–47.

Mahran, Rashīda. *Ṭāhā Ḥusayn bayn al-Sīrah wa al-Tarjamah al-Dhātīyah.* Alexandria: al-Ḥaya'a al-Miṣrīyah al-'Amma lil-Kitāb, 1979.

Makdisi, Georges. *The Rise of Humanism in Classical Islam and the Christian West.* Edinburgh: University of Edinburgh Press, 1990.

Malti-Douglas, Fedwa. *Structures of Avarice: The Bukhalā' in Medieval Arabic Literature.* Leiden: Brill, 1985.

Marcel, Jean-Joseph. *La Décade Égyptienne.* Cairo, 1798–1800.

——. *Les Fables de Lokman.* Éditeurs d'Erpenius et de Golius, Le Caire, 1803.

al-Marṣafī, Ḥusayn. *al-Kalim al-thamān.* Cairo: Maṭba'at al-Jumhūrīyah, 1903.

——. *al-Wasīlah al-adabīyah ilā al-'ulūm al-'Arabīyah.* Cairo: al-Hay'ah al-Miṣrīyah al-'Āmmah li-l-Kitāb, 1981.

Marx, Karl, and Friedrich Engels. *The Communist Manifesto.* 1888. Reprint, London: Penguin, 2002.

Masuzawa, Tomoko. *The Invention of World Religions; or, How European Universalism Was Preserved in the Language of Pluralism.* Chicago: University of Chicago Press, 2005.

McLarney, Ellen. "The Islamic Public Sphere and the Discipline of *Adab.*" *International Journal of Middle East Studies* 43 (2011): 429–49.

Mehrez, Samia. *Egyptian Writers between History and Fiction.* Cairo: AUC Press, 2005.

Meïer, Olivier. *Al-Muqtataf et le débat sur le Darwinisme: Beyrouth, 1876–1885.* Cairo: CEDEJ, 1996.

Melas, Natalie. *All the Difference in the World: Postcoloniality and the Ends of Comparison.* Palo Alto: Stanford University Press, 2006.

Meskell, Lynn, ed. *Archaeology Under Fire.* London: Routledge, 2002.

Metcalf, Barbara Daly, ed. *Moral Conduct and Authority.* Berkeley: University of California Press, 1984.

Michaud, Gabriel. *Gide et l'Afrique.* Paris: Editions de Scorpion, 1961.

Miller, Daniel, ed. *Materiality.* Durham, N.C.: Duke University Press, 2005.

Milner, Alfred. *England in Egypt.* London: E. Arnold, 1894.

Miquel, André. *La littérature arabe.* Paris: Presse universitaire de France, 1969.

al-Misīrī, 'Abd al-Wahhāb Mūḥammad, and 'Azīz al-'Aẓmah. *al-'Ilmānīyah taḥta al-majhar.* Beirut: Dār al-Fikr al-Mu'āsir, 2000.

Mitchell, Timothy. *Colonising Egypt.* Berkeley: University of California Press, 1991.

Mitchell, W.J.T. "Secular Divination: Edward Said's Humanism." In Bhabha and Mitchell, *Edward Said: Continuing the Conversation,* 99–108.

Montesquieu. *Persian Letters.* Translated by C. J. Betts. New York: Penguin, 2004.

Moorhead, J. K., ed. *Conversations of Goethe with Johann Peter Eckermann.* Cambridge: De Capo Press, 1998.

Moosa, Matti. *The Origins of Modern Arabic Fiction.* Boulder, Colo.: Three Continents Press, 1997.

Moretti, Franco. *Atlas of the European Novel, 1800–1900.* New York: Verso, 1999.

——. "Conjectures on World Literature." *New Left Review* (January/February 2000). http://newleftreview.org/II/1/franco-moretti-conjectures-on-world-literature.

Mufti, Aamir. "Auerbach in Istanbul: Edward Said, Secular Criticism, and the Question of Minority Culture." *Critical Inquiry* 25 (Autumn 1998): 95–125.

——, ed. "Critical Secularism." Special issue, *boundary 2* 31, no. 2 (2004).

——. "Orientalism and the Institution of World Literatures." *Critical Inquiry* 36 (2010): 458–93.

al-Mūsawī, Muḥsin Jāsim. *al-Istishrāq fī al-fikr al-ʿArabī.* Beirut: al-Mu'assasah al-ʿArabīyyah lil-Dirāsāt wa-l-Nashr, 1993.

——. *Islam on the Street: Religion in Modern Arabic Literature.* Lanham, Md.: Rowman & Littlefield, 2009.

Nafisi, Azar. *Reading Lolita in Tehran.* New York: Random House, 2003.

Najjar, Fauzi. "The Debate on Islam and Secularism in Egypt." *Arab Studies Quarterly* 18, no. 2 (1996): 1–21.

Nallino, Alfonso. *La littérature arabe des origines à l'époque de la dynastie umayyide.* Translated by Charles Pellat. Paris: Maisonneuve, 1950.

Nancy, Jean-Luc. "Church, State, Resistance." In de Vries and Sullivan, *Political Theologies*, 102–12.

Nancy, Jean-Luc, and Philippe Lacoue-Labarthe. *The Literary Absolute: The Theory of Literature in German Romanticism.* Translated by Philip Barnard and Cheryl Lester. Albany: State University of New York Press, 1988.

Nelson, Victoria. *The Secret Life of Puppets.* Cambridge, Mass.: Harvard University Press, 2001.

Neuman, Justin. *Fiction Beyond Secularism.* Evanston, Ill.: Northwestern University Press, 2014.

Nicholson, Reynold. *A Literary History of the Arabs.* London: T.F. Unwin, 1907.

Olender, Maurice. *The Languages of Paradise.* Cambridge, Mass.: Harvard University Press, 2003.

Orfali, Bilal. "A Sketch Map of Arabic Poetry Anthologies up to the Fall of Baghdad." *Journal of Arabic Literature* 43 (2012): 29–59.

Owen, Roger. *Lord Cromer.* Oxford: Oxford University Press, 2004.

Pamuk, Orhan. *Snow.* Translated by Maureen Freekly. New York: Faber and Faber, 2004.

Parkinson, R. B., ed. *Cracking Codes: The Rosetta Stone and Decipherment.* Berkeley: University of California Press, 1999.

Patel, Abdulrazzak. *The Arab Nahdah: The Making of the Intellectual and Humanist Movement.* Edinburgh: Edinburgh University Press, 2013.

Pellat, Charles. *Études sur l'histoire socio-culturelle de l'Islam (VIIe–XVe s.).* 1964. Reprint, London: Variorum Reprints, 1976.

Penrose, Stephen B. L. *That They May Have Life: The Story of the American University of Beirut, 1866–1941.* Beirut: American University in Beirut, 1970.

Pollock, Sheldon. *Language of the Gods in the World of Men.* Berkeley: University of California Press, 2006.

Powell, Eve Troutt. *A Different Shade of Colonialism: Egypt, Great Britain and the Mastery of the Sudan.* Berkeley: University of California Press, 2003.

Prakash, Gyan. *Another Reason.* Princeton: Princeton University Press, 1999.

Quṭb, Sayyid. *al-Taṣwīr al-fannī fī al-qur'ān.* Cairo: Dār al-Maʿārif, 1945.

al-Rafīʿī, Muṣṭafa Ṣādiq. *Tārīkh ādāb al-ʿArab.* Cairo, 1911.

Reid, Donald. *Cairo University and the Making of Modern Egypt.* Cambridge: Cambridge University Press, 1990.

——. *Whose Pharaohs? Archaeology, Museums and National Identity from Napoleon to World War I.* Berkeley: University of California Press, 2004.

Renfrew, Colin. *Loot, Legitimacy and Ownership: The Ethical Crisis in Archaeology.* London: Duckworth Press, 2000.

Riḍā, Rashīd. "Nazariyat Darwin wa-l-Islām." *al-Manār* 30, no. 8 (March 1930): 593–600.

Russell, Mona. "Competing, Overlapping, and Contradictory Agendas: Egyptian Education under British Occupation, 1882–1922." *Comparative Studies of South Asia, Africa and the Middle East* 21, nos. 1–2 (2001): 50–60.

Sacks, Jeffrey. *Iterations of Loss: Mutilation and Aesthetic Form, al-Shidyaq to Darwish.* New York: Fordham University Press, 2015.

Saghi, Omar. *Figures De L'engagement: Le Militant Dans La Trilogie De Naguib Mahfouz.* Paris: Harmattan, 2003.

Said, Edward W. *Culture and Imperialism.* New York: Knopf, 1993.

——. *Humanism and Democratic Criticism.* New York: Columbia University Press, 2004.

——. *Orientalism.* New York: Vintage, 1978.

——. *Reflections on Exiles and Other Essays.* Cambridge, Mass.: Harvard University Press, 2000.

——. *The World, the Text, and the Critic.* Cambridge, Mass.: Harvard University Press, 1983.

Salama, Mohammad. "Arabic and the Monopoly of Theory." *ARCADE*. https://arcade.stanford.edu/blogs/arabic-and-monopoly-theory. Accessed June 10, 2015.

——. *Islam, Orientalism and Intellectual History: Modernity and the Politics of Exclusion since Ibn Khaldun.* London: I.B. Taurus, 2011.

Salih, Tayeb. *Season of Migration to the North.* Translated by Denys Johnson-Davies. London: Penguin, 2003.

Salvatore, Armando, ed. *Muslim Traditions and Modern Techniques of Power.* Münster: Lit Verlag, 2001.

Ṣarrūf, Yaʿqūb, and Fāris Nimr, eds. "Charles Darwin" [in Arabic]. *al-Muqtaṭaf* 7, no. 1 (June 1882): 4–5.

al-Sayyid, Afaf Lutfi. *Egypt and Cromer: A Study in Anglo-Egyptian Relations.* London: John Murray, 1968.

Schwab, Raymond. *Oriental Renaissance: Europe's Rediscovery of India and the East 1680–1880.* New York: Columbia University Press, 1987.

Scott, David, and Charles Hirschkind. *Powers of the Secular Modern: Talal Asad and His Interlocutors.* Stanford: Stanford University Press, 2006.

Selim, Samah. *The Novel and the Rural Imaginary in Egypt, 1880–1985.* New York: Routledge, 2004.

Seymour-Smith, Martin. *The New Guide to Modern World Literature.* New York: Peter Bedrick Books, 1985.

Sheehan, Jonathan. *The Enlightenment Bible: Translation, Scholarship, Culture.* Princeton: Princeton University Press, 2005.

——. "Enlightenment, Religion, and the Enigma of Secularization." *American Historical Review* 108 (2003): 1061–80.

Sheehi, Stephen. "Arabic Literary-Scientific Journals: Precedence for Globalization and the Creation of Modernity." *Comparative Studies of South Asia, Africa and the Middle East* 25, no. 2 (2005): 418–48.

——. "Towards a Critical Theory of the Nahdah: Epistemology, Ideology, Capital." *Journal of Arabic Literature* 43, nos. 2–3 (2012): 269–98.

Sheridan, Alan. *André Gide: A Life in the Present.* London: Hamish Hamilton, 1998.

Shidyāq, Aḥmad Fāris. *al-Sāq ʻalá al-sāq fī mā huwa al-fāryāq: aw Ayyām wa-shuhūr wa-aʻwām fī ʻajam al-ʻArab wa-al-aʻjām.* Edited by N. W. Khāzin. Beirut: Dār Maktabat al-Ḥayāh, 1966.

Shuger, Deborah. *The Renaissance Bible: Scholarship, Sacrifice and Subjectivity.* Berkeley: University of California Press, 1994.

Siddiq, Muhammad. *Arab Culture and the Novel: Genre, Identity and Agency in Egyptian Fiction.* London: Routledge, 2007.

Silverstein, Michael. "Contemporary Transformations of Local Linguistic Communities." *Annual Review of Anthropology* 27 (1998): 401–26.

Silverstein, Michael, and Greg Urban, eds. *Natural Histories of Discourse.* Chicago: University of Chicago Press, 1996.

Solé, Robert, and Dominique Valbelle. *The Rosetta Stone: The Story of the Decoding of Hieroglyphics.* New York: Profile Books, 2005.

Starkey, Paul. *Modern Arabic Literature.* Edinburgh: University of Edinburgh Press, 2006.

Starrett, Gregory. *Putting Islam to Work: Education, Politics, and Religious Transformation in Egypt.* Berkeley: University of California Press, 1998.

Stock-Morton, Phyllis. *Moral Education for a Secular Society.* Albany: State University Press of New York, 1988.

Sullivan, Winnifred Fallers. *The Impossibility of Religious Freedom.* Princeton: Princeton University Press, 2005.

Tageldin, Shaden. *Disarming Words: Empire and the Seductions of Translation in Egypt.* Berkeley: University of California Press, 2011.

Taha-Hussein, Claude-Moënis, ed. "André Gide: Lettres à Taha Hussein et sa famille." *Bulletin des Amis d'André Gide* 25, nos. 114–15 (April–July 1997): 145–72.

al-Ṭahṭāwī, Rifā'ah Rāfi'. *An Imam in Paris: Account of a Stay in France by an Egyptian Cleric.* Translated by Daniel Newman. London: Saqi, 2004.

——. *Takhlīṣ al-ibrīz fī talkhīṣ Bārīz aw al-dīwān al-nafīs bi-Īwān Bārīz.* Cairo: al-Hay'ah al-Miṣrīyah al-'Āmmah li-l-Kitāb, 1993.

Tambar, Kabir. *The Reckoning of Pluralism: Political Belonging and the Demands of History in Turkey.* Palo Alto: Stanford University Press, 2014.

Taylor, Charles. "Modes of Secularism." In Bhargava, *Secularism and Its Critics*, 31–53.

——. *A Secular Age.* Cambridge, Mass.: Harvard University Press, 2007.

Tignor, Robert. "The 'Indianization' of the Egyptian Administration under British Rule." *American Historical Review* 68, no. 3 (1963): 636–61.

——. *Modernization and British Colonial Rule in Egypt, 1882–1914.* Princeton: Princeton University Press, 1966.

Van Dyck, William. "On the Modification of a Race of Syrian Street Dogs by Means of Sexual Selection." *Proceedings of the Zoological Society of London* 25 (1882): 367–70.

Vatikiotis, P. J. *The History of Modern Egypt: From Muhammad Ali to Mubarak.* Baltimore: Johns Hopkins University Press, 1991.

Viswanathan, Gauri. *Masks of Conquest: Literary Study and British Rule in India.* New York: Columbia University Press, 1989.

Warner, Michael. "Secularism." In Burgett and Hendler, *Keywords for American Cultural Studies*, 220–23.

——. "Uncritical Reading." In Gallop, *Polemic*, 13–38.

Warren, Austin, and René Wellek. *Theory of Literature.* Orlando, Fla.: Harcourt Brace, 1949.

Wellek, René. "The Crisis of Comparative Literature (1959)." In Damrosch, Melas, and Buthelezi, *Princeton Sourcebook in Comparative Literature*, 161–74.

——. "The Name and Nature of Comparative Literature." In *Discriminations*, 1–30. New Haven: Yale University Press, 1970.
Zaydān, Jurjī. "Tadhkirat al-Madrasah." *al-Hilāl* 33 (1924–25).
——. *Tārīkh ādāb al-lughah al-'Arabīyah*. Cairo: Maṭbaʿat al-Hilāl, 1911–14.
Zayyāt, Aḥmad Ḥasan. *Tārīkh al-adab al-'Arabī li-l-madāris al-thānawīyah wa-l-ʿulyā*. 5th ed. Cairo: Lajnat al-Ta'līf wa-l-Tarjamah wa-l-Nashr, 1930.

INDEX

Qur'an: and Gide-Hussein correspondence, 121; as literary text, 7, 50–52, 54; and Mahfouz's *Cairo Trilogy*, 109–11; memorization of, 7
Qur'anic schools, 2, 3, 12, 13, 61, 63–67
Qutb, Sayyid, 52

al-Rafi'i, Mustafa Sadiq, 81
reading, 3–4; and category of literature, 19; and constructing intellect and ignorance, 105–8 (*see also* illiteracy); and debates over Darwin in the Arab world, 96–97, 102–8, 112–13 (*see also* Darwin, Charles); dynamics of a global public, 134–35; and education in colonial Egypt, 15; and equivalence between languages, 53 (*see also* translation); and literary myopia, 135–37; and Mahfouz's *Cairo Trilogy*, 105–8; as "question-raising procedure," 113; reading beyond representation, 7–9; and Rosetta Stone, 39–54; Said and, 14; site of reading in world literature, 14, 19, 131–37
Reading Lolita in Tehran (Nafisi), 132
realism, 97, 105
religion, 4, 131–33, 135–36; and controversy over Haydar's *Walīmah li-a'shāb al-baḥr*, 19–25; and Danish cartoons depicting the prophet Muhammad, 92–93; and debates over Darwin in the Arab world, 94–114 (*see also* Darwin, Charles); and education in colonial Egypt, 62–66; and epistolary exchanges, 115–30 (*see also* epistolary exchanges); and fanaticism, 9, 15, 21–23, 57, 61–63; and Mahfouz's *Cairo Trilogy*, 109–12; religious traditionalism as counterpart to modernity, 58; and secularism, 9–12. *See also* Islam; Qur'anic schools; secularism
The Revolt of Islam (Shelley), 8
Rida, Rashid, 99
romanticism, 4, 11–12
Rosetta Stone, 14–15, 39–54; discovery and announcement of, 41–43, 45–48; entextualization and rise of world literature, 48–54; extraction of text from, 45–48; global dissemination of, 47–48; reading as an object, 39, 41–42, 45, 47; reading as a text, 39, 41–42, 47–52; translation of, 47–48
Rushdie, Salman, 21, 24–25

Said, Edward, 14, 19, 32–37, 77, 89–92; *Orientalism*, 8, 89; translation of "Philologie der Weltliteratur," 138–39; *The World, the Text, and the Critic*, 32–37; worldliness and secular criticism, 32–33, 75, 136, 137, 139
Salama, Mohammad, 56
Salammbô (Flaubert), 8
Salih, Tayeb, 124
Sarruf, Ya'qub, 99
The Satanic Verses (Rushdie), 21, 24–25
Schwab, Raymond, 80–81
science, 10, 94–114. *See also* Darwin, Charles; secularism
A Secular Age (Taylor), 10
secularism, 4, 9–12, 133, 135, 137; Arabic translations of term, 10–11; and controversy over Haydar's *Walīmah li-a'shāb al-baḥr*, 19–25, 37–38; and controversy over Rushdie's *The Satanic Verses*, 24–25; and debates over Darwin in the Arab world, 94–114 (*see also* Darwin, Charles); and demarcation of the place of religion in the world, 10, 23, 25; and education, 23–24; and Mahfouz's *Cairo Trilogy*, 111; secular criticism, 19, 32–37, 111, 137; and worldliness, 10–11, 19, 32–37
Seymour-Smith, Martin, 17
Shelly, Percy, 8
al-Siyāsah al-usbū'īyah (magazine), 26–27
skepticism, and secularism, 11, 111
Soyinka, Wole, 30
Strich, Fritz, 138
al-Sukkarīyah (Mahfouz), 110
Syrian Protestant College, 15, 94, 97–101

Tageldin, Shaden, 56
Tagore, Rabindranath, 29–30
Taha-Hussein, Claude-Moënis, 118
al-Tahtawi, Rifa'a, 55, 118
ta'līm, 15, 65
tarbiyah, 15, 65, 67–68
Tārīkh ādāb al-lughah al-'Arabīyah (Zaydan), 83–87
al-Taṣwīr al-fannī fī al-Qur'ān (Qutb), 52
Taylor, Charles, 10, 12
Taymur, Muhammad, 27
translation: and Arabic poetry, 49–50; Arabic translations of "secularism," 10–11; and Gide-Hussein correspondence, 117–18, 120–21; and Hussein's *Adīb*, 129–30; and linguistic equivalence, 14, 41, 43, 45–48, 53; and Qu'ran, 50–52; and Rosetta Stone, 39–54

Van Dyke, Cornelius, 97
La Vie de Mahomet (Dermenghem), 27

Translation/Transnation

Series Editor Emily Apter

Writing Outside the Nation by Azade Seyhan

The Literary Channel: The Inter-National Invention of the Novel edited by Margaret Cohen and Carolyn Dever

Ambassadors of Culture: The Transamerican Origins of Latino Writing by Kirsten Silva Gruesz

Experimental Nations: Or, the Invention of the Maghreb by Réda Bensmaïa

What Is World Literature? by David Damrosch

The Portable Bunyan: A Transnational History of "The Pilgrim's Progress" by Isabel Hofmeyr

We, the People of Europe? Reflections on Transnational Citizenship by Étienne Balibar

Nation, Language, and the Ethics of Translation edited by Sandra Bermann and Michael Wood

Utopian Generations: The Political Horizon of Twentieth-Century Literature by Nicholas Brown

Guru English: South Asian Religion in a Cosmopolitan Language by Srinivas Aravamudan

Poetry of the Revolution: Marx, Manifestos, and the Avant-Gardes by Martin Puchner

The Translation Zone: A New Comparative Literature by Emily Apter

In Spite of Partition: Jews, Arabs, and the Limits of Separatist Imagination by Gil Z. Hochberg

The Princeton Sourcebook in Comparative Literature: From the European Enlightenment to the Global Present edited by David Damrosch, Natalie Melas, and Mbongiseni Buthelezi

The Spread of Novels: Translation and Prose Fiction in the Eighteenth Century by Mary Helen McMurran

The Event of Postcolonial Shame by Timothy Bewes

The Novel and the Sea by Margaret Cohen

Hamlet's Arab Journey: Shakespeare's Prince and Nasser's Ghost by Margaret Litvin

Archives of Authority: Empire, Culture, and the Cold War by Andrew N. Rubin

Security: Politics, Humanity, and the Philology of Care by John T. Hamilton

Dictionary of Untranslatables: A Philosophical Lexicon edited by Barbara Cassin

Learning Zulu: A Secret History of Language in South Africa by Mark Sanders

In the Shadow of World Literature: Sites of Reading in Colonial Egypt by Michael Allan